SCOTT FORESMAN · ADDISON WESLEY
Mathematics

Grade 6

Assessment Sourcebook

Editorial Offices: Glenview, Illinois • Parsippany, New Jersey • New York, New York

Sales Offices: Parsippany, New Jersey • Duluth, Georgia • Glenview, Illinois
Coppell, Texas • Ontario, California • Mesa, Arizona

ISBN: 0-328-05525-5

Copyright © Pearson Education, Inc.
All Rights Reserved. Printed in the United States of America. This publication, or parts thereof, may be used with appropriate equipment to reproduce copies for classroom use only.

1 2 3 4 5 6 7 8 9 10 V004 12 11 10 09 08 07 06 05 04 03

Table of Contents

Overview of the Assessment Sourcebook vi

Journal Writing viii

Self–Assessment xi

Portfolio Assessment xiii

Performance Assessment xviii
Chapter 1 Performance Assessment 1
Chapter 2 Performance Assessment 3
Chapter 3 Performance Assessment 5
Chapter 4 Performance Assessment 7
Chapter 5 Performance Assessment 9
Chapter 6 Performance Assessment 11
Chapter 7 Performance Assessment 13
Chapter 8 Performance Assessment 15
Chapter 9 Performance Assessment 17
Chapter 10 Performance Assessment 19
Chapter 11 Performance Assessment 21
Chapter 12 Performance Assessment 23

Basic-Facts Timed Tests 25
Basic-Facts Timed Test 1 27
Basic-Facts Timed Test 2 28
Basic-Facts Timed Test 3 29
Basic-Facts Timed Test 4 30
Basic-Facts Timed Test 5 31
Basic-Facts Timed Test 6 32
Basic-Facts Timed Test 7 33
Basic-Facts Timed Test 8 34
Basic-Facts Timed Test 9 35
Basic-Facts Timed Test 10 36
Basic-Facts Timed Test 11 37
Basic-Facts Timed Test 12 38

continued on next page

Table of Contents

Written Tests 39
Tips for Test Taking 40
Response Sheet 41
Diagnosing Readiness for Grade 6 43
Chapter 1 Tests Form A: Mixed Formats 47
       Form B: Mixed Formats 50
Chapter 2 Tests Form A: Mixed Formats 53
       Form B: Mixed Formats 56
Chapter 3 Tests Form A: Mixed Formats 59
       Form B: Mixed Formats 62
Chapters 1–3 Cumulative Test 65
Chapter 4 Tests Form A: Mixed Formats 69
       Form B: Mixed Formats 72
Chapter 5 Tests Form A: Mixed Formats 75
       Form B: Mixed Formats 78
Chapter 6 Tests Form A: Mixed Formats 81
       Form B: Mixed Formats 84
Chapters 1–6 Cumulative Test 87
Chapter 7 Tests Form A: Mixed Formats 91
       Form B: Mixed Formats 94
Chapter 8 Tests Form A: Mixed Formats 97
       Form B: Mixed Formats 100
Chapter 9 Tests Form A: Mixed Formats 103
       Form B: Mixed Formats 106
Chapters 1–9 Cumulative Test 109
Chapter 10 Tests Form A: Mixed Formats 113
       Form B: Mixed Formats 116
Chapter 11 Tests Form A: Mixed Formats 119
       Form B: Mixed Formats 122
Chapter 12 Tests Form A: Mixed Formats 125
       Form B: Mixed Formats 128
Chapters 1–12 Cumulative Test 131

Table of Contents

Answers

Basic-Facts Timed Tests 135
Diagnosing Readiness for Grade 6 138
Chapter 1 Tests Form A and Form B: Mixed Formats 139–140
Chapter 2 Tests Form A and Form B: Mixed Formats 140–141
Chapter 3 Tests Form A and Form B: Mixed Formats 142–143
Chapters 1–3 Cumulative Test 143–144
Chapter 4 Tests Form A and Form B: Mixed Formats 144–145
Chapter 5 Tests Form A and Form B: Mixed Formats 146–147
Chapter 6 Tests Form A and Form B: Mixed Formats 147–148
Chapters 1–6 Cumulative Test 149
Chapter 7 Tests Form A and Form B: Mixed Formats 150–151
Chapter 8 Tests Form A and Form B: Mixed Formats 151–152
Chapter 9 Tests Form A and Form B: Mixed Formats 153–154
Chapters 1–9 Cumulative Test 154–155
Chapter 10 Tests Form A and Form B: Mixed Formats 155–156
Chapter 11 Tests Form A and Form B: Mixed Formats 157–158
Chapter 12 Tests Form A and Form B: Mixed Formats 158–159
Chapters 1–12 Cumulative Test 160

Additional Answers A1

Overview of the Assessment Sourcebook

Assessment and instruction are interwoven strands in the fabric of mathematics education. The primary purpose of assessment is to promote learning, so assessment may be referred to as the glue that holds curriculum and instruction together. As a result, the various instructional methods used in Scott Foresman–Addison Wesley Mathematics are supported by different assessment methods. This overview is a brief introduction to the kinds of assessment available in this Assessment Sourcebook, including both formal and informal types of assessment.

Formal Written Tests

A variety of formal written tests are provided to assess students' mastery of important mathematics concepts and skills.

Materials Provided
Blackline masters (starting on page 1)

- **Diagnosing Readiness** to assess students' understanding of mathematical concepts developed in the previous grade level.

- **Chapter Tests** for use with all individual chapters in the student text. These tests are called Mixed Formats because they contain free-response, multiple-choice, and writing in math questions. There are two forms for each chapter, Form A and Form B.

- **Cumulative Tests** provided for use after Chapters 3, 6, 9, and 12.

- **A bubble-form Answer Sheet** to allow students to practice answering test questions on a separate response sheet.

Journal Writing

Journal Writing encourages students to use mathematical language as they reflect on what they are learning. It also provides an opportunity for you, the teacher, to gain insight as to how students approach problem-solving.

Materials Provided
(Starting on page viii)
- Tips for assessing and responding to journal entries
- Ideas for Journal Prompts

Portfolio Assessment

Portfolio Assessment provides a way of demonstrating a student's growth and progress over time. A portfolio should include many types of assessment.

Materials Provided
(starting on page xiii)
- Tips and ideas for compiling and managing mathematics portfolios
- Inside My Mathematics Portfolio (blackline master) serves as a table of contents for the portfolios
- A Mathematics Portfolio Assessment Sheet (blackline master) to record how student portfolios demonstrate growth in various areas

Performance Assessment

Performance tests give a way to assess students qualities of imagination, creativity, and perseverance. By using performance assessment, you can evaluate how students

- reason through problems,
- make and test conjectures,
- use number sense to predict reasonable answers, and
- utilize alternative strategies.

Materials Provided
(starting on page xviii)
- Performance Assessment tasks to be used after each chapter
- Notes that identify the mathematical concepts and skills needed
- A four point Scoring Rubric

Basic-Facts Timed Tests

Basic-Facts Timed Tests provide students the opportunity to review and practice basic facts.

Materials Provided
(starting on page 25)
- Tips for administering the tests
- Tips on adjusting time limits
- Additional materials
- Basic-Facts Timed Tests to be used before each chapter

Journal Writing

In a mathematics journal, students have the opportunity to explore their thoughts about a particular mathematics topic, to construct and crystallize their understanding of mathematical concepts and procedures, and to explain their ideas about mathematics. As a result, mathematics journals can provide an enormous amount of information about student thinking and are a valuable component of a comprehensive assessment program.

The Purpose of Journal Writing

Journals can be used to reflect, summarize, or generalize about mathematics lessons. They can also be used as a vehicle to apply mathematical concepts or skills. Some other reasons to incorporate journal writing into your mathematics assessment program include

- improving students' skills in communicating their mathematical thinking,
- encouraging application and transfer of previous knowledge to new situations,
- helping students improve creative writing skills,
- helping students explore their thoughts about mathematics,
- providing you with information about students' prior knowledge and what they do or do not understand,
- building and deepening student understanding of mathematical concepts, and
- helping students review and restate just-learned information.

Opportunities for Journal Writing

Journal writing can be incorporated as a natural extension of daily lessons. A few of the opportunities provided throughout the program are listed below.

- Have students respond in their journals to the *Writing in Math* questions presented in most lessons.

- Have students keep a list of new vocabulary that appears in each lesson. Suggest that they include a definition or an example.

- After Problem Solving lessons, suggest that students write about ways in which the skills and strategies they are learning apply to their everyday lives.

Getting Started with Journal Writing

- Discuss the purpose of each mathematics journal entry and the audience for which it is intended. Students should know before beginning an assignment whether or not their entries will be shared with peers.

- Have students begin each assignment with a 3–5 minutes brainstorming session. Then have students free-write about the assignment. During this time, students should jot down ideas, impressions, computations, drawings, or problems they are having with the assignment.

- Allow limited-English-speaking students to first write in the language in which they feel most comfortable. If students are fluent in two languages, encourage them to write in English.

- Include opportunities for students to express their thoughts about assignments in writing.

Assessing Journal Writing and Providing Feedback

When reading student journals, it's important to provide constructive feedback. You may choose to write comments and suggestions right in the journal or on removable note-pad paper. Include questions you have about the entry, and ideas you have about other topics the student might consider. Encourage the student to reply in his or her next entry.

If journal entries are destined for inclusion in the display portfolio, you might wish to have a formal revision stage in the journal writing process in which students revise their entries.

Ideas for Journal Prompts

Periodically during the school year give students a journal prompt and encourage them to write about the subject provided. This activity will provide opportunities for students to communicate their mathematical thinking as well as reinforce their writing skills. Some suggested journal prompts include:

- Today in math I learned…
- My math goals for this year are…
- The math I learned today can be used to…
- You should go back and check your math work because…
- When I need help with my math homework, I…
- My favorite math lesson is…
- I can use a number line to…
- If I had a hundred (thousand, million) dollars, I would…
- All squares are rectangles but not all rectangles are squares because…
- If I were one centimeter tall, I would…
- It is important to read data from a graph because…
- It is important to figure some math problems in your head because…
- Subtraction is the opposite of addition because…
- To find the mean (average) of five numbers, I would…
- It is faster to count to 100 by 10s rather than by 5s because…
- Using coupons at a grocery store can save on the family budget because…
- Since I know that 36 divided by 9 is 4, I can find the quotient of 3,600 divided by 900 by…
- $\frac{1}{2}$ is greater than $\frac{1}{4}$ because…
- When I think about all the possible numbers between 3 and 4, I know that there are…

Name _____

Date _____

Student Self-Assessment

Assignment _____

Write about what you did.

What were you trying to learn? _____
_____
_____

How did you start your work? _____
_____
_____

What materials did you need? _____

What did you learn? _____
_____
_____

Check the sentences that describe your work.

_____ I made a plan before I began my work.

_____ I was able to do the work.

_____ I did not understand the directions.

_____ I followed the directions but got the wrong answer.

_____ I found a different way to do this assignment.

_____ I could explain how to do this to someone else.

_____ The work was easier than I thought it would be.

_____ The work was harder than I thought it would be.

_____ Other: _____

Name_____

Date_____

My Math Experiences

Math that interests me: _____
_____
_____
_____
_____

My math goals: _____
_____
_____
_____
_____

Math skills I just learned and can do: _____
_____
_____
_____
_____

Math skills I need to work on: _____
_____
_____
_____
_____

Math awards I have received: _____
_____

Portfolio Assessment

What is a Portfolio?
A portfolio is a carefully chosen collection of a student's work that exhibits the student's efforts, achievements, and thinking. A portfolio can include many different types of assessment, including formal and informal assessments. Unlike a test, which gives a picture of a student's achievements at one certain point, a portfolio provides evidence of progress over time. Some pieces of work might remain in the portfolio for the entire school year, if you are going to chart progress over time.

Portfolios should only be used for assessment when
- an assessment purpose is defined,
- a method of determining what is to be put into the portfolio, by whom, and when, is detailed, and
- criteria for assessing individual pieces or the collection as a whole are identified.

The Purposes of Portfolio Assessment
Before making a portfolio, have a clear idea of how you want to use it for assessment. For example, a portfolio may be used

- to help you assess student understanding and progress,
- to help your students monitor their own progress, or
- to aid in teacher-student and teacher-parent conferences.

In addition to these basic purposes, the portfolio can also
- give you insight into your students' views of themselves through the specific pieces they choose to include,
- encourage your students to join with you in assessing their work, and
- provide a tool for evaluating your instruction and the mathematics curriculum.

Getting Started Using Portfolio Assessment

Help students understand what a portfolio is and what they will do to build their own portfolios. You may want to discuss with students the differences between types of portfolios. A *working* portfolio contains ALL the student's work for a particular chapter, group of chapters, and other work that is done which relates to the mathematics that the students are learning. An *assessment* or *display* portfolio is a selection of work that is chosen by the student, the teacher, and by teacher and student agreeing together. Parents can also participate in their child's *assessment* or *display* portfolio by choosing a few pieces of work to be included.

- Have students begin by compiling a working portfolio that holds *all* their work for a particular chapter, group of chapters, and other math-related work. Set aside time each week or at the end of a chapter for students to review their working portfolios in order to select pieces they wish to include in a display portfolio of finished products.

- Have students help set the standards for selection of pieces for the display portfolio. Some should be chosen by the teacher, some by the student, and some by mutual agreement. Talk about choosing quality over quantity. You may also invite parents to choose two or three of their child's pieces of work to include.

- Make sure students consider many kinds of work to include, such as artwork, graphics, audio- and videotapes, project results, journal writings, and self-assessments.

- Identify those items which you will require to be in each student's assessment portfolio, such as Chapter Tests and Performance Assessments.

Organizing Pieces for the Display Portfolio

- **Inside my Mathematics Portfolio** (blackline master) provides students a place to list, date, and explain the inclusion of each piece.

- Be sure that each piece in the portfolio is dated. The portfolio then becomes an ongoing record of student progress.

Assessing Portfolios

Decide when you want to assess students' display portfolios. Logical checkpoints might be quarterly, after chapters 3, 6, 9, and 12. Below are some possible criteria to use for assessing math portfolios. The **Mathematics Portfolio Assessment Sheet** (blackline master) helps you summarize how each student's portfolio demonstrates growth in these areas.

Growth Area	Definitions
Reasoning and Problem Solving	Includes interpreting and analyzing problems, choosing successful problem-solving strategies, and using higher-order thinking skills (interpretation, analysis, justification)
Communication	Includes explaining ideas clearly, using mathematical terms and symbols correctly, and organizing mathematical information effectively (models, diagrams, graphs)
Applying Concepts and Procedures	Includes selecting appropriate concepts, procedures, and materials to solve problems, and applying the concepts and procedures correctly

It is helpful to meet with students as you assess their portfolios. Have some leading statements prepared, such as:

Show me something you are proud of and explain why.
Show me something you revised.
Show me something you enjoyed doing and tell why.

Let students know if you plan to use the display portfolios during conferences with family members, other teachers, or school administrators.

Name_____

Inside My Math Portfolio

My work · Why I Kept It

1. _____ · _____

2. _____ · _____

3. _____ · _____

4. _____ · _____

5. _____ · _____

6. _____ · _____

7. _____ · _____

8. _____ · _____

9. _____ · _____

10. _____ · _____

Name_____

Date_____

Mathematics Portfolio Assessment Sheet

Growth Area	How Portfolio Demonstrates Growth
Reasoning and Problem Solving	_____
Communication	_____
Applying Concepts and Procedures	_____
Summary	_____
Additional Comments	_____

Performance Assessment

Performance assessment allows you to assess how well students apply their mathematical knowledge and skills in different contexts and realistic situations.

Performance Assessment Opportunities Provided in Scott Foresman–Addison Wesley Mathematics
- Many of these tests provide information about a realistic situation and ask students to use new information along with their mathematics power to solve problems. Most of the problems are open-ended problems, with an emphasis on finding meaningful solutions rather than calculating only one correct response.

Administering a Performance Assessment Task
Managing performance assessment projects may be more difficult than managing other types of assessment. The following tips may help you with classroom management during performance assessment administration.

- Consider having students work in groups to complete a performance assessment.
- Move among students as they work to collect anecdotal information during the test. Ask questions that will give you information about thought processes.
- Spend time at the beginning of the test to be sure all students understand the purpose.
- Review the Scoring Rubric. These rubrics, customized to each performance task, provide one way of qualifying your assessment of student results. You may wish to distribute this rubric to each student before beginning the assessment task. In this way, they will understand how they will be assessed on their performance.

During the Performance Assessment
- Consider using the **Observation Checklist Group Skills** on page xix as you observe students working on the task.

Assessing Performance
- Answers to the activities and questions included in the task are provided on the Scoring Rubric page.
- Use the Scoring Rubric to evaluate student performance.

Observation Checklist **Group Skills**

Student	Encourages and Listens to Others	Participates in Discussion	Communicates Clearly	Shares Tasks	Takes Initiative	Shares Responsibility/ Accountability	Cooperates with Others
_____	☐	☐	☐	☐	☐	☐	☐
_____	☐	☐	☐	☐	☐	☐	☐
_____	☐	☐	☐	☐	☐	☐	☐
_____	☐	☐	☐	☐	☐	☐	☐
_____	☐	☐	☐	☐	☐	☐	☐
_____	☐	☐	☐	☐	☐	☐	☐
_____	☐	☐	☐	☐	☐	☐	☐
_____	☐	☐	☐	☐	☐	☐	☐
_____	☐	☐	☐	☐	☐	☐	☐
_____	☐	☐	☐	☐	☐	☐	☐
_____	☐	☐	☐	☐	☐	☐	☐
_____	☐	☐	☐	☐	☐	☐	☐
_____	☐	☐	☐	☐	☐	☐	☐
_____	☐	☐	☐	☐	☐	☐	☐
_____	☐	☐	☐	☐	☐	☐	☐
_____	☐	☐	☐	☐	☐	☐	☐
_____	☐	☐	☐	☐	☐	☐	☐
_____	☐	☐	☐	☐	☐	☐	☐
_____	☐	☐	☐	☐	☐	☐	☐
_____	☐	☐	☐	☐	☐	☐	☐
_____	☐	☐	☐	☐	☐	☐	☐
_____	☐	☐	☐	☐	☐	☐	☐
_____	☐	☐	☐	☐	☐	☐	☐
_____	☐	☐	☐	☐	☐	☐	☐

Name _____

Chapter 1 Performance Assessment

You are working at a local store for the summer. Before the start of school, the store ordered the new school supplies shown on the invoice below. The invoice is incomplete. Your boss asks for your help in figuring out the cost of each backpack.

Wholesale Company
2525 Main Street
Hometown, USA 00252

Invoice #	Invoice Date
01012	07/15/04

Bill To: On the Corner

Item Description	Unit Cost	Quantity	
Notebooks	$3	20	
Binders	$2	20	
Backpacks		12	
		Total Due Please pay this amount →	$244.00

1. What is the total cost of the notebooks and binders together? Which property of operations can you use to find the total using mental math? Explain.

   _____

   _____

2. Using a variable, write an expression representing the total cost of 12 backpacks. What does the variable stand for?

   _____

3. Find the total cost of 12 backpacks. Explain what you did.

   _____

   _____

4. Write an equation by putting your expression from Exercise 2 equal to the total cost of the 12 backpacks. Solve the equation. Which property of equality enabled you to find the cost of each backpack?

   _____

   _____

Chapter 1 Performance Assessment

Teacher Notes

Skills and Concepts This activity requires students to:
- use the Distributive Property.
- write an algebraic expression.
- add, subtract, multiply, and divide whole numbers.
- use the Division Property of Equality.

Guiding the Activity
- Tell students to approach the problem in the steps that are outlined in the exercises.

Answers
1. $20 \times 2 + 20 \times 3 = \$100$; Use the Distributive Property to simplify the calculation: $20(2 + 3) = 20 \times 5 = \$100$.
2. $12x$; x stands for the cost of each backpack. (The variable symbol may be different.)
3. $\$244 - \$100 = \$144$; Subtract the cost of binders and notebooks from the total cost on the invoice to get the cost of 12 backpacks.
4. $12x = 144$; $x = \$12$; Each backpack costs $12. I used the Division Property of Equality and divided both sides of the equation by 12.

Scoring Rubric

4	**Full Achievement** The student wrote the expression, solved the equation, and completed calculations without error. The student demonstrated a thorough understanding of the properties of equality and the Distributive Property. Explanations were well written.
3	**Substantial Achievement** The student wrote the expression, solved the equation, and completed calculations with minor errors. The student demonstrated an understanding of the properties of equality and the Distributive Property. Explanations were basically well written.
2	**Partial Achievement** The student wrote the expression, solved the equation, and completed calculations with errors. The student demonstrated a limited understanding of the properties of equality and the Distributive Property. Explanations were fairly complete, but not well written.
1	**Little Achievement** The student wrote the expression, solved the equation, and completed calculations with numerous errors. The student demonstrated little or no understanding of the properties of equality and the Distributive Property. Explanations were missing or unclear.
0	**No Achievement** The student provided a completely incorrect response, one that was not interpretable, or no response at all.

Chapter 2 Performance Assessment

You are put in charge of planning a class party for 30 students. Use the following information.

> A large, 2 topping pizza costs $12 and can feed 5 students.
>
> Tacos cost $1.24 each. One student can eat at least 2 tacos.
>
> Soda costs $0.75 each and juice costs $0.60 each.
>
> Entertainment: The band charges $50 and the magician charges $25.

1. What food and drink will you serve? How much do you need to spend for food and drinks? Explain how you decided what it cost.

2. If each student pays $4.25, how much money will be left for entertainment? Explain how you could write and solve an equation to decide. Can you afford the magician? The band?

3. Write and solve an equation to find how much each student needs to pay to cover the cost of the food, the drinks, and the band. How much will you charge per student? Why?

Chapter 2 Performance Assessment

Teacher Notes

Skills and Concepts This activity requires students to:

- add and subtract decimals.
- multiply and divide decimals.
- write and solve equations.
- interpret remainders.

Guiding the Activity

- Although students may be able to solve the problems without using equations, make sure they understand that writing and solving equations are important parts of the activity.

Answers

Sample answers are given for serving pizza and soda.

1. A large pizza feeds 5 people and costs $12, so the pizza cost per student is 12 ÷ 5 = $2.40. Each soda costs $0.75. The total per student for pizza and soda is $2.40 + $0.75 = $3.15. The total for 30 students is 30 × $3.15 = $94.50.
2. If each student pays $4.25, the total income would be 30 × $4.25 = $127.50. Let c be the cost of entertainment. Then, 94.50 + c = 127.50, and c = 33. There would be $33 for entertainment, enough for the magician, but not the band.
3. The total for pizza, soda, and the band is $94.50 + $50.00 = $144.50. Let a be the amount each student pays. Then, $30a$ = 144.50, and $a \cong 4.82$. Each student needs to pay at least $4.82. The planner would probably charge $5 per student, which would be easy to collect. This would give a little extra money for extra drinks.

Scoring Rubric

Level	Standard to be achieved for performance at specified level
4	**Full Achievement** The student wrote and solved all equations and performed all decimal operations without errors. The student demonstrated full understanding of interpreting remainders. Explanations were thorough and well written.
3	**Substantial Achievement** The student wrote and solved all equations and performed all decimal operations with minor errors. The student demonstrated understanding of interpreting remainders. Explanations were basically well written.
2	**Partial Achievement** The student wrote and solved all equations and performed all decimal operations with errors. The student demonstrated limited understanding of interpreting remainders. Explanations were not well written.
1	**Little Achievement** The student wrote and solved all equations and performed all decimal operations with numerous errors. The student demonstrated little or no understanding of interpreting remainders. Explanations were missing or incomplete.
0	**No Achievement** The student provided a completely incorrect response, one that was not interpretable, or no response at all.

Name _____

Chapter 3 Performance Assessment

Maggie works at Cory's Dog Hotel. Cory's has 20 kennels. Each group kennel can hold a maximum of 4 small dogs or 3 large dogs. Any group kennel can be partitioned into 2 individual kennels, which hold only one dog each. For example, there could be 14 group kennels, with the remaining 6 kennels partitioned to make 12 individual kennels.

This week Cory's Dog Hotel has 15 large dogs and 35 small dogs. Maggie's boss wants each group kennel for small dogs to have the same number of dogs and each group kennel for large dogs to have the same number of dogs. The group kennels for small dogs do not have to have the same number of dogs as the group kennels for large dogs. Maggie must decide how many kennels to partition and how many dogs will go into each group kennel. She must use all 20 kennels.

1. How can Maggie group the dogs? How many kennels should she partition? Complete the following table.

	Group Kennels	Dogs in Each	Total Dogs in Group Kennels	Individual Kennels	Total Dogs
Large Dogs					15
Small Dogs					35
Total Kennels					

2. Complete the following table to show the part of the large dogs in group and individual kennels and the part of the small dogs in each. Round to the nearest hundredth when necessary.

	Part in Group Kennels		Part in Individual Kennels	
	Fraction	Decimal	Fraction	Decimal
Large Dogs	☐/15		☐/15	
Small Dogs	☐/35		☐/35	

3. If owners prefer their dogs in individual kennels, is Maggie's arrangement fair to both large and small dogs? Refer to the decimals in Exercise 2. Explain.

_____

_____

Chapter 3 Performance Assessment **5**

Chapter 3 Performance Assessment

Teacher Notes

Skills and Concepts This activity requires students to:

- use factors, multiples, and divisibility rules.
- find fractions of a set.
- write fractions as decimals.
- compare decimals.

Guiding the Activity

- Encourage students to try, check, and revise to decide how to group the dogs, using the diagram given. If students have difficulty, let them use counters.
- Make sure students understand that the number of group kennels plus half the number of individual kennels must equal 20.

Answers

Answers will vary. Sample answers are given.

1. Maggie could make 10 group kennels and partition 10 kennels to make 20 individual kennels. She could group the dogs as shown in the table.

	Group Kennels	Dogs in Each	Total Dogs in Group Kennels	Individual Kennels	Total Dogs
Large Dogs	1	3	3	12	15
Small Dogs	9	3	27	8	35
Total Kennels	10			20	

2.

	Part in Group Kennels		Part in Individual Kennels	
	Fraction	Decimal	Fraction	Decimal
Large Dogs	$\frac{3}{15}$	0.2	$\frac{12}{15}$	0.8
Small Dogs	$\frac{27}{35}$	0.77	$\frac{8}{35}$	0.23

3. A greater part of the small dogs are in group kennels than in individual kennels (0.77 > 0.23). So, the grouping is not fair to small dogs.

Scoring Rubric

Level	Standard to be achieved for performance at specified level
4	**Full Achievement** The student correctly grouped the dogs to meet all conditions, wrote fractions and decimals, and compared numbers. The student demonstrated a thorough understanding of factors, multiples, and divisibility in order to group the dogs. Explanations were thorough and well written.
3	**Substantial** The student grouped the dogs to meet all conditions, wrote fractions and decimals, and compared numbers with only minor errors. The student demonstrated understanding of factors, multiples, and divisibility in order to group the dogs. Explanations were basically well written.
2	**Partial Achievement** The student wrote fractions and decimals and compared numbers with errors. The student needed help grouping the dogs and demonstrated a limited understanding of factors, multiples, and divisibility. Explanations were not well written.
1	**Little Achievement** The student wrote fractions and decimals and compared numbers with numerous errors. The student needed help grouping the dogs and demonstrated little or no understanding of factors, multiples, and divisibility. Explanations were missing or incomplete.
0	**No Achievement** The student provided a completely incorrect response, one that was not interpretable, or no response at all.

Name _____

Chapter 4 Performance Assessment

Kabir is taking the train from New York City (NYC) to Atlanta. The train will make several stops on the way. Kabir changes trains only once, in Washington, D.C. The table gives the trip times between the different cities. The train spends $\frac{1}{4}$ hour at each stop.

Departure City	Arrival City	Trip Time
New York City	Philadelphia	$2\frac{1}{3}$ hr
Philadelphia	Baltimore	$1\frac{3}{4}$ hr
Baltimore	Washington, D.C.	$\frac{5}{6}$ hr
Washington, D.C.	Charlottesville	$2\frac{1}{4}$ hr
Charlottesville	Atlanta	$11\frac{1}{2}$ hr

1. About how long is the trip from New York City to Washington, D.C.? Explain how you estimated.

   _____

2. Kabir's train leaves New York City, Friday at 2:30 P.M. His train from Washington, D.C. to Atlanta leaves at 8:15 P.M. Is an estimate enough to decide whether or not Kabir can make his connection? Explain why or why not.

   _____

3. If there are no delays in the train schedule, can Kabir make his connection? Explain how you decided.

   _____

4. How much time does Kabir have to make his connection in Washington? Give your answer both as a fraction and in minutes.

   _____

5. What time should Kabir arrive in Atlanta? Explain how you found your answer.

   _____

6. What computation method did you use in Exercise 4? In Exercise 5? Explain why you chose the one you did.

   _____

Chapter 4 Performance Assessment **7**

Chapter 4 Performance Assessment

Teacher Notes

Concepts and Skills This activity requires students to:
- add and subtract mixed numbers.
- estimate with mixed numbers.
- decide whether an estimate or an exact answer is needed.
- choose a computation method.

Materials
- map (optional)

Guiding the Activity
- Draw a line or use a map to help students visualize the time it takes between the different cities.

Answers

1. About 6 hours; The train stops for $\frac{1}{4}$ hour in Philadelphia and $\frac{1}{4}$ hour in Baltimore, or $\frac{1}{2}$ hour in all. So the total trip is $\frac{1}{2} + 2\frac{1}{3} + 1\frac{3}{4} + \frac{5}{6}$ hours. $\frac{1}{2} + 2\frac{1}{3}$ is about 3. Add $3 + 2 + 1 = 6$ hr.

2. 2:30 P.M. to 8:15 P.M. is $5\frac{3}{4}$ hours. Since $5\frac{3}{4}$ is close to 6, an estimate is not enough.

3. $\frac{1}{2} + 2\frac{1}{3} + 1\frac{3}{4} + \frac{5}{6} = 5\frac{5}{12}$ hr. Since $5\frac{5}{12} < 5\frac{3}{4}$, Kabir can make his connection.

4. $5\frac{3}{4} - 5\frac{5}{12} = \frac{1}{3}$ hr; 20 min.

5. 10:15 A.M. Saturday; $2\frac{1}{4} + \frac{1}{4} + 11\frac{1}{2} = 14$ hr; 14 hr after 8:15 P.M. Friday is 10:15 A.M. Saturday.

6. Sample answer: Paper and pencil; To subtract $5\frac{3}{4} - 5\frac{5}{12}$, it is easy to find the common denominator; Mental math; $2\frac{1}{4} + \frac{1}{4} + 11\frac{1}{2}$ is easy to do with mental math because $2\frac{1}{4} + \frac{1}{4} = 2\frac{1}{2}$, and $2\frac{1}{2} + 11\frac{1}{2} = 14$.

Scoring Rubric

Level	Standard to be achieved for performance at specified level
4	**Full Achievement** The student added and subtracted mixed numbers and estimated mixed number sums, without error. The student showed a thorough understanding when deciding whether an estimate is enough and choosing a computation method. Explanations were well written.
3	**Substantial Achievement** The student added and subtracted mixed numbers and estimated mixed number sums, with only minor errors. The student showed understanding when deciding whether an estimate is enough and choosing a computation method. Explanations were basically well written.
2	**Partial Achievement** The student made errors adding and subtracting mixed numbers and estimating mixed number sums. The student showed limited understanding when deciding whether an estimate is enough and choosing a computation method. Explanations were given, but were not well written.
1	**Little Achievement** The student made numerous errors adding and subtracting mixed numbers and estimating mixed number sums. The student showed little or no understanding when deciding whether an estimate is enough and choosing a computation method. Explanations were missing or unclear.
0	**No Achievement** The student provided a completely incorrect response, one that was not interpretable, or no response at all.

Chapter 5 Performance Assessment

For a science project Nadia built a balance scale with a yardstick. She found that the following is true.

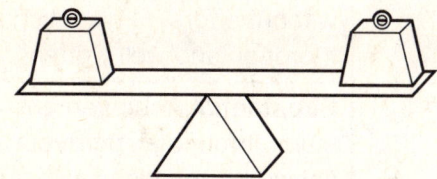

Distance from × Weight = Distance from × Weight
the wedge to   on the left   the wedge to   on the right
the weight   the weight
on the left   on the right

1. Solve the equation $\frac{3}{4} \times 1\frac{1}{2} = 2\frac{1}{4}w$ to find the weight Nadia needs to use to make the scale below balance. _____

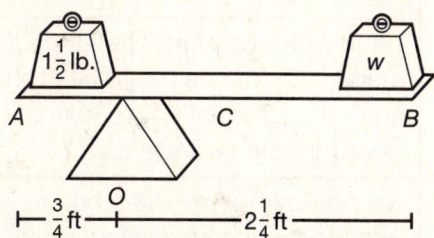

2. Solve the equation $d + \frac{3}{4} = 2\frac{1}{4}$ to find how much farther the weight on the right is from the wedge than the weight on the left is from the wedge. _____

3. Suppose Nadia wants to place a weight at a new location, C, on the right side of the balance scale above. Point C is halfway between O and B. What weight, x, should Nadia put at C to balance the scale? Explain how you decided.

_____

4. With different weights and distances from the wedge, Nadia made four observations. Complete Nadia's table.

Observations	Left		Right	
	Distance	Weight	Distance	Weight
A	$1\frac{3}{4}$ ft	$\frac{2}{3}$ lb	$1\frac{1}{4}$ ft	
B	$2\frac{1}{2}$ ft	$\frac{3}{10}$ lb		$1\frac{1}{2}$ lb
C	$1\frac{1}{2}$ ft		$1\frac{1}{2}$ ft	$\frac{7}{8}$ lb
D		$\frac{4}{5}$ lb	$1\frac{1}{8}$ ft	$1\frac{1}{3}$ lb

Chapter 5 Performance Assessment **9**

Chapter 5 Performance Assessment

Teacher Notes

Concepts and Skills This activity requires students to:
- multiply with fractions and mixed numbers.
- solve equations.
- explain how to find a missing weight with and without calculations.
- explain how to use use proportional reasoning.

Guiding the Activity
- Using the example of a seesaw, help students develop an intuitive understanding of the principle of balance.

Answers
1. $w = \frac{1}{2}$ lb
2. $d = 1\frac{1}{2}$ ft
3. 1 lb; $\frac{1}{2}$ of $2\frac{1}{4}$ is $\frac{9}{8}$; $\frac{3}{4} \times 1\frac{1}{2} = \frac{9}{8}w$, so $w = 1$
4. $\frac{14}{15}$ lb; $\frac{1}{2}$ ft; $\frac{7}{8}$ lb; $1\frac{7}{8}$ ft

Scoring Rubric

4	**Full Achievement** The student found all products and solved all equations without errors. Explanations were thorough and well written.
3	**Substantial Achievement** The student found all products and solved all equations with only minor errors. Explanations were basically well written.
2	**Partial Achievement** The student made errors multiplying and solving equations. Explanations were not well written.
1	**Little Achievement** The student made numerous errors multiplying and solving equations. Explanations were missing or unclear.
0	**No Achievement** The student provided a completely incorrect response, one that was not interpretable, or no response at all.

Name _____

Chapter 6 Performance Assessment

George is planning to publish a cookbook. At the design stage, he needs to decide the total number of pages for the book, including the number of pages with pictures.

George consults with the author, and together they decide to include 150 recipes, one on each page. They also decide to divide the book in three sections: vegetarian dishes, meat dishes, and desserts.

1. After looking at other cookbooks, George decides that 1 out of 6 recipes should be for a dessert. What do you think the ratio of vegetarian recipes to all recipes and the ratio of meat recipes to all recipes should be? Complete the table.

Recipe Type	Vegetarian	Meat	Dessert
Ratio to Total Recipes			1:6
Number of Recipes			

2. After considering the cost of including photos, George decides to include 5 pages with photos for every 15 pages. Write a proportion to find how many photos will be in the cookbook.

_____

3. The printer gives George the cost for printing 5,000, 8,000, and 12,000 copies. George estimates the marketing cost to be $12,000 and the author/photo fee together to be $35,000. Use the printing cost from the table to find the total cost to produce 5,000, 8,000, or 12,000 books. Then explain how to find the cost per book.

	Plan A	Plan B	Plan C
Print Run	5,000	8,000	12,000
Printing Cost	$27,000	$32,040	$37,480

_____

4. George decides to sell the cookbook for $18. For Plan A, he uses the formula $P = 18s - 74{,}000$ to find the total profit, where s is the number of copies sold. How much profit will George make after selling 4,500 copies?

Chapter 6 Performance Assessment

Teacher Notes

Concepts and Skills This activity requires students to:
- write ratios.
- write and solve proportions.
- find unit rates.
- use a formula.

Guiding the Activity
- Tell student to make sure that the sum of the ratios of all the recipes in the table equals 1. Encourage them to use simple ratios.

Answers

1. Sample answer:

Recipe Type	Vegetarian	Meat	Dessert
Ratio to Total Recipes	1:2	1:3	1:6
Number of Recipes	75	50	25

2. $\frac{5}{15} = \frac{x}{150}$; $x = 50$ pages.

3. To find the cost per book, add the printing cost, marketing cost, and author/photo fee. For Plan A, it equals $27,000 + $12,000 + $35,000, or $74,000. Then divide by the number of copies (74,000 ÷ 5,000) to find the cost per copy, $14.80. For Plan B, the total cost is $79,040, so the cost per copy equals $9.88. For Plan C, the total cost is $84,480, so the cost per copy is $7.04.

4. $P = \$7,000$.

Scoring Rubric

Level	Standard to be achieved for performance at specified level
4	**Full Achievement** The student wrote ratios, wrote and solved proportions, found unit rates, and used a formula without error. Explanations were thorough and well written.
3	**Substantial Achievement** The student wrote ratios, wrote and solved proportions, found unit rates, and used a formula with minor errors. Explanations were well written, but not complete.
2	**Partial Achievement** The student made errors writing ratios, writing and solving proportions, finding unit rates, and using a formula. Explanations were basically well written but not complete.
1	**Little Achievement** The student made numerous errors writing ratios, writing and solving proportions, finding unit rates, and using a formula. Explanations were missing or incomplete.
0	**No Achievement** The student provided a completely incorrect response, one that was not interpretable, or no response at all.

Chapter 7 Performance Assessment

Larry borrowed $20,000 from a bank to open a gift shop. The bank charged him simple interest at a rate that depends on the repayment period, as shown in the table below.

1. Complete the table to find the total interest Larry must pay with each option. Then divide the sum of the amount borrowed ($20,000) and the total interest by the total number of months of the loan to find the monthly payment for each option. Round to the nearest dollar.

Annual Interest Rate	Repayment Period	Total Interest	Monthly Payment
7.5%	1 year		
8.2%	2 years		
9%	3 years		

2. The overhead cost to run the shop is $6,000 a month. This amount includes expenses like salaries, rent, and utilities, but not the loan payment. Find Larry's total monthly expenses for each loan option by adding the loan payment to $6,000. Write the sums in the table.

Repayment Period	Avg. Monthly Sales First Year	Total Monthly Expenses	Avg. Monthly Profit	Percent Profit
1 year	$8,500			
2 years	$8,500			
3 years	$8,500			

3. Larry expects to average $8,500 in sales per month the first year. Find Larry's average monthly profit for each loan option by subtracting his average monthly sales minus his total monthly expenses. Then find what percent of his sales is profit for each option. Write your results in the table above. Round to the nearest percent.

4. Which repayment plan should Larry use? Explain your choice.

Chapter 7 Performance Assessment

Teacher Notes

Concepts and Skills This activity requires students to:

- find percent of a number.
- find simple interest.
- find what percent one number is of another.
- write to explain.

Guiding the Activity

- To decide a suitable repayment plan, ask students to consider the total repayment amount and what is an acceptable percent of profit.
- Discuss terms like overhead, expenses, and profit.
- Ask students how many monthly payments there are in a 3-year loan.

Answers

1.

Annual Interest Rate	Repayment Period	Total Interest	Monthly Payment
7.25%	1 year	$1,500	$1,792
8.2%	2 years	$3,280	$970
9%	3 years	$5,400	$706

2.

Repayment Period	Avg. Monthly Sales First Year	Total Monthly Expenses	Avg. Monthly Profit	Percent Profit
1 year	$8,500	$7,792	$708	8%
2 years	$8,500	$6,970	$1,530	18%
3 years	$8,500	$6,706	$1,794	21%

3. See the table above.

4. Sample answer: If Larry repays the loan in 1 year, then the monthly profit in the first year will average only 8% which is very low. If Larry repays the loan in 3 years, he will pay the most interest. So, Larry should repay the loan in 2 years.

Scoring Rubric

Level	Standard to be achieved for performance at specified level
4	**Full Achievement** The student found percent of a number, simple interest, and what percent one number is of another, without error. Explanations were thorough and well written.
3	**Substantial Achievement** The student found percent of a number, simple interest, and what percent one number is of another, with only minor errors. Explanations were well written, but could have been more thorough.
2	**Partial Achievement** The student made a number of errors finding percent of a number, simple interest, and what percent one number is of another. Explanations were basically well written, but not complete.
1	**Little Achievement** The student made numerous errors finding percent of a number, simple interest, and what percent one number is of another. Explanations were missing or incomplete.
0	**No Achievement** The student provided a completely incorrect response, one that was not interpretable, or no response at all.

Name _____

Chapter 8 Performance Assessment

Andrea's Optics specializes in selling binoculars, microscopes, and telescopes. Every quarter of a year, Andrea buys new inventory. The sales in the first three quarters of the year are shown in the table.

Units Sold

Product	Quarter 1	Quarter 2	Quarter 3
Binoculars	73	63	80
Microscopes	8	16	24
Telescopes	5	6	7

1. The number of microscopes sold, m, in quarter, q, is a function. Use the information in the table above to write a rule and an equation to describe the function.

2. Use the equation you wrote in Exercise 1 to predict the number of microscopes that will be sold in the fourth quarter, by finding m when $q = 4$. Write your prediction in the table below.

3. Repeat Exercises 1 and 2 for the number of telescopes, t.

4. At the end of the third quarter, Andrea's Optics has 4 telescopes in stock, 9 back orders for microscopes, and 13 back orders for binoculars. Use integers to indicate the stock for each item at the end of the third quarter. Write your answers in the table below.

5. The table below indicates the stock Andrea would like left at the end of the fourth quarter. Find the number of each item Andrea needs to order at the end of quarter 3 by doing the computation diagrammed. Write your answers in the table below.

Predicted Sales in Quarter 4 + Desired Stock at the End of Quarter 4 − Stock at the End of Quarter 3 = Items to Order at the End of Quarter 3

Product	Predicted Sales in Quarter 4	Desired Stock at the End of Quarter 4	Stock at the End of Quarter 3	Items to Order at the End of Quarter 3
Binoculars	100	25		
Microscopes		8		
Telescopes		2		

Chapter 8 Performance Assessment **15**

Chapter 8 Performance Assessment

Teacher Notes

Concepts and Skills This activity requires students to:

- write a rule and an equation to describe a function given in a table.
- make predictions based on an equation.
- use integers to describe real-world situations.
- add and subtract integers.

Guiding the Activity

- Discuss how businesses often use quarters and that this means a quarter of a year, or three months. Also, make sure students understand the term *back order*.

Answers

1. The number of microscopes sold, m, is 8 times the quarter number, q; $m = 8q$
2. 32 microscopes
3. The number of telescopes sold, t, is 4 plus the quarter number; $t = 4 + q$; 8 telescopes
4. See the table below.
5. binoculars: $100 + 25 - (-13) = 138$; microscopes: $32 + 8 - (-9) = 49$; telescopes: $8 + 2 - 4 = 6$

Product	Predicted Sales in Quarter 4	Desired Stock at the End of Quarter 4	Stock at the End of Quarter 3	Items to Order at the End of Quarter 3
Binoculars	100	25	−13	138
Microscopes	32	8	−9	49
Telescopes	8	2	4	6

Scoring Rubric

Level	Standard to be achieved for performance at specified level
4	**Full Achievement** The student wrote a rule and an equation to describe a function, made predictions, used integers to describe real-world situations, and added and subtracted integers without error. Explanations were thorough and well written.
3	**Substantial Achievement** The student wrote a rule and an equation to describe a function, made predictions, used integers to describe real-world situations, and added and subtracted integers with only minor errors. Explanations were well written but not complete.
2	**Partial Achievement** The student made considerable errors writing a rule and an equation to describe a function, making predictions, using integers to describe real-world situations, and adding and subtracting integers. Explanations were basically well written but not complete.
1	**Little Achievement** The student made numerous errors writing a rule and an equation to describe a function, making predictions, using integers to describe real-world situations, and adding and subtracting integers. Explanations were missing or incomplete.
0	**No Achievement** The student provided a completely incorrect response, one that was not interpretable, or no response at all.

Name _____

Chapter 9 Performance Assessment

Analyze the figure shown and then use it to draw a tessellation.

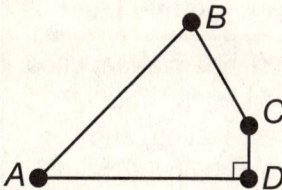

1. Use geometric notation to name a segment, an obtuse angle, and a pair of perpendicular line segments in the figure above.

   _____

2. Find the measure of each angle in the polygon. Explain how to use the sum of the measures to check.

   _____

   _____

3. Draw a tessellation of the figure.

4. Describe two different transformations in your tessellation.

   _____

   _____

Chapter 9 Performance Assessment

Teacher Notes

Concepts and Skills This activity requires students to:
- use geometric notation to name basic geometric figures and relationships.
- measure angles and determine that the sum of the measures of the angles of the quadrilateral is 360°.
- draw a tessellation.
- describe transformations.

Materials
- protractors
- rulers
- scrap paper and scissors (optional)
- colored pencils or markers (optional)

Guiding the Activity
- Some students may need to cut out copies of the quadrilateral that they can arrange in order to figure out the tessellation. However, encourage students to measure angles and sides when they are drawing the tessellation. If they trace around a cutout of the quadrilateral, they are likely to have gaps and overlap.
- Challenge gifted students and early finishers to find a point on their tessellation where four vertices meet and find the sum of the measures of the angles at that vertex.
- You may want to let students color their tessellations, as time allows.

Answers
1. Sample answers: $\overline{AB}$, $\angle BCD$, $\overline{AD} \perp \overline{CD}$.
2. $m\angle A = 45°$; $m\angle B = 75°$; $m\angle C = 150°$; and $m\angle D = 90°$; The sum of the measures of the angles of a quadrilateral is 360°. Since 45 + 90 + 150 + 75 = 360, the measures seem correct.
3.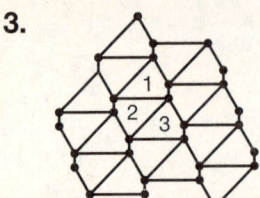
4. Quadrilaterals 1 and 2 are related by a 180° turn and quadrilaterals 1 and 3 are related by a slide.

Scoring Rubic

Level	Standard to be achieved for performance at specified level
4	**Full Achievement** The student used geometric notation, measured angles, drew a tessellation, and described transformations without error. The student knew the sum of the measures of the angles of a quadrilateral. Explanations were well written.
3	**Substantial Achievement** The student used geometric notation, measured angles, drew a tessellation, and described transformations with only minor errors. The student knew the sum of the measures of the angles of a quadrilateral. Explanations were well written but not complete.
2	**Partial Achievement** The student made considerable errors using geometric notation, measuring angles, drawing a tessellation, and describing transformations. The student did not know the sum of the measures of the angles of a quadrilateral. Explanations were not well written.
1	**Little Achievement** The student made numerous errors using geometric notation, measuring angles, drawing a tessellation, and describing transformations. The student did not know the sum of the measures of the angles of a quadrilateral. Explanations were missing or incomplete.
0	**No Achievement** The student provided a completely incorrect response, one that was not interpretable, or no response at all.

Name _____

Chapter 10 Performance Assessment

Jerry designs boxes. Besides the usual shapes, like rectangular prisms, Jerry designs odd-shaped boxes. One of Jerry's customers is designing a wooden wall plaque in the shape of the state of Texas. Jerry has designed a polyhedron-shaped box for the plaque. The dimensions of the bottom of the box are shown. The box is 2 inches thick.

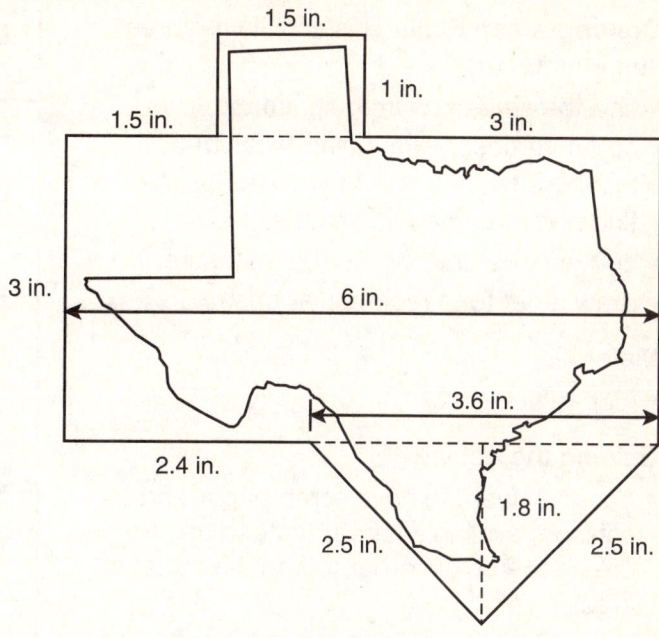

1. Find the area of the bottom of the box. Show your computations.

   _____

2. How many vertices, edges, and faces does the box have?

   _____

3. Excluding overlap, how much cardboard is needed to make the box?

   _____

4. Find the volume of the box and show your computations.

   _____

5. The box might be produced by a company that uses the metric system. Change the outside dimensions to centimeters.

   _____

6. The plaque would also fit in a box shaped like a rectangular prism with a 5.8 inch by 6 inch bottom. Draw a net for this box. Then find how much cardboard is needed to make this box and find the box's volume.

   _____

Chapter 10 Performance Assessment **19**

Chapter 10 Performance Assessment

Teacher Notes

Concepts and Skills This activity requires students to:
- find the area of an irregular shape.
- count vertices, edges, and faces of a polyhedron.
- find surface area and volume.
- convert customary to metric measure.
- draw a net for a rectangular prism.

Materials
- inch rulers

Guiding the Activity
- You may want to have scrap paper and scissors available for students to use to create the box in order to find the surface area.

Answers

1. $1 \times 1.5 + 3 \times 6 + \frac{1}{2} \times 1.8 \times 3.6 = 1.5 + 18 + 3.24 = 22.74$ in^2
2. 20 vertices, 30 edges, and 12 faces
3. SA = $2 \times 22.74 + 2 \times 3 + 2 \times 1.5 + 2 \times 1 + 2 \times 1.5 + 2 \times 1 + 2 \times 3 + 2 \times 3 + 2 \times 2.5 + 2 \times 2.5 + 2 \times 2.4 = 45.48 + 6 + 3 + 2 + 3 + 2 + 6 + 6 + 5 + 5 + 4.8 = 88.28$ in^2
4. $2 \times 22.74 = 45.48$ in^3
5. 1 in. = 2.54 cm; 3 in. = 7.62 cm; 1.5 in. = 3.81 cm; 2.5 in. = 6.35 cm; 2.4 in. = 6.096 cm
6.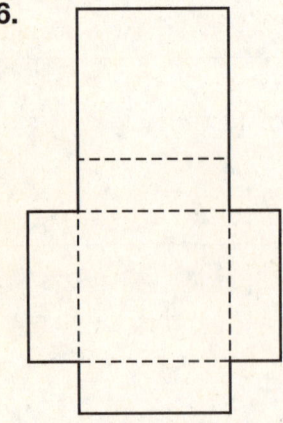

116.8 in^2 of cardboard; 69.6 in^3

Scoring Rubric

Level	Standard to be achieved for performance at specified level
4	**Full Achievement** The student calculated area, surface area, and volume, converted measures, drew a net, and counted vertices, edges, and faces without error.
3	**Substantial Achievement** The student calculated area, surface area, and volume, converted measures, drew a net, and counted vertices, edges, and faces with only minor errors.
2	**Partial Achievement** The student made considerable errors calculating area, surface area, and volume, converting measures, drawing a net, and counting vertices, edges, and faces.
1	**Little Achievement** The student made numerous errors calculating area, surface area, and volume, converting measures, drawing a net, and counting vertices, edges, and faces.
0	**No Achievement** The student provided a completely incorrect response, one that was not interpretable, or no response at all.

Name _____

Chapter 11 Performance Assessment

The students in Mr. Martin's class chose 10 students to be a representative sample of the class. There are 30 students in the class.

1. The table below shows how many students, in the sample, chose each subject as their favorite. Find the percent of students in the sample who chose each favorite subject. Then, approximate the number of students in the entire class who have the same favorite subject.

Favorite Subject	Number of Students (Sample)	Percent of Sample	Approximation of Entire Class
Math	4		
Science	2		
English	1		
History	3		

2. What type of graph would you use to show the different percentages of students who like each subject? Make the graph, and explain why you chose that type of graph.

_____

3. Suppose you randomly select a student from the sample. Find P(Math). Find P(History, Science). Explain how you found each probability.

_____

The table below shows the height of the students in the sample.

Height (in inches)	52	53	54	55	56	57	58	59	60	61
Number of Students (Sample)	1	0	0	1	2	3	0	1	1	1

4. Make a line plot of the height data. Describe any gaps and clusters.

Height (in inches)

←|—|—|—|—|—|—|—|—|—|→
52 53 54 55 56 57 58 59 60 61

_____

5. Find the mean, median, mode, and range of the height data.

_____

Chapter 11 Performance Assessment

Teacher Notes

Concepts and Skills This activity requires students to:

- analyze the results of a survey and make predictions about a population based on a sample.
- choose and make an appropriate graph to represent data.
- find simple and compound probabilities.
- make a line plot.
- describe gaps and clusters.
- find mean, median, mode, and range.

Materials
- straight edge
- compass
- protractor

Guiding the Activity

- The activity may be more interesting if you use real data from your class. The sample should be chosen randomly so that it is not biased. For example, students could count off, and every third student would be part of the sample until ten students are chosen.

Answers

1.

Favorite Subject	Number of Students (Sample)	Percent of Sample	Approximation of Entire Class
Math	4	40%	12
Science	2	20%	6
English	1	10%	3
History	3	30%	9

2. A circle graph is the most appropriate, because it shows how parts are related to a whole.

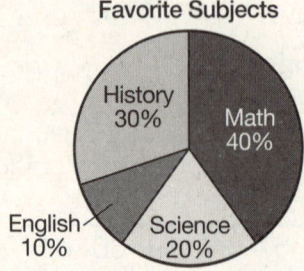

Favorite Subjects

See pages A1–A4 for Additional Answers.

Scoring Rubric

Level	Standard to be achieved for performance at specified level
4	**Full Achievement** The student made plots and graphs, and calculated mean, median, mode, range, and probability without error. The student demonstrated a thorough understanding of samples, surveys, data analysis, and probability. Explanations were thorough and well written.
3	**Substantial Achievement** The student made plots and graphs, and calculated mean, median, mode, range, and probability with only minor errors. The student demonstrated considerable understanding of samples, surveys, data analysis, and probability. Explanations were basically well written but not thorough.
2	**Partial Achievement** The student made considerable errors making plots and graphs, and calculating mean, median, mode, range, and probability. The student demonstrated limited understanding of samples, surveys, data analysis, and probability. Explanations were not well written.
1	**Little Achievement** The student made numerous errors. The student demonstrated little or no understanding of samples, surveys, data analysis, and probability. Explanations were missing or incomplete.
0	**No Achievement** The student provided a completely incorrect response, one that was not interpretable, or no response at all.

Name _____

Chapter 12 Performance Assessment

1. Suppose you are designing a cylindrical-shaped can to hold a maximum of 0.25 liters of pizza sauce. The volume of this can should be 250 cubic centimeters. (1 mL = 1 cm^3) Your first design has a diameter close to 5.64 cm, so the area of the base is 25 cm. Use the inequality $25h \leq 250$, where h is the height of the can. Solve and graph the inequality. Name three possible heights for the can so the volume is close to 250 cm^3.

   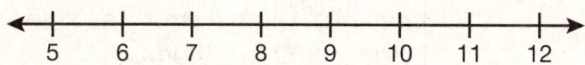

   _____

2. Next, you design a can with a diameter of about 4.37 cm so the area of the base is 15 cm^2. You remember that the can will have 2 cm of air space, which means 30 cm^3 of air. Solve the equation $240 = 15h - 30$ to find the height of a can with 240 cm^3 of pizza sauce and 30 cm^3 of air. Explain how you solved the problem.

   _____

3. Finally, you design a can with a diameter of about 6.18 cm so the area of the base is 30 cm^2. The can will have 60 cm^3 of air. Graph the equation $y = 30x - 60$, where x is the height of the can and y is the volume of pizza sauce. Complete the T-table below. What would be a good height for this can? Explain.

   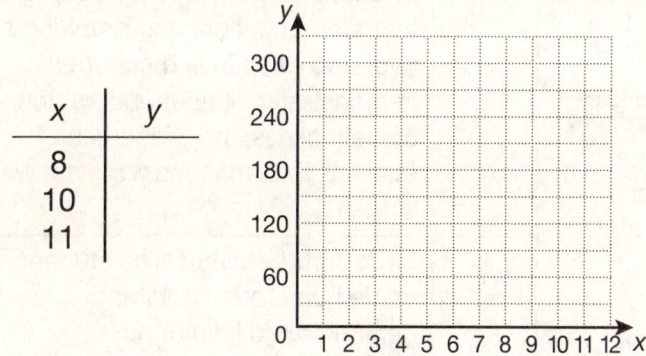

   _____

4. Which of the 3 designs is the best? Explain your choice.

   _____

Chapter 12 Performance Assessment

Teacher Notes

Concepts and Skills This activity requires students to:

- solve and graph an inequality.
- name three solutions to an inequality.
- solve a two-step equation.
- graph a two-step equation.

Guiding the Activity

- You may want to have students measure the diameter and height of several cans to see normal relationships between the diameter and the height.

Answers

1. $h \leq 10$;

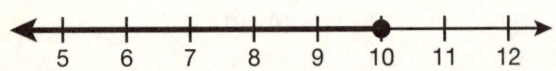

Sample response: 10 cm, 9.5 cm, 9 cm

2. $h = 18$ cm; To solve $240 = 15h - 30$, first add 30 to both sides to get $270 = 15h$. Then, divide both sides by 15 to get $18 = h$.

3.

x	y
8	180
10	240
11	270

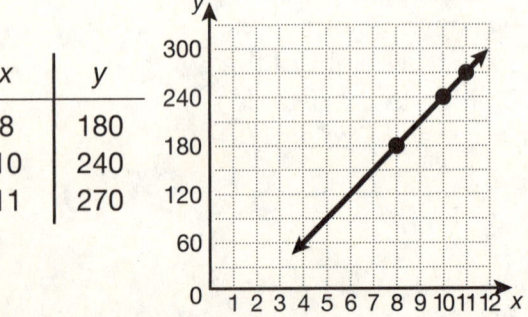

Sample response: A good height for the can would be 10 cm; A height of 10 cm would let the can hold 240 cm³ of pizza sauce which is close to, but less than, 250 cm³.

4. Sample response: The third design is the best; The first design does not allow for the air space. The second design, with a diameter of 4.37 cm and a height of 18 cm, is too tall and thin.

Scoring Rubric

Level	Standard to be achieved for performance at specified level
4	**Full Achievement** The student solved and graphed an inequality, named three solutions to an inequality, solved a two-step equation, and graphed a two-step equation without error. The student demonstrated a thorough understanding of inequalities and properties of equality. Explanations were thorough and well written.
3	**Substantial Achievement** The student solved and graphed an inequality, named three solutions to an inequality, solved a two-step equation, and graphed a two-step equation with only minor errors. The student demonstrated considerable understanding of inequalities and properties of equality. Explanations were well written, but not complete.
2	**Partial Achievement** The student made substantial errors solving and graphing an inequality, naming three solutions to an inequality, solving a two-step equation, and graphing a two-step equation. The student demonstrated limited understanding of inequalities and properties of equality. Explanations were not well written.
1	**Little Achievement** The student made numerous errors and demonstrated little or no understanding of inequalities or properties of inequality. Explanations were missing or incomplete.
0	**No Achievement** The student provided a completely incorrect response, one that was not interpretable, or no response at all.

Basic-Facts Timed Tests

Purpose
The purpose of the Basic-Facts Timed Test is to provide students with practice of the basic facts that they may encounter in the corresponding chapter. Rapid recall of basic addition, subtraction, multiplication, and division facts will give students confidence when learning new material. For instance, being proficient in basic addition and multiplication facts will eliminate frustration and increase accuracy as students learn to do addition and multiplication computation.

The Basic-Facts Timed Tests are designed so that they can be given in a variety of formats and can be used as often as needed.

- Tests can be used as written tests.
- Tests can be given orally and the students respond orally.
- Tests can be given orally and the students record their responses.

When giving the test orally, teachers can state the facts in the order shown on each test, in reverse order or in random order.

Time Limit for the Tests
It is important to consider the amount of time that students should be given to complete each test. You may want to consider your students' proficiency when deciding on how much time to allow.

- If a student is proficient, time how long it initially takes the student to complete a timed test, and use that time as a goal time.
- If a student struggles with rapid recall, allow the student enough time to complete the test so the student gets practice without being frustrated.
- As accuracy increases, challenge the student to a new goal time. Be careful not to make the goal time unattainable.

Additional Material Available
The Core Manipulative Kids contain Basic-Facts Flash Cards on key rings that can be used to supplement the Basic-Facts Timed Tests. The Kit for Grade 1 and Grade 2 contains addition, subtraction, and multiplication flash cards. The Kits for Grade 3 through Grade 6 contain multiplication and division flash cards.

Name _____

Basic-Facts Timed Test 1

Give the answer.

1. $2 + 8 =$ _____
2. $10 - 6 =$ _____
3. $7 + 1 =$ _____
4. $5 + 9 =$ _____
5. $4 + 8 =$ _____
6. $15 - 8 =$ _____
7. $9 - 3 =$ _____
8. $3 + 5 =$ _____
9. $4 + 3 =$ _____
10. $6 + 7 =$ _____
11. $13 - 5 =$ _____
12. $1 + 8 =$ _____
13. $9 - 0 =$ _____
14. $8 - 7 =$ _____
15. $8 + 3 =$ _____
16. $12 - 7 =$ _____
17. $0 + 3 =$ _____
18. $9 + 7 =$ _____
19. $16 - 8 =$ _____
20. $2 + 9 =$ _____
21. $13 - 6 =$ _____
22. $3 - 1 =$ _____
23. $14 - 8 =$ _____
24. $16 - 7 =$ _____
25. $6 + 3 =$ _____

26. $12 - 8 =$ _____
27. $9 + 5 =$ _____
28. $4 + 6 =$ _____
29. $7 - 0 =$ _____
30. $1 + 6 =$ _____
31. $5 + 4 =$ _____
32. $7 + 7 =$ _____
33. $17 - 9 =$ _____
34. $12 - 7 =$ _____
35. $11 - 4 =$ _____
36. $18 - 9 =$ _____
37. $6 + 0 =$ _____
38. $15 - 6 =$ _____
39. $11 - 9 =$ _____
40. $8 + 7 =$ _____
41. $17 - 8 =$ _____
42. $10 - 4 =$ _____
43. $8 + 8 =$ _____
44. $14 - 9 =$ _____
45. $1 + 9 =$ _____
46. $10 - 8 =$ _____
47. $8 + 5 =$ _____
48. $13 - 9 =$ _____
49. $9 + 6 =$ _____
50. $6 + 5 =$ _____

Name _____

Basic-Facts Timed Test 2

Give the answer.

1. $2 \times 8 =$ _____
2. $16 \div 4 =$ _____
3. $4 \times 7 =$ _____
4. $5 \times 9 =$ _____
5. $18 \div 2 =$ _____
6. $15 \div 3 =$ _____
7. $3 \times 6 =$ _____
8. $72 \div 9 =$ _____
9. $7 \times 8 =$ _____
10. $8 \times 9 =$ _____
11. $54 \div 6 =$ _____
12. $36 \div 6 =$ _____
13. $9 \times 2 =$ _____
14. $25 \div 5 =$ _____
15. $8 \times 0 =$ _____
16. $7 \times 7 =$ _____
17. $81 \div 9 =$ _____
18. $6 \times 8 =$ _____
19. $40 \div 5 =$ _____
20. $63 \div 9 =$ _____
21. $9 \times 9 =$ _____
22. $64 \div 8 =$ _____
23. $2 \times 9 =$ _____
24. $24 \div 8 =$ _____
25. $5 \times 8 =$ _____

26. $1 \times 6 =$ _____
27. $7 \times 9 =$ _____
28. $5 \times 4 =$ _____
29. $45 \div 5 =$ _____
30. $6 \times 7 =$ _____
31. $72 \div 8 =$ _____
32. $56 \div 7 =$ _____
33. $42 \div 6 =$ _____
34. $0 \times 8 =$ _____
35. $35 \div 7 =$ _____
36. $48 \div 6 =$ _____
37. $5 \times 0 =$ _____
38. $0 \div 4 =$ _____
39. $6 \times 9 =$ _____
40. $18 \div 6 =$ _____
41. $36 \div 9 =$ _____
42. $3 \times 9 =$ _____
43. $6 \times 4 =$ _____
44. $7 \div 7 =$ _____
45. $30 \div 6 =$ _____
46. $8 \times 7 =$ _____
47. $9 \times 4 =$ _____
48. $7 \div 1 =$ _____
49. $24 \div 6 =$ _____
50. $6 \times 6 =$ _____

Name _____

Basic-Facts Timed Test 3

Give the answer.

1. 3 + 7 = _____
2. 8 + 5 = _____
3. 7 + 3 = _____
4. 4 + 9 = _____
5. 0 + 4 = _____
6. 10 − 3 = _____
7. 11 − 7 = _____
8. 14 − 5 = _____
9. 6 − 2 = _____
10. 12 − 9 = _____
11. 7 + 5 = _____
12. 6 + 6 = _____
13. 8 + 9 = _____
14. 6 + 4 = _____
15. 4 + 7 = _____
16. 15 − 7 = _____
17. 10 − 7 = _____
18. 15 − 9 = _____
19. 13 − 4 = _____
20. 12 − 6 = _____
21. 6 + 8 = _____
22. 7 + 9 = _____
23. 8 + 6 = _____
24. 4 + 5 = _____
25. 9 + 9 = _____

26. 3 × 4 = _____
27. 8 × 8 = _____
28. 5 × 3 = _____
29. 9 × 7 = _____
30. 2 × 7 = _____
31. 49 ÷ 7 = _____
32. 54 ÷ 9 = _____
33. 14 ÷ 2 = _____
34. 27 ÷ 3 = _____
35. 42 ÷ 7 = _____
36. 1 × 9 = _____
37. 7 × 4 = _____
38. 7 × 6 = _____
39. 3 × 3 = _____
40. 6 × 2 = _____
41. 0 ÷ 7 = _____
42. 32 ÷ 4 = _____
43. 48 ÷ 8 = _____
44. 63 ÷ 7 = _____
45. 21 ÷ 7 = _____
46. 4 × 5 = _____
47. 8 × 1 = _____
48. 8 × 5 = _____
49. 2 × 3 = _____
50. 9 × 8 = _____

Name _____

Basic-Facts Timed Test 4

Give the answer.

1. 4 + 4 = _____
2. 6 + 9 = _____
3. 5 + 6 = _____
4. 2 + 7 = _____
5. 3 + 9 = _____
6. 4 − 3 = _____
7. 12 − 3 = _____
8. 12 − 5 = _____
9. 11 − 8 = _____
10. 9 − 6 = _____
11. 1 + 6 = _____
12. 5 + 7 = _____
13. 8 + 4 = _____
14. 5 + 8 = _____
15. 9 + 1 = _____
16. 5 − 3 = _____
17. 14 − 7 = _____
18. 12 − 8 = _____
19. 16 − 9 = _____
20. 14 − 6 = _____
21. 7 + 8 = _____
22. 3 + 2 = _____
23. 9 + 8 = _____
24. 2 + 5 = _____
25. 8 + 0 = _____

26. 8 × 2 = _____
27. 4 × 9 = _____
28. 6 × 5 = _____
29. 8 × 4 = _____
30. 3 × 8 = _____
31. 8 ÷ 1 = _____
32. 12 ÷ 2 = _____
33. 45 ÷ 9 = _____
34. 56 ÷ 8 = _____
35. 20 ÷ 4 = _____
36. 7 × 0 = _____
37. 9 × 6 = _____
38. 9 × 5 = _____
39. 3 × 7 = _____
40. 8 × 6 = _____
41. 6 ÷ 6 = _____
42. 9 ÷ 3 = _____
43. 16 ÷ 8 = _____
44. 40 ÷ 8 = _____
45. 28 ÷ 7 = _____
46. 9 × 7 = _____
47. 7 × 2 = _____
48. 4 × 3 = _____
49. 5 × 7 = _____
50. 2 × 4 = _____

Name _____

Basic-Facts Timed Test 5

Give the answer.

1. $8 \times 3 =$ _____
2. $9 \times 4 =$ _____
3. $7 \times 8 =$ _____
4. $6 \times 2 =$ _____
5. $5 \times 9 =$ _____
6. $7 \times 4 =$ _____
7. $2 \times 1 =$ _____
8. $3 \times 2 =$ _____
9. $9 \times 9 =$ _____
10. $8 \times 4 =$ _____
11. $2 \times 9 =$ _____
12. $8 \times 5 =$ _____
13. $7 \times 7 =$ _____
14. $7 \times 2 =$ _____
15. $9 \times 3 =$ _____
16. $1 \times 6 =$ _____
17. $3 \times 0 =$ _____
18. $5 \times 7 =$ _____
19. $7 \times 9 =$ _____
20. $9 \times 2 =$ _____
21. $3 \times 3 =$ _____
22. $6 \times 5 =$ _____
23. $5 \times 5 =$ _____
24. $8 \times 2 =$ _____
25. $5 \times 8 =$ _____

26. $16 \div 4 =$ _____
27. $30 \div 5 =$ _____
28. $10 \div 5 =$ _____
29. $24 \div 3 =$ _____
30. $42 \div 7 =$ _____
31. $16 \div 2 =$ _____
32. $6 \div 6 =$ _____
33. $81 \div 9 =$ _____
34. $35 \div 5 =$ _____
35. $0 \div 2 =$ _____
36. $21 \div 3 =$ _____
37. $7 \div 1 =$ _____
38. $56 \div 8 =$ _____
39. $8 \div 2 =$ _____
40. $27 \div 3 =$ _____
41. $48 \div 6 =$ _____
42. $28 \div 4 =$ _____
43. $10 \div 2 =$ _____
44. $15 \div 5 =$ _____
45. $18 \div 3 =$ _____
46. $24 \div 6 =$ _____
47. $2 \div 2 =$ _____
48. $24 \div 4 =$ _____
49. $63 \div 7 =$ _____
50. $36 \div 4 =$ _____

Name _____

Basic-Facts Timed Test 6

Give the answer.

1. 7 × 9 = _____
2. 9 × 6 = _____
3. 9 × 9 = _____
4. 9 × 1 = _____
5. 4 × 9 = _____
6. 6 × 9 = _____
7. 7 × 3 = _____
8. 3 × 5 = _____
9. 3 × 6 = _____
10. 8 × 9 = _____
11. 5 × 3 = _____
12. 9 × 2 = _____
13. 2 × 3 = _____
14. 5 × 5 = _____
15. 2 × 7 = _____
16. 2 × 2 = _____
17. 7 × 5 = _____
18. 6 × 3 = _____
19. 7 × 7 = _____
20. 2 × 5 = _____
21. 7 × 6 = _____
22. 8 × 8 = _____
23. 9 × 4 = _____
24. 9 × 3 = _____
25. 6 × 7 = _____
26. 8 × 4 = _____
27. 4 × 2 = _____
28. 9 × 5 = _____
29. 8 × 3 = _____
30. 3 × 7 = _____
31. 8 × 5 = _____
32. 4 × 1 = _____
33. 4 × 6 = _____
34. 3 × 9 = _____
35. 3 × 2 = _____
36. 1 × 8 = _____
37. 5 × 6 = _____
38. 7 × 4 = _____
39. 4 × 5 = _____
40. 4 × 8 = _____
41. 6 × 8 = _____
42. 1 × 6 = _____
43. 8 × 2 = _____
44. 2 × 8 = _____
45. 1 × 3 = _____
46. 4 × 0 = _____
47. 1 × 5 = _____
48. 4 × 4 = _____
49. 2 × 6 = _____
50. 1 × 4 = _____

Name _____

Basic-Facts Timed Test 7

Give the answer.

1. 8 + 2 = _____
2. 3 + 7 = _____
3. 8 + 8 = _____
4. 3 + 6 = _____
5. 5 + 1 = _____
6. 7 + 6 = _____
7. 9 + 2 = _____
8. 7 + 7 = _____
9. 5 + 3 = _____
10. 6 + 2 = _____
11. 4 + 7 = _____
12. 3 + 8 = _____
13. 1 + 1 = _____
14. 9 − 1 = _____
15. 11 − 7 = _____
16. 12 − 5 = _____
17. 9 − 4 = _____
18. 11 − 3 = _____
19. 8 − 4 = _____
20. 13 − 7 = _____
21. 6 − 2 = _____
22. 12 − 9 = _____
23. 6 − 4 = _____
24. 11 − 6 = _____
25. 3 − 1 = _____

26. 2 × 6 = _____
27. 3 × 4 = _____
28. 8 × 2 = _____
29. 6 × 2 = _____
30. 3 × 9 = _____
31. 7 × 2 = _____
32. 8 × 8 = _____
33. 4 × 6 = _____
34. 8 × 7 = _____
35. 7 × 8 = _____
36. 2 × 5 = _____
37. 5 × 5 = _____
38. 5 × 1 = _____
39. 4 ÷ 4 = _____
40. 0 ÷ 4 = _____
41. 12 ÷ 4 = _____
42. 21 ÷ 3 = _____
43. 14 ÷ 2 = _____
44. 5 ÷ 1 = _____
45. 24 ÷ 4 = _____
46. 54 ÷ 6 = _____
47. 20 ÷ 4 = _____
48. 45 ÷ 5 = _____
49. 63 ÷ 7 = _____
50. 18 ÷ 2 = _____

Name _____

Basic-Facts Timed Test 8

Give the answer.

1. 4 + 9 = _____
2. 2 + 5 = _____
3. 8 + 2 = _____
4. 13 − 9 = _____
5. 9 − 1 = _____
6. 12 − 4 = _____
7. 9 + 4 = _____
8. 8 − 8 = _____
9. 7 + 1 = _____
10. 3 − 3 = _____
11. 12 − 8 = _____
12. 6 − 5 = _____
13. 5 + 5 = _____
14. 7 + 4 = _____
15. 8 + 9 = _____
16. 4 + 1 = _____
17. 2 − 2 = _____
18. 1 + 7 = _____
19. 7 + 6 = _____
20. 2 + 1 = _____
21. 8 − 7 = _____
22. 2 + 7 = _____
23. 16 − 9 = _____
24. 13 − 4 = _____
25. 5 + 1 = _____

26. 7 + 2 = _____
27. 4 + 8 = _____
28. 9 + 3 = _____
29. 15 − 7 = _____
30. 14 − 7 = _____
31. 7 − 3 = _____
32. 9 − 7 = _____
33. 5 − 0 = _____
34. 8 + 7 = _____
35. 4 + 4 = _____
36. 8 + 3 = _____
37. 11 − 2 = _____
38. 6 + 6 = _____
39. 2 + 6 = _____
40. 7 + 7 = _____
41. 7 − 4 = _____
42. 5 + 9 = _____
43. 5 − 2 = _____
44. 11 − 5 = _____
45. 5 + 3 = _____
46. 4 − 1 = _____
47. 4 + 5 = _____
48. 11 − 9 = _____
49. 8 − 2 = _____
50. 3 − 0 = _____

Name _____

Basic-Facts Timed Test 9

Give the answer.

1. 6 × 6 = _____
2. 4 × 5 = _____
3. 5 × 2 = _____
4. 8 × 9 = _____
5. 5 × 9 = _____
6. 7 × 2 = _____
7. 8 × 0 = _____
8. 4 × 7 = _____
9. 9 × 6 = _____
10. 8 × 3 = _____
11. 8 × 6 = _____
12. 5 × 8 = _____
13. 1 × 1 = _____
14. 1 × 0 = _____
15. 2 × 7 = _____
16. 5 × 4 = _____
17. 5 × 3 = _____
18. 6 × 4 = _____
19. 7 × 7 = _____
20. 2 × 9 = _____
21. 7 × 5 = _____
22. 5 × 5 = _____
23. 4 × 4 = _____
24. 4 × 3 = _____
25. 7 × 3 = _____

26. 9 ÷ 9 = _____
27. 9 ÷ 3 = _____
28. 12 ÷ 4 = _____
29. 9 ÷ 1 = _____
30. 4 ÷ 2 = _____
31. 63 ÷ 9 = _____
32. 27 ÷ 9 = _____
33. 0 ÷ 8 = _____
34. 36 ÷ 6 = _____
35. 36 ÷ 4 = _____
36. 35 ÷ 5 = _____
37. 32 ÷ 8 = _____
38. 72 ÷ 8 = _____
39. 8 ÷ 4 = _____
40. 3 ÷ 1 = _____
41. 10 ÷ 5 = _____
42. 18 ÷ 3 = _____
43. 21 ÷ 7 = _____
44. 8 ÷ 2 = _____
45. 6 ÷ 1 = _____
46. 20 ÷ 5 = _____
47. 30 ÷ 5 = _____
48. 6 ÷ 2 = _____
49. 40 ÷ 8 = _____
50. 28 ÷ 7 = _____

Name _____

Basic-Facts Timed Test 10

Give the answer.

1. 9 × 0 = _____
2. 7 × 6 = _____
3. 5 × 9 = _____
4. 3 × 1 = _____
5. 3 × 9 = _____
6. 8 × 9 = _____
7. 6 × 9 = _____
8. 8 × 7 = _____
9. 4 × 6 = _____
10. 7 × 4 = _____
11. 3 × 3 = _____
12. 6 × 7 = _____
13. 1 × 3 = _____
14. 5 × 5 = _____
15. 2 × 8 = _____
16. 9 × 2 = _____
17. 4 × 8 = _____
18. 3 × 8 = _____
19. 7 × 2 = _____
20. 2 × 2 = _____
21. 5 × 6 = _____
22. 0 × 2 = _____
23. 3 × 4 = _____
24. 8 × 3 = _____
25. 3 × 7 = _____

26. 9 × 4 = _____
27. 3 × 2 = _____
28. 3 × 5 = _____
29. 6 × 3 = _____
30. 2 × 7 = _____
31. 7 × 5 = _____
32. 7 × 1 = _____
33. 1 × 2 = _____
34. 5 × 7 = _____
35. 4 × 2 = _____
36. 8 × 8 = _____
37. 9 × 8 = _____
38. 6 × 4 = _____
39. 2 × 5 = _____
40. 4 × 7 = _____
41. 6 × 6 = _____
42. 1 × 9 = _____
43. 8 × 5 = _____
44. 6 × 8 = _____
45. 7 × 3 = _____
46. 4 × 4 = _____
47. 6 × 5 = _____
48. 4 × 9 = _____
49. 2 × 4 = _____
50. 0 × 4 = _____

Name _____

Basic-Facts Timed Test 11

Give the answer.

1. 5 + 2 = _____
2. 6 + 5 = _____
3. 16 − 7 = _____
4. 18 − 9 = _____
5. 6 − 4 = _____
6. 16 − 8 = _____
7. 6 + 9 = _____
8. 9 − 9 = _____
9. 2 + 9 = _____
10. 17 − 9 = _____
11. 14 − 9 = _____
12. 6 − 3 = _____
13. 9 + 2 = _____
14. 1 + 5 = _____
15. 4 + 8 = _____
16. 5 + 7 = _____
17. 8 − 6 = _____
18. 1 + 9 = _____
19. 6 + 8 = _____
20. 2 + 7 = _____
21. 9 − 3 = _____
22. 2 + 6 = _____
23. 15 − 7 = _____
24. 9 − 2 = _____
25. 7 + 9 = _____

26. 0 + 9 = _____
27. 4 + 2 = _____
28. 4 + 3 = _____
29. 14 − 6 = _____
30. 10 − 7 = _____
31. 9 − 8 = _____
32. 9 + 9 = _____
33. 8 − 6 = _____
34. 9 + 7 = _____
35. 6 + 4 = _____
36. 2 + 8 = _____
37. 10 − 5 = _____
38. 7 + 3 = _____
39. 9 + 8 = _____
40. 9 + 6 = _____
41. 8 − 8 = _____
42. 7 + 8 = _____
43. 15 − 9 = _____
44. 10 − 9 = _____
45. 6 + 7 = _____
46. 2 − 1 = _____
47. 9 + 5 = _____
48. 13 − 6 = _____
49. 4 + 6 = _____
50. 7 − 4 = _____

Name _____

Basic-Facts Timed Test 12

Give the answer.

1. 6 × 1 = _____
2. 8 × 6 = _____
3. 4 × 9 = _____
4. 5 × 2 = _____
5. 5 × 4 = _____
6. 6 × 9 = _____
7. 6 × 0 = _____
8. 7 × 8 = _____
9. 6 × 6 = _____
10. 4 × 2 = _____
11. 1 × 5 = _____
12. 3 × 7 = _____
13. 9 × 3 = _____
14. 1 × 4 = _____
15. 4 × 7 = _____
16. 6 × 3 = _____
17. 8 × 4 = _____
18. 8 × 7 = _____
19. 3 × 8 = _____
20. 9 × 9 = _____
21. 2 × 9 = _____
22. 4 × 4 = _____
23. 9 × 5 = _____
24. 9 × 8 = _____
25. 9 × 7 = _____

26. 8 ÷ 4 = _____
27. 30 ÷ 5 = _____
28. 15 ÷ 3 = _____
29. 21 ÷ 7 = _____
30. 42 ÷ 6 = _____
31. 10 ÷ 2 = _____
32. 64 ÷ 8 = _____
33. 12 ÷ 2 = _____
34. 27 ÷ 9 = _____
35. 35 ÷ 5 = _____
36. 72 ÷ 9 = _____
37. 18 ÷ 3 = _____
38. 8 ÷ 1 = _____
39. 20 ÷ 5 = _____
40. 48 ÷ 8 = _____
41. 32 ÷ 4 = _____
42. 28 ÷ 4 = _____
43. 36 ÷ 6 = _____
44. 56 ÷ 7 = _____
45. 54 ÷ 6 = _____
46. 16 ÷ 2 = _____
47. 20 ÷ 4 = _____
48. 32 ÷ 8 = _____
49. 12 ÷ 4 = _____
50. 45 ÷ 9 = _____

Written Tests

Scott Foresman–Addison Wesley Mathematics provides you with written tests for each chapter of your mathematics program. The Form A and Form B tests contain free-response, multiple-choice, and Writing in Math questions. In addition, cumulative tests and Performance Assessments are provided. You may also want to distribute and discuss **"Tips for Test Taking"** (blackline master) with your students.

Diagnosing Readiness for Grade 6

This multiple-choice test may be used at the beginning of the school year to assess student mastery of the previous grade. The test items address

- Place Value, Addition, and Subtraction
- Whole Number Multiplication and Division
- Fractions
- Decimals, Ratios, and Percent
- Integers and Algebra
- Measurement and Geometry
- Statistics, Data Analysis, and Probability
- Problem Solving

Chapter Test: Mixed Format

Both Form A and Form B chapter tests parallel the corresponding test in the Pupil Edition, item for item. See the Chapter Tests in the Teacher Edition for an item analysis.

Cumulative Tests

There is a Cumulative Test after every three chapters in the Pupil Edition. Each test is a four-page long multiple-choice test.

Tips for Test Taking

Following Instructions
- Listen carefully as your teacher explains the test.

Budget Your Time
- Do the questions in order if you can.
- If a question seems very hard, skip it and go back to it later.

Read Carefully
- Watch for extra information in a problem.
- Watch for words like *not*.
- Be sure to answer the questions asked.

Make Smart Choices
- Estimate when you can so that you have a better idea what the answer might be.
- Eliminate answer choices that are not reasonable or are clearly wrong.
- Check an answer that you think is correct by working backward.

Mark Answers Carefully
- If you are using a "bubble" answer sheet or a grided response form, be careful to match each question number with the correct number of the answer row.
- If you skip a question, be sure to leave that question's answer space blank.

Name_____

Date_____

1.	Ⓐ	Ⓑ	Ⓒ	Ⓓ		21.	Ⓐ	Ⓑ	Ⓒ	Ⓓ
2.	Ⓐ	Ⓑ	Ⓒ	Ⓓ		22.	Ⓐ	Ⓑ	Ⓒ	Ⓓ
3.	Ⓐ	Ⓑ	Ⓒ	Ⓓ		23.	Ⓐ	Ⓑ	Ⓒ	Ⓓ
4.	Ⓐ	Ⓑ	Ⓒ	Ⓓ		24.	Ⓐ	Ⓑ	Ⓒ	Ⓓ
5.	Ⓐ	Ⓑ	Ⓒ	Ⓓ		25.	Ⓐ	Ⓑ	Ⓒ	Ⓓ
6.	Ⓐ	Ⓑ	Ⓒ	Ⓓ		26.	Ⓐ	Ⓑ	Ⓒ	Ⓓ
7.	Ⓐ	Ⓑ	Ⓒ	Ⓓ		27.	Ⓐ	Ⓑ	Ⓒ	Ⓓ
8.	Ⓐ	Ⓑ	Ⓒ	Ⓓ		28.	Ⓐ	Ⓑ	Ⓒ	Ⓓ
9.	Ⓐ	Ⓑ	Ⓒ	Ⓓ		29.	Ⓐ	Ⓑ	Ⓒ	Ⓓ
10.	Ⓐ	Ⓑ	Ⓒ	Ⓓ		30.	Ⓐ	Ⓑ	Ⓒ	Ⓓ
11.	Ⓐ	Ⓑ	Ⓒ	Ⓓ		31.	Ⓐ	Ⓑ	Ⓒ	Ⓓ
12.	Ⓐ	Ⓑ	Ⓒ	Ⓓ		32.	Ⓐ	Ⓑ	Ⓒ	Ⓓ
13.	Ⓐ	Ⓑ	Ⓒ	Ⓓ		33.	Ⓐ	Ⓑ	Ⓒ	Ⓓ
14.	Ⓐ	Ⓑ	Ⓒ	Ⓓ		34.	Ⓐ	Ⓑ	Ⓒ	Ⓓ
15.	Ⓐ	Ⓑ	Ⓒ	Ⓓ		35.	Ⓐ	Ⓑ	Ⓒ	Ⓓ
16.	Ⓐ	Ⓑ	Ⓒ	Ⓓ		36.	Ⓐ	Ⓑ	Ⓒ	Ⓓ
17.	Ⓐ	Ⓑ	Ⓒ	Ⓓ		37.	Ⓐ	Ⓑ	Ⓒ	Ⓓ
18.	Ⓐ	Ⓑ	Ⓒ	Ⓓ		38.	Ⓐ	Ⓑ	Ⓒ	Ⓓ
19.	Ⓐ	Ⓑ	Ⓒ	Ⓓ		39.	Ⓐ	Ⓑ	Ⓒ	Ⓓ
20.	Ⓐ	Ⓑ	Ⓒ	Ⓓ		40.	Ⓐ	Ⓑ	Ⓒ	Ⓓ

Bubble Answer Sheet

Name_____

Diagnosing Readiness for Grade 6

Circle the letter of the correct answer.

1. What is the value of the underlined digit in 12.094?

   A. nine
   B. nine tenths
   C. nine hundredths
   D. nine thousandths

2. What is the measure of the angle?

   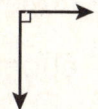

   A. 180°   C. 90°
   B. 150°   D. 60°

3. Which is the best estimate for 61,089 + 3,112?

   A. 64,000   C. 74,000
   B. 65,000   D. 75,000

4. Find 23.1 − 2.56.

   A. 21.5   C. 20.55
   B. 20.6   D. 20.54

5. Solve $24 = x - 8$.

   A. $x = 3$ C. $x = 24$
   B. $x = 16$ D. $x = 32$

6. What instrument do most of the members of the orchestra play?

   A. Brass   C. Woodwinds
   B. Strings   D. Percussion

7. Simone is decorating her bedroom. She can buy a red bedspread, a blue bedspread, or an orange bedspread. She can choose either white pillows or black pillows. From how many different combinations of bedspreads and pillows can Simone choose?

   A. 3 combinations
   B. 6 combinations
   C. 9 combinations
   D. 12 combinations

Diagnosing Readiness for Grade 6   **43**

8. You spin the spinner once. Which of the following best describes the chances that the spinner will land on gray?

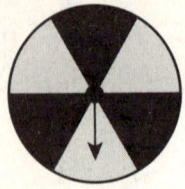

A. certain

B. more likely

C. equally likely as black

D. impossible

9. Which is the most reasonable estimate for 8,914 ÷ 3?

A. 2,800 C. 3,500

B. 3,000 D. 4,000

10. Which number is NOT divisible by 3?

A. 42 C. 243

B. 139 D. 291

11. Which fraction equals 0.8?

A. $\frac{1}{80}$ C. $\frac{1}{8}$

B. $\frac{8}{100}$ D. $\frac{8}{10}$

12. Evaluate $x + 5$ for $x = 4$.

A. 45 C. 9

B. 20 D. 1

For 13–14, use the solid.

13. Which of the following is the top view of the solid?

A. ▯▯▯ C.

B.   D. ▯▯

14. Find the volume of the solid.

A. 6 cubes C. 12 cubes

B. 10 cubes D. 27 cubes

15. Which is the most reasonable estimate for 551 ÷ 63?

A. 8 C. 80

B. 9 D. 90

16. Find the area of a square with each side measuring $4\frac{1}{2}$ feet.

A. $16\frac{1}{4}$ ft² C. 18 ft²

B. $16\frac{1}{2}$ ft² D. $20\frac{1}{4}$ ft²

17. Find 912 ÷ 38.

A. 204 C. 24

B. 26 D. 2.4

18. Find the perimeter of the figure.

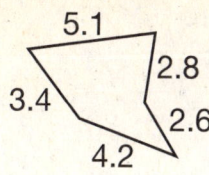

A. 18.1 in.²   C. 19.1 in.²
B. 18.1 in.   D. 19.1 in.

19. Which polygon has 4 sides?

A. pentagon   C. octagon
B. hexagon   D. quadrilateral

20. Find 5.3 × 100.

A. 5.3   C. 530
B. 53   D. 5,300

21. What fraction of the figure is shaded?

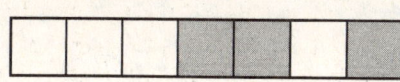

A. $\frac{3}{7}$ C. $\frac{4}{7}$
B. $\frac{1}{2}$ D. $\frac{7}{3}$

22. Write a ratio to compare the number of striped triangles to the number of circles.

A. 5:7   C. 7:5
B. 5:5   D. 5:12

23. Which is a prime number?

A. 72   C. 35
B. 53   D. 27

24. Write $\frac{18}{8}$ as a mixed number in simplest form.

A. $3\frac{1}{4}$ C. $2\frac{1}{4}$
B. $2\frac{8}{18}$ D. $2\frac{4}{18}$

25. Find $\frac{7}{10} - \frac{3}{5}$.

A. $\frac{1}{10}$ C. $\frac{4}{5}$
B. $\frac{5}{10}$ D. $\frac{10}{10}$

26. Multiply $\frac{3}{4}$ and 24.

A. 6   C. 12
B. 9   D. 18

27. Which unit would be most appropriate to measure the width of a house?

A. millimeter   C. meter
B. centimeter   D. kilometer

28. Round 8.9̲71 to the underlined place.

A. 9.0   C. 8.8
B. 8.9   D. 8.09

Diagnosing Readiness for Grade 6

29. Find 5,600 ÷ 80.

A. 60 C. 600
B. 70 D. 700

30. Which solid figure does this object resemble?

A. prism C. pyramid
B. cylinder D. cone

31. 5,300 mL = ☐

A. 5,300,000 L C. 5.3 L
B. 53 L D. 0.53 L

32. Find $14.80 ÷ 4.

A. $0.35 C. $3.45
B. $0.37 D. $3.70

33. Find 3(15 − 9) + 2.

A. 38 C. 24
B. 30 D. 20

34. Which decimal is less than 7.805?

A. 78.05 C. 7.815
B. 7.850 D. 7.58

35. Find the least common denominator of $\frac{1}{10}$ and $\frac{5}{6}$.

A. 6 C. 50
B. 30 D. 60

36. Find the measure of ∠S.

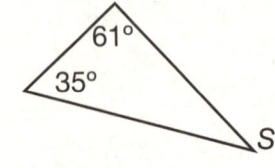

A. 35°
B. 55°
C. 84°
D. 96°

37. What percent is shaded?

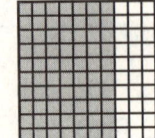

A. 7%
B. 35%
C. 70%
D. 140%

38. Estimate $2\frac{1}{5} + 4\frac{5}{6}$ to the nearest whole number.

A. 5 C. 7
B. 6 D. 8

39. Which is the most reasonable estimate for 4.15 × 3.9?

A. 8 C. 16
B. 12 D. 20

40. Name the ordered pair for Point H.

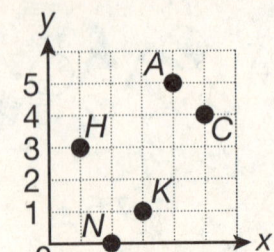

A. (3, 1)
B. (1, 3)
C. (0, 3)
D. (3, 0)

Name _____

Chapter 1 Test Form A: Mixed Formats

MULTIPLE CHOICE

Circle the letter of the correct answer.

1. Which is the standard form for
   $6 \times 100{,}000 + 8 \times 10{,}000 + 2 \times 100 + 4$?

   A. 6,824 C. 680,024
   B. 608,204 D. 680,204

2. Which is 10^7 written in the standard form?

   A. 100,000
   B. 1,000,000
   C. 10,000,000
   D. 1,000,000,000

3. Which list shows numbers in order from least to greatest?

   A. 3,906; 3,609; 3,096; 3,960
   B. 3,096; 3,609; 3,906; 3,960
   C. 3,906; 3,960; 3,609; 3,096
   D. 3,960; 3,906; 3,096; 3,609

4. Which is 6,120,888 rounded to the nearest thousand?

   A. 6,000,000 C. 6,120,900
   B. 6,120,800 D. 6,121,000

5. Estimate $239 + 1{,}058 + 560$ by rounding to the nearest hundred.

   A. 1,000 C. 1,900
   B. 1,800 D. 2,000

6. Which is the best estimate for 159×208?

   A. 30,000 C. 50,000
   B. 32,000 D. 60,000

7. Calculate the value of $2^3 \times 3 \div (6 - 3)$.

   A. 1 C. 7
   B. 6 D. 8

8. The sentence $8(5 - 3) = 8(5) - 8(3)$ illustrates which property?

   A. Distributive Property
   B. Identity Property of Multiplication
   C. Commutative Property of Addition
   D. Associative Property of Addition

9. Which algebraic expression represents 7 less than 3 times a number n?

   A. $7 - 3n$ C. $7 + 3n$
   B. $n - 3(7)$ D. $3n - 7$

10. How can you get the variable alone in the equation $5x = 10$?

    A. Divide both sides by 5.
    B. Divide both sides by 2.
    C. Multiply both sides by 5.
    D. Multiply both sides by 2.

Chapter 1 Test Form A

11. Which equation does NOT have the solution $b = 6$?

  A. $6b = 36$

  B. $b - 2 = 4$

  C. $\frac{b}{3} = 2$

  D. $3b = 9$

FREE RESPONSE

For 12–13, write the place and the value of each underlined digit.

12. 1,0<u>2</u>6,417

_____

_____

13. 81<u>7</u>,204,106,000

_____

_____

14. Write the short-word form and the expanded form for 61,420,185.

_____

_____

_____

_____

_____

_____

For 15–16, write as a product and evaluate.

15. 2^4 _____

16. seven squared

_____

17. Find $33 + 17 + 11$ using mental math.

_____

18. Use the Distributive Property to find $3(20 + 4)$. _____

Estimate each answer.

19. $3{,}406 - 2{,}914$ _____

20. $629 \div 32$ _____

21. $6{,}081 \times 49$ _____

22. $18 + 21 + 19 + 22 + 23$ _____

23. For Exercise 20, tell what method you used.

_____

_____

Evaluate each expression for $a = 3$ and 6.

24. $\frac{36}{a}$ _____, _____

25. $21 - 2a$ _____, _____

Solve each equation. Check your answer.

26. $x + 4 = 12$ $x =$ _____

27. $y - 8 = 10$ $y =$ _____

28. $3m = 27$ $m =$ _____

29. $\frac{n}{4} = 7$ $n =$ _____

30. For Exercise 29, explain how to get n alone.

_____

_____

31. State the Identity Property of Multiplication in your own words.

_____

_____

_____

32. Evaluate $30 - 24 \div (2 + 4)$ _____

WRITING IN MATH

For 33–35, use the Quiz Game problem.

Quiz Game In a quiz game, every correct answer wins 10 points. For every incorrect answer, 5 points are subtracted from a player's total score. Samia had a total score of 95 points for 17 questions. How many correct and incorrect answers did Samia have?

33. Write what you are trying to find.

_____

_____

_____

_____

34. Solve the problem and write your answer in a complete sentence. What strategy did you use to complete the problem?

_____

_____

_____

_____

_____

_____

_____

35. Check your answer. Did you answer the right question? Explain.

_____

_____

_____

_____

_____

_____

Chapter 1 Test Form A

Name _____

Chapter 1 Test Form B: Mixed Formats

MULTIPLE CHOICE

Circle the letter of the correct answer.

1. Which is the standard form for
   $3 \times 1,000,000 + 5 \times 100,000 + 2 \times 1,000$?

   A. 3,520 C. 3,502,000

   B. 3,250,000 D. 3,520,000

2. Which is 10^4 written in standard form?

   A. 10,000

   B. 100,000

   C. 1,000,000

   D. 1,000,000,000

3. Which list shows numbers in order from least to greatest?

   A. 5,149; 5,419; 5,914; 5,491

   B. 5,914; 5,149; 5,491; 5,419

   C. 5,149; 5,419; 5,491; 5,914

   D. 5,491; 5,914; 5,419; 5,149

4. Which is 240,689 rounded to the nearest ten-thousand?

   A. 200,000

   B. 240,000

   C. 240,700

   D. 250,000

5. Estimate $267 + 2,689 + 389$ by rounding to the nearest hundred.

   A. 3,000 C. 3,300

   B. 3,100 D. 3,400

6. Which is the best estimate for 407×156?

   A. 40,000 C. 60,000

   B. 50,000 D. 75,000

7. Calculate the value of $18 \div (3 + 3) \times 2^3$.

   A. 4 C. 36

   B. 24 D. 72

8. The sentence $2 + (6 + 5) = (2 + 6) + 5$ illustrates which property?

   A. Associative Property of Addition

   B. Identity Property of Multiplication

   C. Commutative Property of Addition

   D. Distributive Property

9. Which algebraic expression represents 4 less than a number n divided by 5?

   A. $\frac{n}{5} - 4$ C. $4 + \frac{n}{5}$

   B. $\frac{n}{5} + 4$ D. $4 - \frac{n}{5}$

10. How can you get the variable alone in the equation $\frac{y}{4} = 2$?

    A. Divide both sides by 4.

    B. Divide both sides by 2.

    C. Multiply both sides by 4.

    D. Multiply both sides by 2.

11. Which equation does NOT have the solution $a = 5$?

   A. $a + 7 = 12$

   B. $a - 3 = 2$

   C. $\frac{a}{5} = 2$

   D. $2a = 10$

FREE RESPONSE

For 12–13, write the place and value of each underlined digit.

12. <u>6</u>1,234,906,000

_____

13. 491,28<u>3</u>,004

_____

14. Write the short-word form and the expanded form for 7,240,130.

_____

_____

_____

For 15–16, write as a product and evaluate.

15. 3^3

_____

16. four squared

_____

17. Find $19 + 31 + 15$ using mental math.

_____

18. Use the Distributive Property to find $2(8 + 15)$.

_____

Estimate each answer.

19. $2{,}109 - 1{,}817$

_____

20. $711 \div 68$

_____

21. $5{,}141 \times 57$

_____

22. $43 + 38 + 41 + 35 + 40$

_____

23. For Exercise 21, tell what method you used.

_____

Evaluate each expression for $c = 4$ and 8.

24. $\frac{16}{c}$ _____, _____

25. $3c - 9$ _____, _____

Solve each equation. Check your answer.

26. $x + 7 = 11$ $x =$ _____

27. $y - 1 = 0$ $y =$ _____

28. $2n = 18$ $n =$ _____

29. $\frac{m}{3} = 6$ $m =$ _____

30. For Exercise 28, explain how to get n alone.

_____

Chapter 1 Test Form B

31. State the Commutative Property of Addition in your own words.

_____

_____

_____

_____

_____

32. Evaluate $10 + 8 \div (14 - 12)$.

_____

WRITING IN MATH

For 33–35, use the Language Time problem.

Language Time Frank bought a German language course with 12 audio taped lessons. There are two lessons on each 45-minute audio tape. What is the total playing time on the tapes?

33. Write what you are trying to find.

_____

_____

_____

_____

_____

34. Solve the problem and write your answer in a complete sentence. What strategy did you use to complete the problem?

_____

_____

_____

_____

_____

_____

_____

35. Check your answer. Did you answer the right question? Explain.

_____

_____

_____

_____

_____

_____

Name_____

Chapter 2 Test Form A: Mixed Formats

MULTIPLE CHOICE

Circle the letter of the correct answer.

1. Find $9 - 3.28$.
   - A. 6.72
   - B. 6.28
   - C. 5.72
   - D. 5.28

2. Find $15.6 \div 0.3$.
   - A. 520
   - B. 52
   - C. 5.2
   - D. 0.52

3. Find 0.9×0.13.
   - A. 0.117
   - B. 1.17
   - C. 11.7
   - D. 117

4. Find $11.9 + 33.406$.
   - A. 34.596
   - B. 44.415
   - C. 45.306
   - D. 45.415

5. Find $47.32 \div 14$.
   - A. 33.8
   - B. 3.38
   - C. 0.338
   - D. 0.0338

6. Which symbol will make the statement below true?

   3.465 _____ 3.456
   - A. $=$
   - B. $>$
   - C. $<$
   - D. $\cong$

7. Which is the best estimate of $5.91 + 22.39$?
   - A. 26
   - B. 27
   - C. 28
   - D. 30

8. Round 7.407 to the nearest hundredth.
   - A. 7
   - B. 7.40
   - C. 7.408
   - D. 7.41

For 9–10, use the following information:

At school, Jack spends $3.75 for lunch every day.

9. About how many lunches can Jack buy with $12?
   - A. about 5
   - B. about 4
   - C. about 3
   - D. about 2

10. About how much money would Jack spend in 7 days?
    - A. about $28
    - B. about $24
    - C. about $22
    - D. about $20

11. Fencing is sold in two-meter lengths. How many lengths will Carrie have to buy to fence the perimeter of her yard?

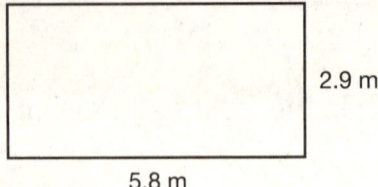

A. 8   C. 11
B. 9   D. 12

12. Solve for n. $2.7n = 16.2$

A. $n = 0.9$ C. $n = 6$
B. $n = 5.9$ D. $n = 60$

FREE RESPONSE

Simplify.

13. 3.12×10^2 _____

14. $9.6 \div 0.8$ _____

15. $\$14.23 - \$11.94$ _____

16. $2.695 \div 10^{-3}$ _____

17. 124.9×1.2 _____

18. $7 - 2.161$ _____

Solve each equation.

19. $\frac{n}{2.6} = 1.4$ $n =$ _____

20. $x + 1.49 = 9.76$ $x =$ _____

21. $0.4y = 3.46$ $y =$ _____

22. $z - 3.8 = 4$ $z =$ _____

Estimate each answer.

23. $15.82 \div 4.03$ _____

24. 7.5×3.1 _____

25. $38.19 + 21.88$ _____

26. $37.41 - 19.47$ _____

27. $188.19 \div 3.011$ _____

28. 8.14×3.29 _____

Write each number in scientific notation.

29. 0.00028 _____

30. $1{,}290$ _____

31. 36.95 _____

32. 895 _____

Solve.

33. Karen bought two sandwiches and a bag of chips for lunch for $8.25. The bag of chips cost $0.79. Write and solve an equation to find the cost of the two sandwiches.

34. Chen works at a local farmer's market. His boss asked him to put 6 bananas in each bag. If all 82 bananas must be put in a bag, how many bags does he need?

_____

WRITING IN MATH

35. To divide a decimal number by another decimal number, what is the first step?

_____

_____

_____

_____

36. Tell how you know which inverse operation to use when solving the equation below.

    $5.4x = 16.2$

_____

_____

_____

_____

37. Terome solved the word problem below. Did he interpret the remainder correctly? Explain why or why not.

    A bag of peanuts should contain 3 ounces of peanuts. There are 29 ounces of peanuts. How many bags of peanuts can be made?

_____

_____

_____

_____

_____

_____

_____

_____

Chapter 2 Test Form A **55**

Name _____

Chapter 2 Test Form B: Mixed Formats

MULTIPLE CHOICE

Circle the letter of the correct answer.

1. Find 7 − 3.52.
   A. 4.52   C. 3.52
   B. 4.48   D. 3.48

2. Find 15.3 ÷ 0.3.
   A. 0.51   C. 51
   B. 5.1   D. 510

3. Find 0.7 × 0.24.
   A. 0.168 C. 16.8
   B. 1.68   D. 168

4. Find 9.7 + 21.064.
   A. 31.34   C. 30.071
   B. 30.764 D. 22.034

5. Find 54.86 ÷ 13.
   A. 422   C. 4.22
   B. 42.2   D. 0.422

6. Which symbol will make the statement below true?

   0.9231 _____ 0.9251
   A. =   C. <
   B. >   D. ≅

7. Which is the best estimate of 13.68 + 19.19?
   A. 33   C. 32
   B. 32.2 D. 30

8. Round 13.4072 to the nearest thousandth.
   A. 13.41   C. 13.407
   B. 13.408 D. 13

For 9–10, use the following information:

Each paper cup holds 8.5 ounces.

9. About how many cups can Nora fill with 63 ounces?
   A. about 7 cups   C. about 5 cups
   B. about 6 cups   D. about 4 cups

10. About how many ounces are in 5 cups?
    A. about 25 ounces
    B. about 30 ounces
    C. about 35 ounces
    D. about 45 ounces

11. Picture-framing wood is sold in two-foot lengths. How many lengths will Joseph need to buy to frame his picture?

    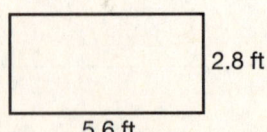

    A. 8 lengths   C. 10 lengths
    B. 9 lengths   D. 11 lengths

12. Solve for m.

    $1.9m = 15.2$

    A. $m = 0.8$ C. $m = 8$
    B. $m = 7.9$ D. $m = 80$

FREE RESPONSE

Simplify.

13. 1.06×10^3

14. $8.825 \div 10^{-2}$

Solve each equation.

15. $\frac{x}{3.3} = 0.7$ $x =$ _____

16. $y + 0.27 = 3.16$ $y =$ _____

17. $1.8n = 9.9$ $n =$ _____

18. $z - 1.77 = 3$ $z =$ _____

Estimate each answer.

19. $27.84 + 19.41$

20. $28.66 - 14.32$

21. $146.28 \div 1.84$

22. 5.71×4.25

Write each number in scientific notation.

23. 0.00104

24. $21{,}020$

Solve.

25. Shakil bought a dozen eggs and a loaf of bread for $4.65. The eggs were $1.99. Write and solve an equation to find the cost of the bread.

26. Mary's science teacher asked her to make packets containing two ounces of salt. The salt jar contains 23 ounces of salt. How many complete packets can she make?

WRITING IN MATH

27. Explain how to add a whole number and a decimal number using the example below.

    $27 + 2.67$

Chapter 2 Test Form B **57**

28. Tell how you know which inverse operation to use when solving the equation $x + 8.4 = 16.8$.

29. Larry solved the word problem below. Did he interpret the remainder correctly? Explain why or why not.

For a party, Faiz ordered 52 muffins. They were delivered in boxes. Each box holds up to 12 muffins. How many boxes were delivered?

$52 \div 12 \approx 4.3$;
4 boxes were delivered.

Name _____

Chapter 3 Test Form A: Mixed Formats

MULTIPLE CHOICE

Circle the correct letter for each answer.

1. Which number is divisible by 6?
   A. 108 C. 301
   B. 223 D. 514

2. Which number is a multiple of 4?
   A. 362 C. 1,202
   B. 864 D. 2,458

3. Which of the following is a prime number?
   A. 19 C. 129
   B. 45 D. 216

4. What is the prime factorization of 117?
   A. $2 \times 3 \times 13$
   B. $3^2 \times 13$
   C. $3 \times 5 \times 9$
   D. 9×13

5. Find the GCF for 21 and 42.
   A. 7 C. 21
   B. 14 D. 42

6. Find the LCM for 3, 5, and 6.
   A. 15 C. 30
   B. 18 D. 90

7. Which fraction has a decimal equivalent of $0.\overline{3}$?
   A. $\frac{3}{100}$
   B. $\frac{1}{6}$
   C. $\frac{1}{4}$
   D. $\frac{1}{3}$

8. What fraction does the shaded part of this figure represent?
   A. $\frac{1}{8}$
   B. $\frac{3}{8}$
   C. $\frac{1}{2}$
   D. $\frac{5}{8}$

   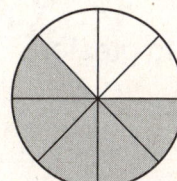

9. Which fraction is NOT equivalent to $\frac{2}{3}$?
   A. $\frac{10}{18}$ C. $\frac{8}{12}$
   B. $\frac{4}{6}$ D. $\frac{6}{9}$

10. What is $1\frac{2}{5}$ written as an improper fraction?
    A. $\frac{3}{5}$
    B. $\frac{5}{5}$
    C. $\frac{7}{5}$
    D. $\frac{9}{5}$

11. Which of the following is the best estimate for $\frac{402}{600}$?
    A. $\frac{3}{4}$ C. $\frac{1}{2}$
    B. $\frac{2}{3}$ D. $\frac{1}{3}$

Chapter 3 Test Form A

12. Which is 0.6 as a fraction in simplest form?

   A. $\frac{1}{8}$

   B. $\frac{1}{2}$

   C. $\frac{6}{10}$

   D. $\frac{3}{5}$

FREE RESPONSE

Compare using >, <, or =.

13. $\frac{2}{6}$ ◯ $\frac{1}{2}$

14. $\frac{7}{8}$ ◯ $\frac{4}{5}$

15. $\frac{3}{15}$ ◯ $\frac{2}{5}$

16. $\frac{4}{12}$ ◯ $\frac{3}{9}$

Order from least to greatest.

17. $\frac{9}{7}$, $1\frac{1}{4}$, 1.3 _____

18. $\frac{4}{5}$, 0.75, $\frac{2}{3}$, 0.5

   _____

Find the LCM and GCF for each pair of numbers.

19. 7 and 9 LCM: _____ GCF: _____

20. 40 and 10 LCM: _____ GCF: _____

Write each fraction in simplest form.

21. $\frac{9}{4}$ _____   22. $\frac{6}{14}$ _____

23. $\frac{45}{60}$ _____

24. Tamara and her family picked 108 apples during a day trip to an orchard. She wants to divide all the apples into groups of 5, 7, or 9 and give them to her friends. Which group size can she use?

   _____

25. A box of nails contains four different sizes: $\frac{5}{8}$ inch, $\frac{3}{4}$ inch, $\frac{7}{8}$ inch, and $\frac{2}{3}$ inch. Which size nail is the greatest?

   _____

   _____

26. Which letter on the number line below corresponds to $1\frac{1}{4}$? _____

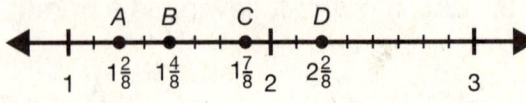

27. Make a table to solve this problem.

   Suppose the population of a city doubled every 25 years between the years 1900 and 2000. In the year 2000, the population of the city was 256,000. What was the population of the city in the year 1900?

   _____

WRITING IN MATH

28. Explain how to write nine-twelfths as a simplified fraction and as a decimal.

_____
_____
_____
_____
_____

29. Without dividing, explain how you can tell whether 143 pencils can be shared equally by 3 people.

_____
_____
_____
_____

30. Identify and answer any hidden questions in the problem. Then, solve the problem.

Josh is shopping for tank-top shirts for his school basketball team. The team has five players and three substitutes. Josh wants to get each player two shirts. The shirts come in packs of 8 for $45. How much will the shirts cost?

_____
_____
_____
_____
_____
_____

What is the cost for 16 shirts? _____

Chapter 3 Test Form A

Name _____

Chapter 3 Test Form B: Mixed Formats

MULTIPLE CHOICE

Circle the letter of the correct answer.

1. Which number is divisible by 9?
   A. 147   C. 335
   B. 225   D. 614

2. Which number is a multiple of 7?
   A. 1,157
   B. 775
   C. 324
   D. 63

3. Which of the following is a prime number?
   A. 15   C. 184
   B. 23   D. 213

4. What is the prime factorization of 189?
   A. $3^3 \times 7$
   B. $3 \times 5 \times 11$
   C. $2 \times 3^2 \times 5$
   D. $2^2 \times 27$

5. Find the GCF for 15 and 27.
   A. 1   C. 5
   B. 3   D. 9

6. Find the LCM for 2, 7, and 10.
   A. 140   C. 35
   B. 70   D. 20

7. Which fraction has a decimal equivalent of 0.$\overline{8}$?
   A. $\frac{8}{100}$ C. $\frac{1}{5}$
   B. $\frac{1}{8}$ D. $\frac{8}{9}$

8. What fraction does the shaded part of this figure represent?

   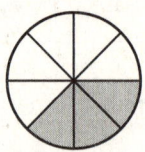

   A. $\frac{1}{8}$ C. $\frac{1}{2}$
   B. $\frac{3}{8}$ D. $\frac{5}{8}$

9. Which fraction is NOT equivalent to $\frac{6}{10}$?
   A. $\frac{3}{5}$ C. $\frac{12}{20}$
   B. $\frac{9}{15}$ D. $\frac{12}{15}$

10. What is $2\frac{2}{3}$ written as an improper fraction?
    A. $\frac{8}{3}$ C. $\frac{6}{6}$
    B. $\frac{6}{3}$ D. $\frac{3}{8}$

11. Which of the following is the best estimate for $\frac{284}{600}$?
    A. $\frac{1}{4}$ C. $\frac{1}{2}$
    B. $\frac{1}{3}$ D. $\frac{3}{4}$

12. Write 0.4 as a fraction in simplest form.
    A. $\frac{1}{5}$ C. $\frac{2}{5}$
    B. $\frac{1}{4}$ D. $\frac{4}{10}$

FREE RESPONSE

Compare using >, <, or =.

13. $\frac{3}{9}$ ◯ $\frac{4}{12}$

14. $\frac{4}{7}$ ◯ $\frac{2}{9}$

15. $\frac{2}{3}$ ◯ $\frac{3}{4}$

16. $\frac{3}{8}$ ◯ $\frac{2}{6}$

Order from least to greatest.

17. $\frac{4}{3}$, 1.1, $1\frac{2}{3}$

_____

18. $\frac{5}{6}$, 0.9, 0.7, $\frac{3}{4}$

_____

Find the LCM and GCF for each pair of numbers.

19. 3 and 10   LCM: _____   GCF: _____

20. 12 and 20   LCM: _____   GCF: _____

Write each fraction in simplest form.

21. $\frac{11}{4}$ _____

22. $\frac{7}{21}$ _____

23. $\frac{15}{55}$ _____

24. Deepak works in a bookstore where they received a shipment of 78 copies of a recent bestseller. He has been asked to arrange the books in equal stacks of 6, 7, or 9. Which stack size can he use?

_____

25. Dr. Jones, an entomologist, collected four butterflies during a recent trip. She measured and labeled the length of each butterfly. Butterfly A is $1\frac{7}{8}$ in. long, butterfly B is $1\frac{9}{16}$ in. long, butterfly C is $1\frac{1}{2}$ in. long, and butterfly D is $1\frac{13}{16}$ in. long. Which butterfly is the longest?

_____

26. Which letter on the number line corresponds to $2\frac{1}{2}$?

_____

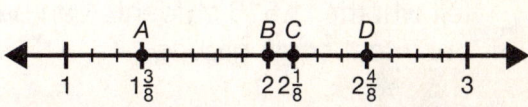

27. Make a table to solve this problem.

Susan saves $3.50 a week from her pocket money to buy a shirt that costs $21. In how many weeks can she save enough money to buy the shirt?

_____

WRITING IN MATH

28. Explain how to write fifteen twenty-fifths as a simplified fraction and as a decimal.

29. Without dividing, explain how you can tell whether 1,516 students can be put into 4 equal groups.

30. Identify and answer any hidden questions in the problem. Then, solve the problem.

Eugenia is going on a 210-mile car trip. Her gas budget is $12. Gas costs $1.39/gallon and the car gets 30 miles/gallon. Does she have enough money budgeted for gas?

Name _____

Chapters 1–3 Cumulative Test: Multiple Choice

Circle the letter of the correct answer.

1. Which is the standard form for
   $3 \times 1,000,000 + 2 \times 1,000 + 7 \times 100 + 2$?

   A. 3,002,702

   B. 3,020,072

   C. 3,020,720

   D. 3,207,002

2. What is the place value of 6 in 1.02364?

   A. tenths

   B. hundredths

   C. thousandths

   D. ten-thousandths

3. Which number is divisible by 6?

   A. 70   C. 214

   B. 108   D. 482

4. Write 10^5 in standard form.

   A. 10,000,000

   B. 1,000,000

   C. 100,000

   D. 10,000

5. Which symbol makes this statement true?

   2.409 ◯ 2.490

   A. =   C. <

   B. >   D. ≅

6. Round 1.21895 to the nearest ten-thousandth.

   A. 1.2189   C. 1.2191

   B. 1.2190   D. 1.2195

7. Which of the following is a prime number?

   A. 21   C. 111

   B. 47   D. 302

8. Round 11,617,264 to the nearest ten thousand.

   A. 11,615,000

   B. 11,617,000

   C. 11,620,000

   D. 11,620,300

9. Nikki sold 12 boxes of cookies for $3.25 each to raise money for her soccer team. About how much money did she raise?

   A. about $30   C. about $44

   B. about $36   D. about $50

10. What is the prime factorization of 144?

    A. $2^4 \times 3^2$

    B. $2^3 \times 3^2$

    C. $2^4 \times 3$

    D. $2 \times 3 \times 5$

11. Estimate 841 + 1,107 + 1,479 to the nearest hundred.
    A. 3,600
    B. 3,550
    C. 3,500
    D. 3,400

12. Find 8 − 5.19.
    A. 2.91
    B. 2.81
    C. 2.69
    D. 2.19

13. Find the GCF for 18 and 27.
    A. 54
    B. 36
    C. 27
    D. 9

14. Which is the best estimate for 132 × 206?
    A. 26,000
    B. 30,000
    C. 32,000
    D. 35,000

15. Find 0.8 × 0.21.
    A. 16.8
    B. 1.68
    C. 0.168
    D. 0.108

16. Devon bought 3 jars of spaghetti sauce for $11.25. Which equation could you use to find the cost, x, of each jar?
    A. $3x = 11.25$
    B. $\frac{x}{3} = 11.25$
    C. $x + 3 = 11.25$
    D. $x − 3 = 11.25$

17. Which is the best estimate for 254 ÷ 27?
    A. 9
    B. 10
    C. 11
    D. 12

18. Find 31.56 ÷ 12.
    A. 263
    B. 26.3
    C. 2.63
    D. 0.238

19. One day Mary missed 2 classes and attended 5 classes. What fraction of the school day did she miss?
    A. $\frac{1}{5}$
    B. $\frac{2}{7}$
    C. $\frac{2}{5}$
    D. $\frac{5}{7}$

20. Calculate the value of $4^2 \div 2 \times (3 + 1)$.
    A. 2
    B. 12
    C. 32
    D. 40

21. Mira, who owns a local bakery, puts all the unsold cookies in packets of 3 at the end of the day. How many packets can she make if she has 32 cookies left?
    A. 9
    B. 10
    C. 11
    D. 12

22. Which property does the following number sentence illustrate?
    (2 × 3) + (4 + 3) = (4 + 3) + (2 × 3)
    A. Distributive Property
    B. Identity Property of Multiplication
    C. Commutative Property of Addition
    D. Associative Property of Addition

23. Find 9.81 ÷ 0.3.
    A. 32.7
    B. 3.27
    C. 2.27
    D. 0.227

24. Which fraction is NOT equivalent to $\frac{2}{5}$?
    A. $\frac{2}{10}$
    B. $\frac{6}{15}$
    C. $\frac{10}{25}$
    D. $\frac{8}{20}$

25. Which algebraic expression represents the sum of 13 and x?
    A. $13 - x$
    B. $x - 13$
    C. $13x$
    D. $13 + x$

26. Find 2.80451×10^3.
    A. 280,451
    B. 28,045.1
    C. 2,804.51
    D. 28.0451

27. Write $2\frac{3}{5}$ as an improper fraction.
    A. $\frac{13}{5}$
    B. $\frac{7}{3}$
    C. $\frac{5}{5}$
    D. $\frac{3}{7}$

28. How can you get the variable alone in the equation $2x = 8$?
    A. Divide both sides by 8.
    B. Divide both sides by 2.
    C. Multiply both sides by 8.
    D. Multiply both sides by 2.

29. Estimate the shaded part of the rectangle.
    A. $\frac{3}{4}$
    B. $\frac{2}{3}$
    C. $\frac{1}{2}$
    D. $\frac{1}{4}$

30. Solve for x: $x - 3 = 11$.
    A. $x = 8$
    B. $x = 14$
    C. $x = 15$
    D. $x = 33$

31. Solve for p: $1.8p = 23.4$
    A. $p = 10$
    B. $p = 11$
    C. $p = 12$
    D. $p = 13$

32. What is 0.8 written as a fraction in simplest form?
    A. $\frac{4}{5}$
    B. $\frac{3}{5}$
    C. $\frac{1}{2}$
    D. $\frac{3}{6}$

33. Find the LCM for 4, 7, and 12.
    A. 84
    B. 64
    C. 42
    D. 36

34. Which symbol makes this statement true?
    $\frac{7}{9}$ ◯ $\frac{2}{3}$
    A. $=$
    B. $>$
    C. $<$
    D. $\cong$

35. Which properties are used to simplify $(39 + 14) + 11 = (39 + 11) + 14$?
    A. Distributive Property
    B. Associative Property of Multiplication
    C. Identity Property of Addition
    D. Commutative and Associative Properties of Addition

36. Peter wants to plant trees every 2.7 meters along the square perimeter of his yard. The perimeter of the yard is 13.5 meters. How many trees can Peter plant?
    A. 7
    B. 6
    C. 5
    D. 4

37. Which list shows numbers in order from least to greatest?
    A. 0.7; $\frac{2}{3}$; $\frac{1}{5}$; 0.6
    B. $\frac{1}{5}$; 0.6; 0.7; $\frac{2}{3}$
    C. $\frac{1}{5}$; 0.6; $\frac{2}{3}$; 0.7
    D. $\frac{2}{3}$; 0.6; $\frac{1}{5}$; 0.7

Chapters 1–3 Cumulative Test

38. Which equation does NOT have the solution $x = 4$?

    A. $2x = 10$

    B. $10 - x = 6$

    C. $3x = 12$

    D. $\frac{12}{x} = 3$

39. Which is the best estimate of $3.22 + 18.69$?

    A. 20   **C.** 22

    B. 21   **D.** 23

40. Why is 3,627 divisible by 9?

    A. The sum of the digits is divisible by 3.

    B. The sum of the digits equals 9.

    C. The sum of the digits is divisible by 9.

    D. The last two digits make a number divisible by 9.

41. Find $3{,}380 \times 10^{-2}$.

    A. 338   **C.** 3.380

    B. 33.80   **D.** 0.3380

42. Write 0.01975 in scientific notation.

    A. 19.75×10^{2} **C.** 1.975×10^{-2}

    B. 19.75×10^{-2} **D.** 1.975×10^{-3}

Use the following information for 43–44.

Video Brad plans on renting at least 5 DVDs. Should he join the Video Club or just rent the DVDs from Video Market?

Video Club
$10.00 membership
$1.25 per DVD rented

Video Market
$3.50 per DVD rented
No membership

43. What question is being asked in the video problem?

    A. How much does it cost to rent 5 DVDs from the Video Club?

    B. How much does it cost to rent 5 DVDs from the Video Market?

    C. Is it cheaper to rent 5 DVDs from Video Club or Video Market?

    D. How many video DVDs will Brad rent?

Katie solved the video problem as shown below.

Number of Videos	1	2	3	4	5
Video Club	$11.25	$12.50	$13.75	$15.00	$16.25
Video Market	$3.50	$7.00	$10.50	$14.00	$17.50

Brad should join the Video Club.

44. What strategy did Katie use to solve the video problem?

    A. Try, Check, and Revise

    B. Write an Equation

    C. Draw a Picture

    D. Make a Table

Name _____

Chapter 4 Test Form A: Mixed Formats

MULTIPLE CHOICE

Circle the correct letter for each answer.

1. Find $\frac{5}{6} + \frac{5}{6}$.
   A. $\frac{5}{12}$
   B. $\frac{5}{6}$
   C. $1\frac{1}{6}$
   D. $1\frac{2}{3}$

2. Find $\frac{7}{9} - \frac{1}{3}$.
   A. $\frac{4}{9}$
   B. $\frac{5}{9}$
   C. $\frac{2}{3}$
   D. 1

3. Choose the best estimate for $3\frac{1}{3} + 6\frac{3}{4}$.
   A. 8
   B. 9
   C. 10
   D. 11

4. Choose the best estimate for $7\frac{4}{5} - 2\frac{1}{4}$.
   A. 7
   B. 6
   C. 5
   D. 4

5. Find $4\frac{8}{9} + 2\frac{4}{9}$.
   A. $7\frac{4}{9}$
   B. $7\frac{1}{3}$
   C. $6\frac{1}{3}$
   D. $2\frac{4}{9}$

6. Find the sum of $2\frac{2}{3}$ and $2\frac{1}{2}$.
   A. $1\frac{1}{6}$
   B. $4\frac{3}{5}$
   C. $5\frac{1}{6}$
   D. $5\frac{1}{3}$

7. Find the difference between $2\frac{5}{8}$ and $\frac{1}{4}$.
   A. $2\frac{3}{8}$
   B. $3\frac{1}{8}$
   C. $3\frac{3}{8}$
   D. $3\frac{7}{8}$

8. Find $11\frac{1}{3} - 6\frac{2}{3}$.
   A. $3\frac{1}{3}$
   B. $3\frac{2}{3}$
   C. $4\frac{2}{3}$
   D. $5\frac{1}{3}$

9. Find the difference $6 - 5\frac{4}{7}$.
   A. $\frac{2}{7}$
   B. $\frac{3}{7}$
   C. $\frac{4}{7}$
   D. $1\frac{3}{7}$

10. Which number is NOT a common denominator for $\frac{2}{3}$, $\frac{5}{6}$, and $\frac{5}{12}$?
    A. 36
    B. 24
    C. 12
    D. 6

11. What are the next 3 numbers in the pattern 1, 4, 6, 9, 11, …?
    A. 13, 15, 17
    B. 14, 17, 20
    C. 14, 16, 19
    D. 22, 44, 88

Chapter 4 Test Form A **69**

For 12–14, refer to the table below.

County Fair Ticket Sales Rides $4.50—Games $2.50		
	Ride Tickets Sold	Game Tickets Sold
Day 1	50	37
Day 2	102	65
Day 3	75	73
Day 4	96	89

12. What was the total income for Day 2? Is an exact answer or an estimate needed?

    A. $750.00; estimate

    B. $547.50; exact

    C. $621.50; exact

    D. $600.00; estimate

13. For all four days, were more tickets sold for rides or games? About how many more? Is an exact answer or an estimate needed?

    A. Rides; 59; exact

    B. Rides; 60; estimate

    C. Games; 59; exact

    D. Games; 50; estimate

14. What would it cost to ride 3 rides and play 2 games? Is an exact answer or estimate needed?

    A. $19.00; estimate

    B. $18.50; exact

    C. $21.50; exact

    D. $24.00; estimate

FREE RESPONSE

Estimate each answer.

15. $6\frac{1}{8} + 3\frac{2}{3}$ _____

16. $12\frac{7}{9} - 6\frac{1}{4}$ _____

Find each answer. Simplify if possible.

17. $\frac{5}{8} + \frac{7}{12}$ _____

18. $\frac{7}{8} - \frac{3}{8}$ _____

19. $4\frac{1}{2} + 5\frac{7}{12}$ _____

20. $6\frac{2}{3} - \frac{1}{5}$ _____

21. Tell what computation method you would use to find $3 - 1\frac{5}{8}$.

    _____

Chapter 4 Test Form A

WRITING IN MATH

22. In the pattern below, how many squares are formed at the 5th stage? Explain the strategy you used.

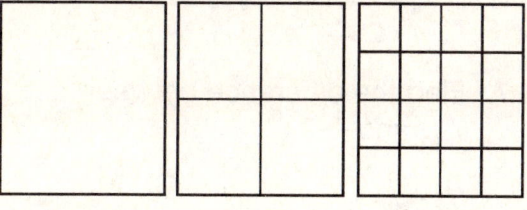

Stage 1   Stage 2   Stage 3

23. Explain how to subtract $6\frac{1}{3}$ from $8\frac{1}{6}$.

24. Explain how you could use mental math to add $6\frac{2}{7} + 3\frac{5}{7}$.

Name _____

Chapter 4 Test Form B: Mixed Formats

MULTIPLE CHOICE

Circle the letter of the correct answer.

1. Find $\frac{8}{9} + \frac{7}{9}$.
   A. $1\frac{7}{9}$
   B. $1\frac{2}{3}$
   C. $\frac{5}{6}$
   D. $\frac{8}{18}$

2. Find $\frac{5}{8} - \frac{1}{2}$.
   A. $\frac{1}{8}$
   B. $\frac{1}{4}$
   C. $\frac{1}{2}$
   D. $\frac{3}{4}$

3. Choose the best estimate for $4\frac{7}{8} + 6\frac{1}{5}$.
   A. 12
   B. 11
   C. 10
   D. 9

4. Choose the best estimate for $5\frac{1}{4} - 1\frac{5}{6}$.
   A. 4
   B. 3
   C. 2
   D. 1

5. Find $3\frac{9}{10} + 1\frac{7}{10}$.
   A. $2\frac{1}{5}$
   B. $4\frac{1}{5}$
   C. $5\frac{3}{10}$
   D. $5\frac{3}{5}$

6. Find the sum of $3\frac{2}{5}$ and $4\frac{2}{3}$.
   A. $1\frac{4}{15}$
   B. $7\frac{1}{2}$
   C. $8\frac{1}{15}$
   D. $8\frac{1}{5}$

7. Find the difference between $7\frac{7}{12}$ and $\frac{1}{6}$.
   A. $8\frac{3}{4}$
   B. $8\frac{5}{12}$
   C. $8\frac{1}{12}$
   D. $7\frac{5}{12}$

8. Find $12\frac{1}{5} - 4\frac{4}{5}$.
   A. $8\frac{3}{5}$
   B. $7\frac{2}{5}$
   C. $6\frac{2}{5}$
   D. $6\frac{1}{5}$

9. Find the difference $5 - 4\frac{5}{9}$.
   A. $1\frac{4}{9}$
   B. $\frac{5}{9}$
   C. $\frac{4}{9}$
   D. $\frac{1}{3}$

10. Which number is NOT a common denominator for $\frac{1}{2}$, $\frac{3}{5}$, and $\frac{7}{10}$?
    A. 10
    B. 15
    C. 20
    D. 30

11. Name the next 3 numbers in the pattern 3, 6, 12, 24, 48, ____, ____, ____.
    A. 50, 52, 54
    B. 72, 120, 192
    C. 96, 192, 384
    D. 58, 70, 84

For 12-14, refer to the table below.

Movie Ticket Sales Adult $6.50 Children $4.50		
Day	Tickets Sold Adults	Tickets Sold Children
1	40	27
2	104	75
3	65	63
4	79	86

12. What was the total of the ticket sales for Day 2? Is an exact answer or an estimate needed?

   A. $1,013.50; exact

   B. $1,113.50; exact

   C. $970.00; estimate

   D. $1,100.00; estimate

13. For all four days, were more children or adult tickets sold? About how many more? Is an exact answer or an estimate needed?

   A. Children; 37; exact

   B. Children; 40; estimate

   C. Adults; 47; exact

   D. Adults; 50; estimate

14. What would it cost for 2 adults and 3 children to see the movie? Is an exact answer or estimate needed?

   A. $26.50; exact

   B. $30.50; exact

   C. $24.00; estimate

   D. $29.00; estimate

FREE RESPONSE

Estimate each answer.

15. $3\frac{1}{3} + 5\frac{3}{4}$ _____

16. $11\frac{5}{6} - 8\frac{1}{4}$ _____

Find each answer. Simplify if possible.

17. $\frac{3}{4} + \frac{2}{3}$ _____

18. $\frac{5}{6} - \frac{1}{6}$ _____

19. $2\frac{4}{5} + 2\frac{7}{15}$ _____

20. $4\frac{5}{6} - \frac{1}{4}$ _____

21. Tell what computation method you would use to find $6 - 1\frac{3}{4}$.

   _____

WRITING IN MATH

22. In the pattern below, how many circles are formed at the 6th stage? Explain the strategy you used.

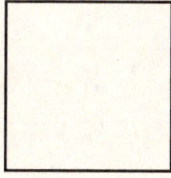 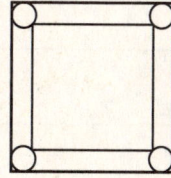 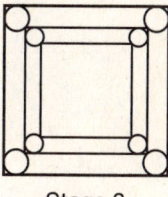

Stage 1   Stage 2   Stage 3

_____
_____
_____
_____

Chapter 4 Test: Form B **73**

23. Explain how to subtract $4\frac{1}{5}$ from $9\frac{1}{10}$.

24. Explain how you could use mental math to find $5\frac{3}{8} + 3\frac{2}{5} + 4\frac{5}{8} + 1\frac{1}{5}$.

Name _____

Chapter 5 Test Form A: Mixed Formats

MULTIPLE CHOICE

Circle the correct letter for each answer.

1. What is $\frac{5}{7} \times 63$?
   A. 9
   B. 45
   C. 60
   D. 72

2. Darren spends $\frac{5}{8}$ of his allowance on baseball cards and school supplies. He spends $\frac{4}{5}$ of this amount on baseball cards. What fraction of his allowance is spent on baseball cards?
   A. $\frac{1}{40}$
   B. $\frac{1}{2}$
   C. $\frac{5}{8}$
   D. $\frac{4}{5}$

3. Estimate $\frac{3}{4} \times 27$ using compatible numbers.
   A. 81
   B. 21
   C. 12
   D. 7

4. Find $2\frac{1}{5} \times 6\frac{2}{3}$.
   A. $8\frac{1}{4}$
   B. $12\frac{2}{15}$
   C. $14\frac{2}{3}$
   D. $14\frac{3}{4}$

5. The shadow of a tree is $1\frac{1}{4}$ times as tall as the tree. The tree is 8 feet tall. How tall is the shadow?
   A. 12 feet
   B. 10 feet
   C. 5 feet
   D. 2 feet

6. Find $5\frac{1}{4} \div 3\frac{1}{2}$.
   A. $15\frac{1}{8}$
   B. $2\frac{1}{4}$
   C. $1\frac{2}{3}$
   D. $1\frac{1}{2}$

7. Which is the reciprocal of $3\frac{2}{5}$?
   A. $\frac{5}{17}$
   B. $\frac{5}{6}$
   C. $1\frac{7}{5}$
   D. $3\frac{5}{2}$

8. Peter has saved $35 to buy a radio. This is only $\frac{5}{7}$ of what the radio costs. How much does the radio cost?
   A. $25
   B. $45
   C. $48
   D. $49

9. Which expression represents 9 less than $\frac{4}{5}$ of a number, p?
   A. $\frac{4}{5}p \times 9$
   B. $\frac{4}{5}p - 9$
   C. $9p - \frac{4}{5}$
   D. $p \div \frac{4}{5} - 9$

10. Solve $x \div \frac{9}{2} = 5$.
    A. $x = \frac{9}{10}$
    B. $x = 5\frac{5}{9}$
    C. $x = 5\frac{9}{2}$
    D. $x = 22\frac{1}{2}$

For 11–12, use the ingredient list below.

Blueberry Pancakes
Ingredients:
- $1\frac{1}{3}$ cups milk
- 2 eggs
- $\frac{1}{4}$ tsp salt
- $2\frac{3}{4}$ cups flour
- 1 tsp baking soda
- $\frac{3}{4}$ cup blueberries

11. If you tripled the recipe, how much flour would you need?

   A. $8\frac{1}{2}$ cups   C. $6\frac{3}{4}$ cups
   B. $8\frac{1}{4}$ cups   D. $5\frac{3}{4}$ cups

12. Justin only wants to make $\frac{1}{3}$ the amount of pancake batter. How much of the blueberries will he need?

   A. $\frac{1}{4}$ cup   C. $\frac{1}{6}$ cup
   B. $\frac{1}{3}$ cup   D. $\frac{1}{12}$ cup

FREE RESPONSE

Find each product. Simplify if possible.

13. $\frac{1}{5} \times \frac{5}{12}$ _____

14. $40 \times \frac{3}{8}$ _____

15. $3\frac{2}{3} \times 5\frac{1}{6}$ _____

16. $4\frac{1}{5} \times 5$ _____

Write the reciprocal of each.

17. $\frac{2}{7}$ _____

18. 9 _____

Estimate.

19. $\frac{7}{10} \times 37$ _____

20. $5\frac{6}{7} \div 2\frac{1}{5}$ _____

For 21–24, find each quotient. Simplify if possible.

21. $\frac{4}{9} \div \frac{1}{3}$ _____

22. $8\frac{2}{3} \div 3\frac{7}{9}$ _____

23. $1\frac{3}{8} \div \frac{3}{4}$ _____

24. $\frac{6}{11} \div 3$ _____

25. Write 5 more than $\frac{2}{3}$ of a number, k, as an algebraic expression.

   _____

26. Evaluate $\frac{2}{3}m + 5\frac{1}{2}$ for $m = \frac{1}{4}$.

   _____

Solve each equation and check your answer.

27. $2\frac{4}{7}n = \frac{3}{5}$ $n =$ _____

28. $x + \frac{8}{9} = 4\frac{1}{3}$ $x =$ _____

WRITING IN MATH

29. Explain why $\frac{3}{7}$ and $2\frac{1}{3}$ are reciprocals.

_____

_____

30. A computer password uses the letters A, B, C, and D. Each letter is used only once. How many different combinations are possible? Solve by making an organized list.

_____

31. In a parking garage, each parking space is $6\frac{1}{4}$ ft wide. There are 20 spaces along a 132-foot wall of the garage. Each space is separated by a line of equal width. There is also a line of the same width at both ends. What is the width of each line? Explain your solution and show your work.

_____

_____

_____

_____

_____

_____

_____

_____

Chapter 5 Test Form A

Name _____

Chapter 5 Test Form B: Mixed Formats

MULTIPLE CHOICE

Circle the letter of the correct answer.

1. What is $\frac{5}{8} \times 48$?

   A. 6   C. 40

   B. 30   D. 56

2. Courtney spends $\frac{4}{9}$ of her allowance on parts for her bike. Her new brakes cost $\frac{1}{4}$ of this amount. What fraction of her allowance is spent on brakes?

   A. $\frac{4}{9}$ C. $\frac{1}{9}$

   B. $\frac{1}{4}$ D. $\frac{1}{12}$

3. Estimate $\frac{3}{5} \times 41$ using compatible numbers.

   A. 123   C. 15

   B. 24   D. 8

4. Find $2\frac{1}{3} \times 6\frac{3}{4}$.

   A. $9\frac{1}{12}$ C. $15\frac{3}{4}$

   B. $\frac{3}{12}$ D. $15\frac{5}{6}$

5. Maria's puppy weighs $1\frac{3}{4}$ times more than her cat. Her cat weighs 8 pounds. How much does Maria's puppy weigh?

   A. 14 pounds   C. 6 pounds

   B. 12 pounds   D. 4 pounds

6. Find $8\frac{1}{6} \div 2\frac{1}{3}$.

   A. $3\frac{1}{2}$ C. $6\frac{1}{3}$

   B. $3\frac{2}{3}$ D. $16\frac{1}{18}$

7. Which is the reciprocal of $5\frac{3}{4}$?

   A. $5\frac{4}{3}$ C. $\frac{4}{15}$

   B. $2\frac{3}{4}$ D. $\frac{4}{23}$

8. Janice has read 42 pages of a book. This is only $\frac{7}{9}$ of the book. How many pages is the entire book?

   A. 45 pages   C. 54 pages

   B. 49 pages   D. 63 pages

9. Which expression represents four less than $\frac{5}{6}$ of a number, n?

   A. $\frac{5}{6}n \times 4$ C. $n \div \frac{5}{6} - 4$

   B. $4n - \frac{5}{6}$ D. $\frac{5}{6}n - 4$

10. Solve $x \div \frac{4}{3} = 7$.

    A. $x = \frac{4}{21}$ C. $x = 7\frac{4}{3}$

    B. $x = 7\frac{4}{7}$ D. $x = 9\frac{1}{3}$

For 11–12, use the ingredient list below.

Soap
Ingredients:
- $7\frac{1}{2}$ ounces lye
- 8 ounces cocoa butter
- $8\frac{3}{4}$ ounces olive oil
- $9\frac{2}{3}$ ounces coconut oil
- 4 drops rose oil
- $\frac{3}{4}$ teaspoon grapefruit extract

11. If you tripled the recipe, how much lye would you need?

   A. $22\frac{1}{2}$ ounces C. $21\frac{1}{2}$ ounces
   B. $22\frac{1}{4}$ ounces D. $10\frac{1}{2}$ ounces

12. Manuel only wants to make $\frac{2}{3}$ the amount of soap. How much of the grapefruit extract will he need?

   A. $\frac{2}{3}$ teaspoon C. $\frac{1}{2}$ teaspoon
   B. $\frac{1}{2}$ teaspoon D. $\frac{1}{6}$ teaspoon

FREE RESPONSE

Find each product. Simplify if possible.

13. $3\frac{1}{4} \times 7\frac{2}{3}$ _____

14. $3\frac{1}{4} \times 4$ _____

Write the reciprocal of each.

15. $\frac{8}{9}$ _____

16. 7 _____

Estimate.

17. $\frac{3}{10} \times 58$ _____

18. $8\frac{2}{9} \div 1\frac{4}{5}$ _____

For 19–20, find each quotient. Simplify if possible.

19. $8\frac{1}{3} \div 5\frac{5}{6}$ _____

20. $\frac{10}{13} \div 5$ _____

21. Write 3 more than $\frac{2}{5}$ a number, k, as an algebraic expression.

   _____

22. Evaluate $\frac{1}{2}m + 6\frac{1}{2}$ for $m = \frac{3}{4}$.

   _____

Solve each equation and check your answer.

23. $1\frac{1}{4}n = \frac{3}{16}$ $n =$ _____

24. $x + \frac{5}{8} = 6\frac{1}{4}$ $x =$ _____

WRITING IN MATH

25. Explain why $\frac{4}{9}$ and $2\frac{1}{4}$ are reciprocals.

   _____
   _____
   _____

26. Amelia wants to make a 4-digit password with her four favorite numbers: 2, 3, 7, and 9. Each number is used only once. How many different combinations are possible? Solve by making an organized list.

   _____

Chapter 5 Test Form B

27. A $102\frac{1}{4}$ inch ladder has 8 steps. There are no steps at the top or the bottom, and each step is $2\frac{3}{8}$ inches thick. What is the distance of the space between any two steps? Explain.

_____

_____

_____

_____

_____

_____

Name _____

Chapter 6 Test Form A: Mixed Formats

MULTIPLE CHOICE

Circle the letter of the correct answer.

1. Which ratio compares the number of squares to the number of circles?

   A. 3 to 4   C. 2 to 1
   B. 4 to 3   D. 4 to 2

2. Which ratio is equal to 9:3?

   A. 16:3   C. 12 to 4
   B. $\frac{10}{2}$ D. $\frac{1}{3}$

3. Which pair below are equal ratios?

   A. $\frac{2}{9}$; 18:4   C. 3 to 2; $\frac{6}{3}$
   B. $\frac{4}{6}$; 2:3   D. 14 to 8; 7 to 2

4. Find the unit rate for running 20 miles in 5 hours.

   A. $\frac{4 \text{ mi}}{1 \text{ hr}}$ C. $\frac{10 \text{ mi}}{2 \text{ hr}}$
   B. $\frac{5 \text{ mi}}{1 \text{ hr}}$ D. $\frac{8 \text{ mi}}{1 \text{ hr}}$

5. A fruit basket contains 25 pieces of fruit. Two pieces of fruit out of every 5 are oranges. How many oranges are in the fruit basket?

   A. 2   C. 8
   B. 5   D. 10

6. Which proportion is written correctly?

   A. $\frac{5 \text{ in.}}{3 \text{ ft}} = \frac{2 \text{ ft}}{60 \text{ in.}}$
   B. $\frac{4 \text{ oz}}{2 \text{ lb}} = \frac{12 \text{ oz}}{6 \text{ lb}}$
   C. $\frac{2 \text{ hr}}{10 \text{ min}} = \frac{20 \text{ min}}{1 \text{ hr}}$
   D. $\frac{4 \text{ ft}}{6 \text{ yd}} = \frac{2 \text{ yd}}{15 \text{ yd}}$

7. Solve the proportion $\frac{180 \text{ mi}}{x \text{ hr}} = \frac{240 \text{ mi}}{4 \text{ hr}}$

   A. $x = 10$ hr   C. $x = 3$ hr
   B. $x = 5$ hr   D. $x = 2.5$ hr

8. Which is the best buy?

   A. 6 lb for $3.00
   B. 9 lb for $4.50
   C. 5 lb for $2.60
   D. 7 lb for $3.36

9. Darren types 55 words per minute. At this rate, how many words will he type in 15 minutes?

   A. 610 words   C. 900 words
   B. 825 words   D. 1,025 words

10. Kayla can jump 27 inches high. Using the formula $y = \frac{i}{36}$, where y is the number of yards, and i is the number of inches, find how high Kayla can jump in yards.

    A. $y = 0.75$ yd   C. $y = 7.5$ yd
    B. $y = 0.8$ yd   D. $y = 972$ yd

11. What is the actual distance between Percentville and Fractiontown along the road?

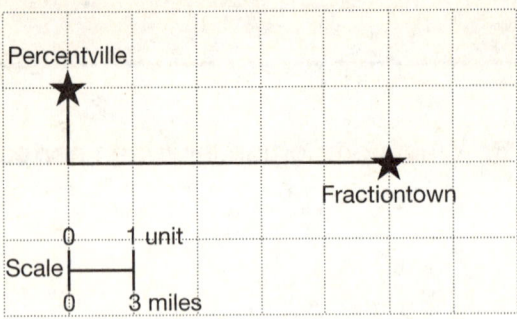

A. 6 miles C. 18 miles
B. 15 miles D. 21 miles

FREE RESPONSE

Write a ratio for each comparison.

Color	black	brown	white	red
Number of horses	17	3	15	13

12. white to brown

13. red to all colors

14. black to all other colors

Give three ratios that are equal to each ratio.

15. $\frac{4}{5}$ _____ _____ _____

16. 6 to 16 _____

17. 18:3 _____ _____ _____

18. $\frac{14}{8}$ _____ _____ _____

Write each ratio in simplest form.

19. $\frac{234}{104}$ _____

20. 4.8 to 0.6 _____

Write each as a unit rate.

21. 18 mi in 3 hr

22. $4.64 for 8 gal

23. 36 cans in 4 cases

24. 364 mi on 14 gal

Decide if the ratios form a proportion.

25. $\frac{3 \text{ ft}}{8 \text{ mi}}, \frac{12 \text{ ft}}{18 \text{ mi}}$ _____

26. $\frac{15 \text{ oz}}{3 \text{ lb}}, \frac{10 \text{ oz}}{2 \text{ lb}}$ _____

Solve each proportion.

27. $\frac{176 \text{ mi}}{8 \text{ gal}} = \frac{x \text{ mi}}{14 \text{ gal}}$ $x =$ _____

28. $\frac{6 \text{ min}}{21 \text{ ft}} = \frac{24 \text{ min}}{y \text{ ft}}$ $y =$ _____

29. $\frac{28}{16} = \frac{n}{12}$ $n =$ _____

30. $\frac{18}{32} = \frac{27}{z}$ $z =$ _____

31. Josh drives at a rate of 35 miles per hour for 5 hours. How far does he drive? Use the formula $d = rt$.

_____

32. There are about 28.35 grams in an ounce. How many grams are in 1 pound?

_____

33. The scale on a map is 1.5 in. to 24 mi. If two cities are 7 in. apart on the map, what is the actual distance between the two cities?

_____

WRITING IN MATH

34. Beginning with the ratio $\frac{2 \text{ in.}}{3 \text{ hr}}$, make a table of quantities that vary proportionally. Tell how you know that the values in the table vary proportionally.

Inches	2				
Hours	3				

_____

_____

_____

35. The ratio of fish to turtles in the pond is 26 to 7. If there are 21 turtles, how many fish are there? Solve and explain your reasoning.

_____

_____

_____

36. Use objects to solve this problem. Give the answer in a complete sentence.

Three out of every 5 players on a 20-person basketball team can slam dunk. How many players can slam dunk?

_____

_____

_____

Chapter 6 Test Form A

Name _____

Chapter 6 Test Form B: Mixed Formats

MULTIPLE CHOICE

Circle the letter of the correct answer.

1. Which ratio compares the number of triangles to the number of hexagons?

   A. 3 to 4 C. 4 to 3
   B. 1 to 2 D. 4 to 2

2. Which ratio is equal to 6:2?
   A. 12 to 2 C. 3 to 9
   B. 9:3 D. $\frac{1}{3}$

3. Which pair below are equal ratios?
   A. 6 to 21; $\frac{4}{14}$ C. 3 to 2; 5 to 4
   B. 8:4; $\frac{4}{8}$ D. 12 to 6; $\frac{4}{3}$

4. Find the unit rate for 16 miles in 4 hours.
   A. $\frac{6 \text{ mi}}{1 \text{ hr}}$ C. $\frac{8 \text{ mi}}{2 \text{ hr}}$
   B. $\frac{4 \text{ mi}}{1 \text{ hr}}$ D. $\frac{1 \text{ mi}}{4 \text{ hr}}$

5. There are 56 passengers on a plane. Five out of every 8 passengers are carrying a suitcase. How many passengers are carrying a suitcase?
   A. 35 C. 16
   B. 30 D. 7

6. Which proportion is written correctly?
   A. $\frac{7 \text{ ft}}{3 \text{ in.}} = \frac{35 \text{ ft}}{15 \text{ in.}}$
   B. $\frac{30 \text{ min}}{2 \text{ hr}} = \frac{45 \text{ min}}{240 \text{ min}}$
   C. $\frac{3 \text{ yd}}{4 \text{ ft}} = \frac{9 \text{ ft}}{4 \text{ yd}}$
   D. $\frac{3 \text{ lb}}{15 \text{ oz}} = \frac{3{,}000 \text{ lb}}{2 \text{ T}}$

7. Solve the proportion $\frac{280 \text{ mi}}{x \text{ hr}} = \frac{210 \text{ mi}}{3 \text{ hr}}$.
   A. $x = 10$ hr C. $x = 4.5$ hr
   B. $x = 5$ hr D. $x = 4$ hr

8. Which is the best buy?
   A. 4 oz for $3.76 C. 3 oz for $2.88
   B. 6 oz for $5.70 D. 2 oz for $1.92

9. A toy robot walks 42 inches per minute. At this rate, how many inches will it walk in 7 minutes?
   A. 6 in. C. 294 in.
   B. 49 in. D. 840 in.

10. Matt put 2 milliliters of chocolate syrup into a cup of milk. Using the formula $t = 4.93m$, where t is the number of teaspoons, and m is the number of milliliters, find the amount of syrup Matt used in teaspoons.
    A. $t = 98.6$ tsp C. $t = 10$ tsp
    B. $t = 9.86$ tsp D. $t = 2.465$ tsp

11. What is the actual distance between Percentville and Fractiontown?

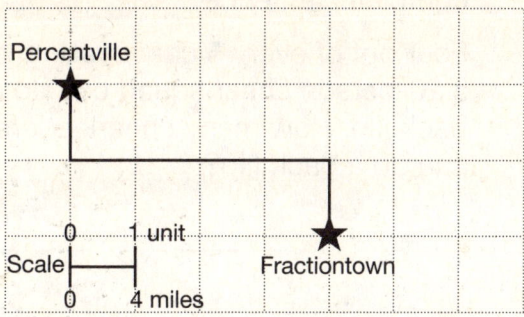

A. 6 miles   C. 20 miles
B. 16 miles D. 24 miles

FREE RESPONSE

Write a ratio for each comparison.

Size	Small	Medium	Large	Extra-large
Number of T-shirts	10	8	21	17

12. small to extra-large

_____

13. large to all sizes

_____

14. medium to all other sizes

_____

Give three ratios that are equal to each ratio.

15. 9:15 _____, _____, _____

16. $\frac{5}{6}$ _____, _____, _____

Write each ratio in simplest form.

17. 184:115 _____

18. 5.6 to 0.8 _____

Write each as a unit rate.

19. $4.48 for 8 oz _____

20. 357 mi on 17 gal _____

Decide if the ratios form a proportion.

21. $\frac{49 \text{ mi}}{14 \text{ hr}}, \frac{21 \text{ mi}}{6 \text{ hr}}$ _____

22. $\frac{8 \text{ m}}{20 \text{ min}}, \frac{4 \text{ m}}{5 \text{ min}}$ _____

Solve each proportion.

23. $\frac{234 \text{ mi}}{9 \text{ hr}} = \frac{x \text{ mi}}{15 \text{ hr}}$ $x = $ _____

24. $\frac{19}{57} = \frac{10}{z}$ $z = $ _____

25. Carol drives at a rate of 45 miles per hour for 3 hours. How far does she drive? Use the formula $d = rt$.

_____

26. There are 0.473 liters in a pint. How many liters are in 1 gallon?

_____

27. The scale of a model car is 1.2 cm to 20 cm. If the model car is 18 cm long, what is the length of the real car?

_____

Chapter 6 Test Form B

WRITING IN MATH

28. Beginning with the ratio $\frac{3 \text{ ft}}{4 \text{ hr}}$, make a table of quantities that vary proportionally. Tell how you know that the values in the table vary proportionally.

Feet	3			
Hours	4			

_____

_____

29. The ratio of kittens to puppies is 14 to 9. If there are 27 puppies, how many kittens are there? Solve and explain your reasoning.

_____

_____

30. Explain how to use objects to solve this problem. Give the answer in a complete sentence.

Four out of every 5 cheerleaders on a 20-person cheer squad can do a back flip. How many cheerleaders can do a back flip?

_____

_____

_____

_____

_____

_____

_____

_____

_____

_____

_____

Chapters 1–6 Cumulative Test

Circle the letter of the correct answer.

1. Find $\frac{13}{15} - \frac{1}{3}$.
   - A. $\frac{5}{12}$
   - B. $\frac{8}{15}$
   - C. $\frac{12}{15}$
   - D. 1

2. What is the prime factorization of 189?
   - A. $2^2 \times 7$
   - B. $2 \times 3 \times 7$
   - C. $3^3 \times 7$
   - D. $3^2 \times 7^2$

3. Which ratio compares the number of triangles to the number of circles?

   - A. 3 to 4
   - B. 2 to 3
   - C. 4 to 3
   - D. 5 to 3

4. In the pattern below, how many squares are needed to build the 6th shape?

   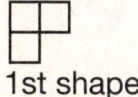 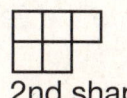
   1st shape   2nd shape

   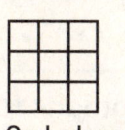 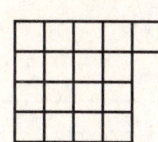
   3rd shape   4th shape

   - A. 65 squares
   - B. 45 squares
   - C. 39 squares
   - D. 33 squares

5. Trish saves $\frac{2}{9}$ of her income every month. She uses $\frac{3}{5}$ of it to buy savings bonds. What fraction of her income does she use to buy savings bonds?
   - A. $\frac{1}{2}$
   - B. $\frac{1}{3}$
   - C. $\frac{2}{15}$
   - D. $\frac{1}{10}$

6. Which ratio is equal to 3:7?
   - A. 13 to 9
   - B. $\frac{12}{7}$
   - C. 9:12
   - D. 6 to 14

7. Choose the best estimate for $6\frac{1}{5} - 2\frac{7}{8}$.
   - A. 5
   - B. 4
   - C. 3
   - D. 2

8. Round 24.1266 to the nearest thousandth.
   - A. 24.137
   - B. 24.13
   - C. 24.127
   - D. 24.126

9. Which computation method would be most appropriate to find $2\frac{3}{4} - 1\frac{5}{6}$?
   - A. Use paper and pencil.
   - B. Use a number line.
   - C. Use a calculator.
   - D. Use mental math.

10. Find the sum of $4\frac{1}{3}$ and $3\frac{5}{6}$.
    - A. $8\frac{5}{12}$
    - B. $8\frac{1}{6}$
    - C. $7\frac{11}{12}$
    - D. $7\frac{2}{3}$

11. Find the unit rate of a bicycle wheel that turns 240 times in 3 minutes.

   A. $\frac{40 \text{ turns}}{1 \text{ min}}$

   B. $\frac{60 \text{ turns}}{1 \text{ min}}$

   C. $\frac{120 \text{ turns}}{2 \text{ min}}$

   D. $\frac{80 \text{ turns}}{1 \text{ min}}$

12. Find $\frac{3}{4} + \frac{2}{5}$.

   A. $\frac{3}{20}$ C. $1\frac{1}{5}$

   B. $1\frac{3}{20}$ D. $\frac{7}{20}$

13. Estimate $708 + 1{,}289 + 1{,}311$ by rounding to the nearest hundred.

   A. 3,000   C. 3,400

   B. 3,300   D. 3,600

14. Which is the best way to estimate $\frac{3}{7} \times 30$ using compatible numbers?

   A. Multiply $\frac{3}{8}$ by 32.

   B. Multiply $\frac{3}{7}$ by 28.

   C. Multiply $\frac{3}{7}$ by 21.

   D. Multiply $\frac{1}{3}$ by 30.

15. Find the GCF for 12 and 42.

   A. 6   C. 12

   B. 10   D. 84

16. In a class, 7 out of 9 students play a sport. There are 36 students in the class. How many students play a sport?

   A. 8   C. 28

   B. 20   D. 32

17. Find $2\frac{2}{3} \times 5\frac{1}{4}$.

   A. $7\frac{11}{12}$ C. 14

   B. $10\frac{1}{6}$ D. $14\frac{5}{12}$

18. Ming bought 8 gallons of juice. The total was $19.12 before tax. Which equation would you use to find the cost, x, of each gallon?

   A. $8x = 19.12$

   B. $\frac{x}{8} = 19.12$

   C. $x + 19.12 = 8$

   D. $x + 8 = 19.12$

19. Find $4\frac{1}{3} \div 8\frac{2}{3}$.

   A. $37\frac{5}{9}$ C. $\frac{1}{2}$

   B. $\frac{3}{4}$ D. $\frac{1}{4}$

20. Which proportion is written correctly?

   A. $\frac{10 \text{ ft}}{6 \text{ ft}} = \frac{30 \text{ in}}{15 \text{ in}}$

   B. $\frac{3 \text{ yd}}{2 \text{ ft}} = \frac{9 \text{ yd}}{6 \text{ ft}}$

   C. $\frac{100 \text{ min}}{2 \text{ hr}} = \frac{1 \text{ hr}}{10 \text{ min}}$

   D. $\frac{3 \text{ tsp}}{10 \text{ tsp}} = \frac{3 \text{ tsp}}{12 \text{ tsp}}$

21. Write 6.24×10^{-4} in standard form.

   A. 0.000624   C. 62.4

   B. 0.00624   D. 62,400

22. Calculate the value of $27 \div 3^2 \times (6 - 3)$.

   A. 15   C. 12

   B. $13\frac{1}{2}$ D. 9

23. David needs to buy 92 hotdogs for the concession stand. If 8 hotdogs are in a package, how many packages does he need?

   A. 10 packages

   B. 11 packages

   C. 12 packages

   D. 13 packages

24. How many different ways can you make $0.50 without using pennies or half dollars?

   A. 7 ways   C. 15 ways
   B. 10 ways D. 50 ways

25. Which property does the following number sentence illustrate?

   $(36 + 46) + 0 = 36 + 46$

   A. Distributive Property
   B. Identity Property of Addition
   C. Commutative Property of Addition
   D. Associative Property of Addition

26. Which is the reciprocal of $2\frac{1}{5}$?

   A. $\frac{1}{4}$ C. $\frac{11}{5}$
   B. $\frac{5}{11}$ D. $2\frac{5}{1}$

27. Solve the proportion.

   $\frac{20 \text{ ft}}{2 \text{ min}} = \frac{x \text{ ft}}{20 \text{ min}}$

   A. $x = 10$ ft   C. $x = 40$ ft
   B. $x = 20$ ft   D. $x = 200$ ft

28. How can you get the variable alone in the equation $24 = \frac{n}{6}$?

   A. Divide both sides by 24.
   B. Divide both sides by 6.
   C. Multiply both sides by 24.
   D. Multiply both sides by 6.

For 29, refer to the sign below.

Zoo Admission Prices	
Infant 0–2 years	Free
Children 3–18 years	$4.25
Adults 19–54 years	$6.00
Seniors 55 and over	$4.00

29. What would it cost for 1 infant, 5 children, 2 adults, and 1 senior to attend the zoo? Is an exact answer or estimate needed?

   A. $30.25; exact
   B. $36.00; estimate
   C. $37.25; exact
   D. $40.00; estimate

30. Nicole drove at a rate of 60 miles per hour for 4 hours. How far did she drive? Use the formula $d = rt$.

   A. 604 miles   C. 56 miles
   B. 240 miles   D. 15 miles

31. Which expression represents 4 fewer than $\frac{3}{4}$ of a number, x?

   A. $4\frac{3}{4}x$ C. $4 - \frac{3}{4}x$
   B. $\frac{3}{4}x + 4$ D. $\frac{3}{4}x - 4$

32. Choose the best estimate for $4\frac{5}{7} + 2\frac{1}{4}$.

   A. 9   C. 7
   B. 8   D. 6

33. Solve $\frac{5}{6}y = 5$.

   A. $y = 6$ C. $y = 4\frac{1}{6}$
   B. $y = 5\frac{5}{6}$ D. $y = 2\frac{5}{6}$

Chapters 1–6 Cumulative Test

Which list shows the numbers in order from least to greatest?

A. 0.2; $\frac{1}{3}$; $\frac{3}{5}$; 0.4

B. $\frac{3}{5}$; 0.2; $\frac{1}{3}$; 0.4

C. 0.4; $\frac{3}{5}$; 0.2; $\frac{1}{3}$

D. 0.2; $\frac{1}{3}$; 0.4; $\frac{3}{5}$

35. What is the actual distance between Perry and Frank along the road?

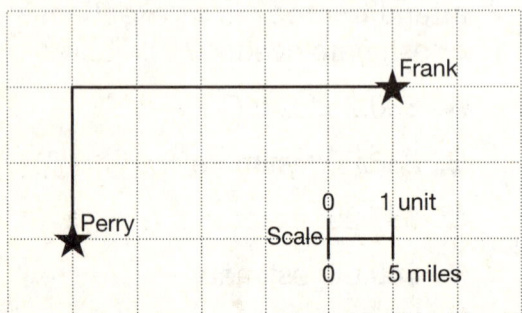

A. 28 miles C. 35 miles

B. 30 miles D. 40 miles

36. Find $\frac{3}{7} + \frac{5}{7}$.

A. $2\frac{3}{7}$ C. 1

B. $1\frac{1}{7}$ D. $\frac{6}{7}$

37. Write the cross products for the proportion below.

$\frac{7}{8} = \frac{x}{12}$

A. $7x = 8 \cdot 12$

B. $12x = 7 \cdot 8$

C. $8x = 7 \cdot 12$

D. $8x = \frac{7}{12}$

38. Find the LCM for 3, 7, and 21.

A. 42 C. 7

B. 21 D. 3

39. Evaluate $\frac{2}{5}m + 3\frac{1}{2}$ for $m = \frac{1}{2}$.

A. $5\frac{1}{2}$ C. $3\frac{1}{7}$

B. $4\frac{2}{5}$ D. $3\frac{7}{10}$

40. In a fruit salad, 3 apples are used for every 5 bananas. How many apples are needed if 15 bananas are used?

Apples	3	6		
Bananas	5			

A. 9 C. 15

B. 12 D. 20

Name _____

Chapter 7 Test Form A: Mixed Formats

MULTIPLE CHOICE

Choose the correct letter for each answer.

1. Which is 40% of 20?
   - A. 6
   - B. 8
   - C. 20
   - D. 800

2. A $45 telephone is on sale for $36. Which is the percent of decrease?
   - A. 5%
   - B. 15%
   - C. 20%
   - D. 33%

3. Which is 42% of 28?
   - A. 0.1176
   - B. 1.176
   - C. 11.76
   - D. 117.6

4. Estimate 30% of 51.
   - A. 15
   - B. 19
   - C. 27
   - D. 30

5. Which percent is equivalent to $\frac{3}{8}$?
   - A. 3.75%
   - B. 6%
   - C. 24%
   - D. 37.5%

6. Denise bought sneakers that were discounted 25%. If the original price was $84, how much did Denise pay for the sneakers?
   - A. $63
   - B. $42
   - C. $25
   - D. $21

7. Jason invested $4,000 for 2 years at a simple interest rate of 3% a year. How much interest did he earn?
   - A. $24
   - B. $120
   - C. $200
   - D. $240

8. Kamil's dinner bill is $40. If he wants to leave a 15% tip, how much should he leave?
   - A. $12
   - B. $18
   - C. $6
   - D. $4

Thelis bought a pair of headphones. The original price was $36. The headphones were discounted 25%. She also paid a sales tax of 5%.

9. How much were the headphones discounted?
   - A. $4.50
   - B. $9
   - C. $18
   - D. $25

10. How much did Thelis pay for the headphones, including sales tax?
    - A. $9.45
    - B. $14.18
    - C. $28.35
    - D. $37.80

11. Corey sorted his coins. He collected the data below. What percent of the coins are nickels?

Coin Type	Number of Coins
Pennies	53
Nickels	12
Dimes	10
Quarter	5
Total	80

A. 12% C. 40%

B. 15% D. 80%

FREE RESPONSE

Write each in two other ways.

12. 73% _____ _____

13. 60% _____ _____

14. 0.84 _____ _____

15. $\frac{17}{20}$ _____ _____

16. 4.5% _____ _____

17. 0.03 _____ _____

Find the percent of each number.

18. 33% of 410 _____

19. 90% of 70 _____

20. 40% of 260 _____

21. 30% of 65 _____

22. 27% of 675 _____

23. 2% of 55 _____

Find the percent of increase or decrease. If necessary, round to the nearest tenth of a percent.

24. The temperature drops from 24°F to 16°F.

_____

25. The worm population in Soren's compost bin increases from 75 to 105.

_____

26. A calf weighs 90 pounds when it is born and grows into a 1,800 pound adult cow.

_____

27. The price of a watermelon is $3 in the summer and increases to $7 in the winter.

_____

For Exercises 28–29, write the percent of the figure that is shaded.

28.

_____

29. [grid showing 5 of 25 squares shaded]

_____

30. Maya deposited $450 into a savings account with a simple interest rate of 6.1% per year. How much money did she have after 4 years?

_____

31. What is the total cost of a $23 item with a sales tax of 4.75%?

_____

WRITING IN MATH

32. Can 50% of Jack's allowance be something less than 25% of Marcia's allowance? Why or why not?

_____
_____
_____
_____
_____

33. Explain how to use the strategy solve a simpler problem to find 35% of $24,000.

_____
_____
_____
_____
_____
_____
_____
_____

34. Nate bought the following items at the store. If he received a discount of 15% off each item and then paid a sales tax of 3%, what was his total bill? Explain how you found the total amount.

batteries	$6.75
notebook	$2.50
box of pens	$5.25
calendar	$12.50
Subtotal	$27.00
Discount: 15%	
Sales Tax: 3%	
Total	

_____
_____
_____
_____
_____
_____
_____
_____

Chapter 7 Test Form A

Name _____

Chapter 7 Test Form B: Mixed Formats

MULTIPLE CHOICE

Circle the letter of the correct answer.

1. Which is 30% of 40?
   A. 1,200 C. 12
   B. 120   D. 7

2. A $55 jacket is on sale for $33. Which is the percent of decrease?
   A. 45% C. 35%
   B. 40% D. 22%

3. Which is 36% of 47?
   A. 169.2 C. 1.692
   B. 16.92 D. 0.1692

4. Estimate 20% of 69.
   A. 20 C. 16
   B. 19 D. 14

5. Which percent is equivalent to $\frac{7}{8}$?
   A. 87.5% C. 8.55%
   B. 56%   D. 5.6%

6. Don bought a shirt that was discounted 20%. If the original price was $45, how much did Don pay for the shirt?
   A. $9   C. $36
   B. $20 D. $54

7. Kristine invested $3,000 for 3 years at a simple interest rate of 5% a year. How much interest did she earn?
   A. $45   C. $300
   B. $150 D. $450

8. Rochelle's cab fare is $20. If she wants to give the driver a 15% tip, how much should she give?
   A. $2 C. $6
   B. $3 D. $9

9. Victor bought a desk lamp. The original price was $28. The desk lamp was discounted 25%. He also paid a sales tax of 6%. How much was the desk lamp discounted?
   A. $21 C. $7
   B. $14 D. $3.50

10. How much did Victor pay for the desk lamp, including sales tax?
    A. $40.28 C. $11.28
    B. $22.26 D. $7.42

94 Chapter 7 Test Form B

11. Julia sorted her stamps. She collected the data below. What percent of her stamps are from Africa?

Julia's Stamp Collection

Stamp Origin	Number of Stamps
Africa	11
Asia	12
Australia	6
Europe	8
North and South America	13
Total	50

A. 50%   C. 22%
B. 33%   D. 11%

FREE RESPONSE

Write each in two other ways.

12. 40% _____ _____

13. $\frac{13}{20}$ _____ _____

14. 3.2% _____ _____

15. 0.07 _____ _____

Find the percent of each number.

16. 40% of 40 _____

17. 20% of 59 _____

18. 92% of 115 _____

19. 1% of 55 _____

Find the percent of increase or decrease. If necessary, round to the nearest tenth of a percent.

20. The temperature decreases from 52°F to 46°F.
    _____

21. Tony's savings account increases from $85 to $136.
    _____

22. The auditorium sat 80 people last year; now it seats 480 people.
    _____

23. The price of admission was raised from $3 to $4.
    _____

Write the percent of the figure that is shaded.

24.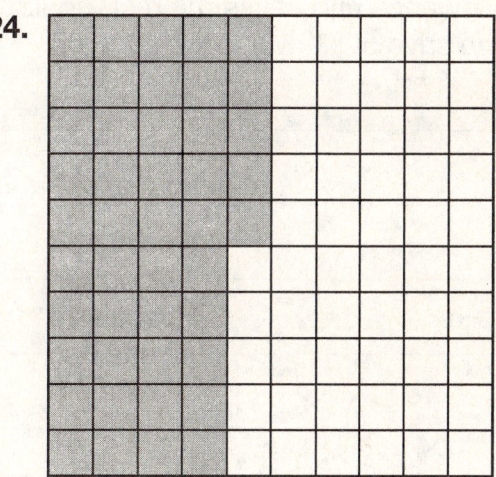

_____

25.

_____

26. Avery deposited $250 into a savings account with a simple interest rate of 3.5% per year. How much money did he have after 5 years?

_____

27. What is the total cost of a $64 item with a sales tax of 5.25%?

_____

WRITING IN MATH

28. If Isabelle spends 60% of her allowance and saves the rest, could she save 50%? Why or why not?

_____
_____
_____
_____
_____

29. Explain how to use the problem-solving strategy Solve a Simpler Problem to find 51% of $32,000.

_____
_____
_____
_____
_____
_____

30. Jessica bought the items listed below at the store. If she received a discount of 30% off each item and then paid a sales tax of 7%, what was her total bill? Explain how you found the total amount.

Big Mart	
We sell everything!	
address book	$4.75
notebooks	$2.50
markers	$2.25
calculator	$15.50
Subtotal	$25.00
Discount: 30%	
Sales Tax: 7%	
Total:	

_____
_____
_____
_____
_____
_____
_____
_____
_____

Name _____

Chapter 8 Test Form A: Mixed Formats

MULTIPLE CHOICE

Circle the letter of the correct answer.

1. Which point is the opposite of −4?

   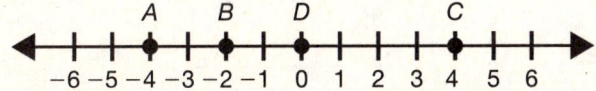

   A. A   C. C
   B. B   D. D

2. Which integer is the greatest?

   A. −8   C. −4
   B. 1   D. −1

3. Which of the following sets of numbers is in order from least to greatest?

   A. $3\frac{2}{3}, -0.7, -2\frac{1}{5}, -3.2$
   B. $-0.6, -1.5, -3\frac{1}{10}, 0$
   C. $-1.9, 2\frac{3}{4}, -4\frac{1}{7}, 5.3$
   D. $-1\frac{2}{5}, -0.4, \frac{1}{4}, 1.8$

4. Find −16 + 9.

   A. 25   C. −7
   B. 7   D. −25

5. Find 4 × (−8).

   A. −32   C. 24
   B. −24   D. 32

6. Which answer is a negative integer?

   A. 5 − (−8)   C. 14 + (−10)
   B. −72 ÷ (−9) D. 6 × (−3)

7. Find −6 − (−20).

   A. −26   C. 14
   B. −14   D. 26

8. Solve $n + 7 = -3$.

   A. $n = -10$ C. $n = 10$
   B. $n = -4$ D. $n = 4$

9. The temperature at noon was 67°F. This was 8°F warmer than at 7:00 A.M. The temperature had risen 12°F from 1:00 A.M. to 7:00 A.M. What was the temperature at 1:00 A.M.?

   A. 68°F   C. 59°F
   B. 47°F   D. 54°F

10. Which point is NOT located on the line with the equation $y = x - 7$?

    A. M(4, −3)   C. O(−3, −10)
    B. N(1, −6)   D. P(−5, 2)

11. Which point is located at (−3, 1)?

    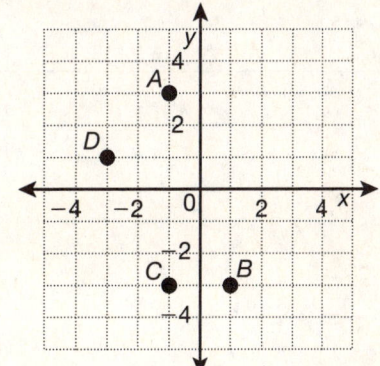

    A. A   C. C
    B. B   D. D

FREE RESPONSE

For 12–14, use the number line below. Write the integer for each point. Then give its opposite and absolute value.

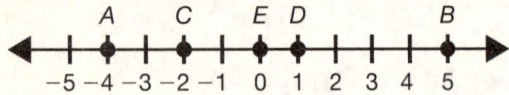

12. C _____

13. B _____

14. E _____

Use <, >, or = to compare.

15. −13 ◯ 7

16. −2 ◯ −6

17. |−4| ◯ −4

18. −7.3 ◯ 6.7

19. −8.5 ◯ −8$\frac{4}{5}$

20. −1.99 ◯ −1$\frac{7}{10}$

Order from least to greatest.

21. 5, −8, |−2|, 3, |9|

_____

22. −2.6, −2$\frac{5}{7}$, 2.33

Add or subtract.

23. −5 + 9 _____

24. −8 − (−7) _____

25. 6 − (−4) _____

26. 2 + (−25) _____

27. −13 + (−6) _____

28. −17 + 28 _____

Multiply or divide.

29. −5 × (−8) _____

30. 144 ÷ (−12) _____

31. −11 × 7 _____

32. −24 ÷ 6 _____

33. 12 × (−4) _____

34. −21 ÷ (−3) _____

Solve each equation.

35. $\frac{-k}{-3} = 8$ k = _____

36. g − (−25) = 17   g = _____

37. n + 14 = −2   n = _____

38. −6i = 90   i = _____

Graph and label the points on the same coordinate plane.

39. A(3, −2)   **40.** B(−3, 0)

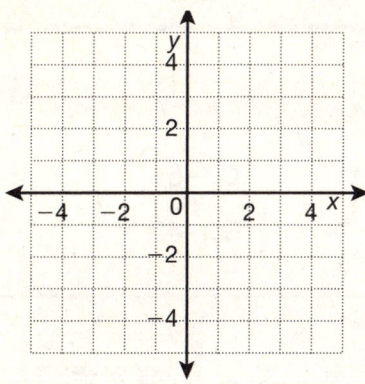

Make a T-table. Then graph each equation.

41. $y = -2x$ **42.** $y = 3 + x$

x	y

x	y

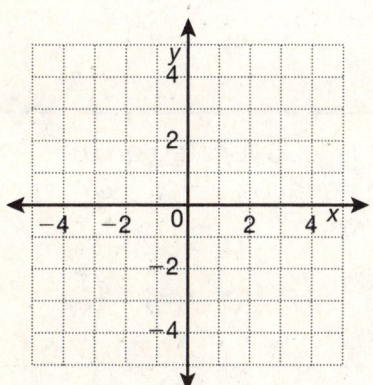

43. Write a rule and an equation for the table below.

x	1	−1	−4
y	−3	−5	−8

_____

_____

WRITING IN MATH

44. Write a word problem. Draw a picture to show the main idea and give the solution in a complete sentence.

_____

_____

_____

_____

45. Explain when the answer to an addition problem uses the difference of the absolute values.

_____

_____

_____

_____

46. Pizza costs $1.50 per slice. How many slices of pizza can Sergio buy with $12.50, the cost of a medium pizza? Explain.

_____

_____

_____

_____

Chapter 8 Test Form A

Name _____

Chapter 8 Test Form B: Mixed Formats

MULTIPLE CHOICE

Circle the letter of the correct answer.

1. Which point is the opposite of –2?

   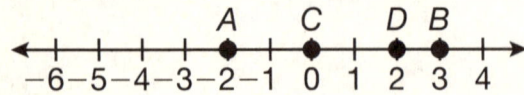

   A. A   C. C
   B. B   D. D

2. Which integer is the greatest?
   A. 0   C. –6
   B. –3   D. –2

3. Which of the following sets of numbers is in order from least to greatest?
   A. $1\frac{1}{4}, -\frac{3}{5}, -1.5, -2.9$
   B. $-2.7, -1, -1\frac{1}{2}, 5.2$
   C. $-\frac{4}{5}, -2.7, -4\frac{1}{10}, 0$
   D. $-4.6, -2\frac{1}{3}, 0, 2\frac{1}{2}$

4. Find –14 + 8.
   A. 22   C. –6
   B. 6   D. –22

5. Find 6 × (–7).
   A. –48   C. 42
   B. –42   D. 48

6. Which answer is a negative integer?
   A. 8 ÷ (–2)   C. 3 – (–4)
   B. 30 + (–5)   D. –7 × –9

7. Find –18 – (–24).
   A. 42   C. –6
   B. 6   D. –42

8. Solve $n + 9 = -8$.
   A. –17   C. 1
   B. –1   D. 17

9. The temperature at 6:00 P.M. was 73°F. This was 12°F cooler than at 4:00 P.M. Earlier that same day, the temperature rose 15°F from 10:00 A.M. to noon. Then it rose 8°F from noon to 4:00 P.M. What was the temperature at 10:00 A.M.?
   A. 87°F   C. 77°F
   B. 85°F   D. 62°F

10. Which point is NOT located on the line with the equation $y = x - 9$?
    A. Q(1, –8)   C. S(–2, –11)
    B. R(3, –12)   D. T(–4, –13)

11. Which point is located at (1, –3)?

    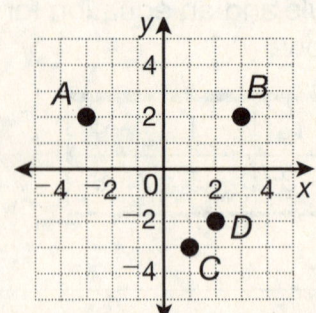

    A. A   C. C
    B. B   D. D

100 Chapter 8 Test Form B

FREE RESPONSE

For 12–14, use the number line below. Write the integer for each point. Then give its opposite and absolute value.

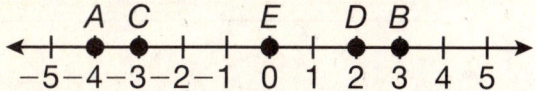

12. E _____

13. C _____

14. D _____

Use <, >, or = to compare.

15. –6 ◯ –7

16. –2 ◯ |–2|

17. 4.5 ◯ –8.2

18. $-7\frac{1}{5}$ ◯ –7.44

Order from least to greatest.

19. |–5|, 9, |4|, –6, 2

_____

20. 4.15, –4.8, $-4\frac{2}{3}$

_____

Add or subtract.

21. –8 – (–6) _____

22. 5 + (–39) _____

23. –22 + (–4) _____

24. –13 + 29 _____

Multiply or divide.

25. –3 × –7 _____

26. –54 ÷ 6 _____

27. 12 × –5 _____

28. –42 ÷ –7 _____

Solve each equation.

29. $\frac{m}{-3} = 9$ m = _____

30. w – (–12) = 5   w = _____

31. e + 3 = –5   e = _____

32. –5v = 65   v = _____

Graph and label the points on the same coordinate plane.

33. N(0, –3)   34. M(–4, 2)

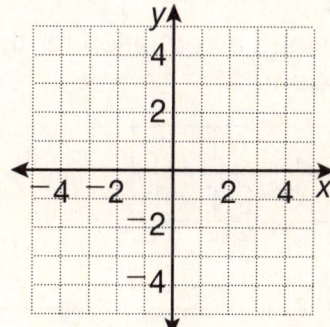

Make a T-table. Then graph each equation.

35. $y = -4x$

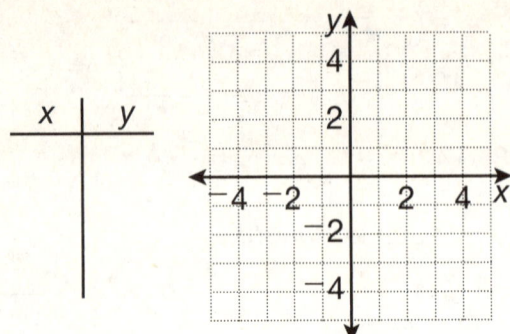

36. $y = 2 + x$

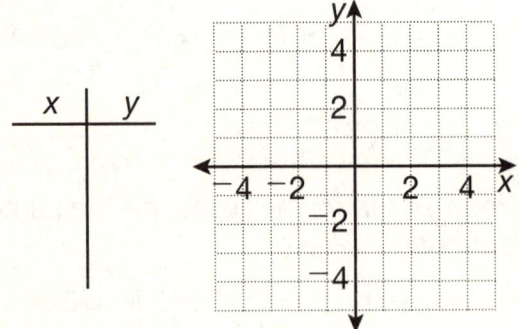

37. Write a rule and an equation for the function below.

x	1	−1	−3
y	0	−2	−4

_____

_____

_____

WRITING IN MATH

38. Write a word problem. Draw a picture to show the main idea and give the solution in a complete sentence.

_____

_____

_____

39. Explain how you can tell if the answer to a multiplication problem with two factors will be positive or negative.

_____

_____

_____

_____

_____

_____

_____

_____

40. Chris is going to a coin shop. He wants to buy mounted coin sets that cost $2.50 each. How many coin sets can he buy if he has $22? Explain how you found your answer.

_____

_____

_____

_____

_____

_____

Name _____

Chapter 9 Test Form A: Mixed Formats

MULTIPLE CHOICE

Circle the letter of the correct answer.

1. Which is true of the picture?

   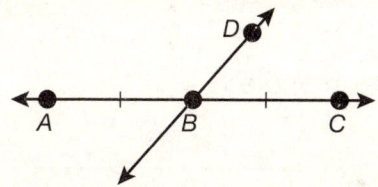

   A. $\overleftrightarrow{AC} \perp \overleftrightarrow{DB}$
   B. $\overleftrightarrow{AC}$ and $\overleftrightarrow{DB}$ are intersecting lines.
   C. $\overline{AC} \cong \overline{DB}$
   D. $\overleftrightarrow{AC} \parallel \overleftrightarrow{DB}$

2. Which angle below is acute?

   A.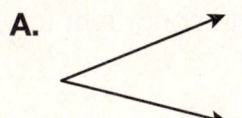

   B.

   C.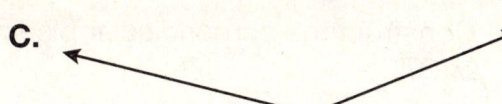

   D.

3.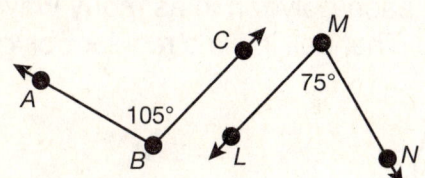

   ∠ABC and ∠LMN are
   A. supplementary.   C. adjacent.
   B. complementary.   D. vertical.

4. Find x.

   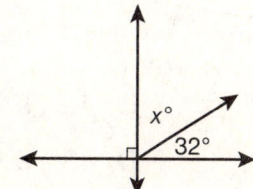

   A. 32°   C. 58°
   B. 45°   D. 148°

5. Two angles of a triangle measure 56° and 28°. What is the measure of the third angle?

   A. 152°   C. 96°
   B. 124°   D. 6°

6. How many sides does a nonagon have?

   A. 12   C. 8
   B. 9   D. 7

7. Which statement is false?
   A. All trapezoids are quadrilaterals.
   B. All rectangles are parallelograms.
   C. All squares are rhombuses.
   D. All rectangles are squares.

8. Identify the shaded region of the figure.

   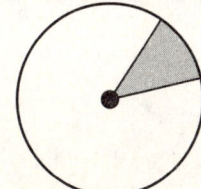

   A. sector
   B. central angle
   C. arc
   D. radius

Chapter 9 Test Form A **103**

9. The two triangles are similar. Find $m\angle C$ and $\overline{YZ}$.

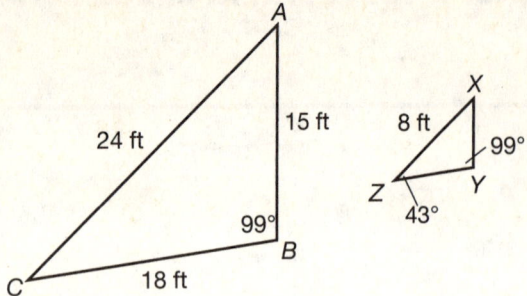

   A. 38°, 36 ft   C. 43°, 6 ft
   B. 38°, 18 ft   D. 43°, 9 ft

10. Which figure tessellates?

   A. 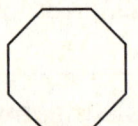   C.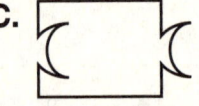

   B. 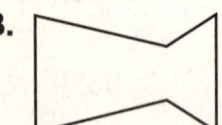   D.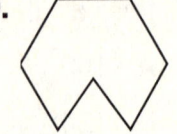

11. A triangle on a coordinate grid has vertices at (−1, −1), (3, 5), and (4, −2). If the triangle is translated 2 units to the left and flipped over the y-axis, what would be the coordinates of the new triangle's vertices?

   A. (−3, 1); (1, 5); (2, −2)
   B. (3, −1); (1, −5); (−2, 2)
   C. (3, −1); (−1, 5); (−2, −2)
   D. (1, 1); (−3, 5); (−4, −2)

FREE RESPONSE

Draw a diagram to illustrate each.

12. $\overleftrightarrow{XY}$ is the perpendicular bisector of $\overline{GH}$.

13. Lines $\overleftrightarrow{AB}$, $\overleftrightarrow{CD}$, and $\overleftrightarrow{EF}$ intersect at one point.

Classify each angle.

14. 61°   _____

15. 97°   _____

16. 180°   _____

17. Find the measure of an angle supplementary to an angle with a measure of 56°.   _____

18. Construct an angle congruent to $\angle B$.

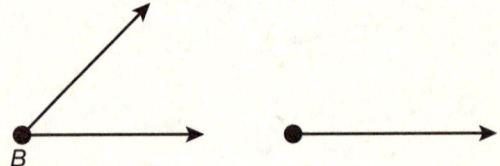

19. Construct the perpendicular bisector of $\overline{ST}$.

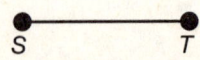

Classify each polygon in as many ways as possible. Then tell if it is a regular polygon.

20.

21.

22. 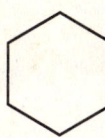 23.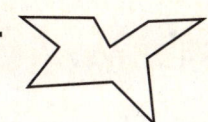

Tell whether the figures in each pair are related by a slide, a flip, or a turn. If a turn, describe it.

24.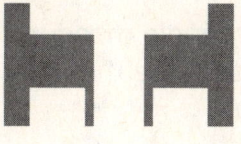

25.

Tell if each figure has reflection symmetry, rotational symmetry, or both.

26.

27. **Z**

WRITING IN MATH

28. If 2 quadrilaterals are similar and one is a parallelogram, is the other one also a parallelogram? Explain.

29. Compare the figures below. Write two statements about how the figures are alike and one statement about how the figures are different.

    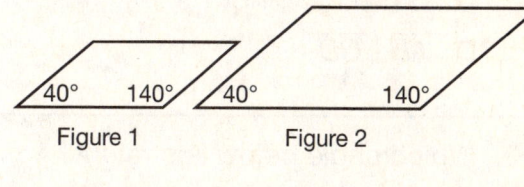
    Figure 1   Figure 2

30. Draw a picture to solve the problem.

    A river has 3 major tributaries. Each major tributary has 4 smaller tributaries. Each of the smaller tributaries has 2 feeder streams. How many streams of all sizes are there?

Chapter 9 Test Form A **105**

Name _____

Chapter 9 Test Form B: Mixed Formats

MULTIPLE CHOICE

Circle the letter of the correct answer.

1. Which is true of the picture?

   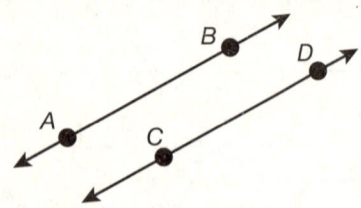

   A. $\overleftrightarrow{AB} \perp \overleftrightarrow{CD}$
   B. $\overleftrightarrow{AB}$ and $\overleftrightarrow{CD}$ are intersecting lines
   C. C is a midpoint
   D. $\overleftrightarrow{AB} \parallel \overleftrightarrow{CD}$

2. Which angle below is straight?

   A.

   B.

   C.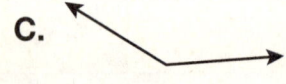

   D.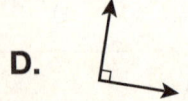

3.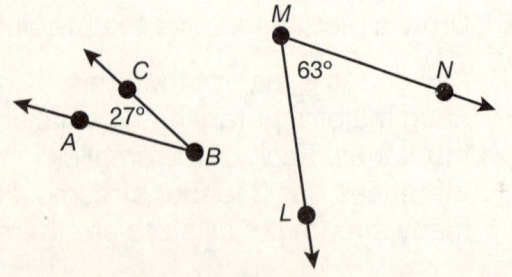

   ∠ABC and ∠LMN are
   A. adjacent.
   B. complementary.
   C. supplementary.
   D. vertical.

4. Find y.

   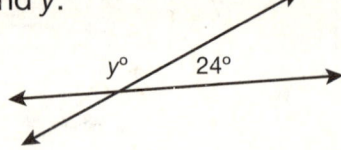

   A. 24°   C. 66°
   B. 42°   D. 156°

5. Two angles of a triangle measure 96° and 71°. What is the measure of the third angle?

   A. 13°   C. 109°
   B. 33°   D. 167°

6. How many sides does a decagon have?

   A. 12   C. 7
   B. 10   D. 6

7. Which statement is false?

   A. All squares are parallelograms.
   B. All rhombuses are quadrilaterals.
   C. All polygons are closed plane figures.
   D. All isosceles triangles are similar.

8. Identify the figure shown in bold.

   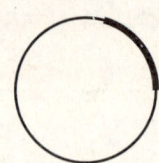

   A. semicircle   C. arc
   B. central angle   D. radius

106 Chapter 9 Test Form B

9. The two parallelograms are similar. Find $m\angle A$ and MN.

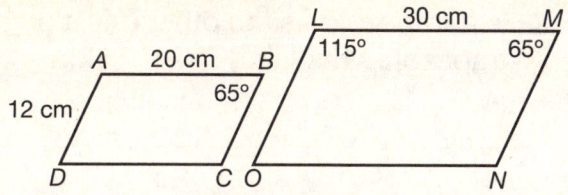

   A. 115°, 18 cm   C. 65°, 15 cm
   B. 115°, 24 cm   D. 65°, 30 cm

10. Which figure tessellates?

   A.    C.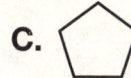
   B. 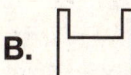   D.

11. A triangle on a coordinate grid has vertices at (0, 5), (3, 4), and (−2, −1). If the triangle is translated 3 units to the right and flipped over the x-axis, what would be the coordinates of the new triangle's vertices?

   A. (0, −5); (3, −4); (−2, 1)
   B. (3, −5); (6, −4); (1, 1)
   C. (3, −5); (−6, 4); (1, −1)
   D. (−3, 5); (−6, −4); (−1, 1)

FREE RESPONSE

Draw a diagram to illustrate each.

12. Point N is the midpoint of $\overline{RS}$.

13. $\overrightarrow{QR}$ intersects perpendicular lines $\overleftrightarrow{ST}$ and $\overleftrightarrow{UV}$.

Classify each angle.

14. 129° _____

15. 57° _____

16. 89° _____

17. Find the measure of an angle supplementary to an angle with a measure of 83°.

   _____

18. Construct a segment congruent to $\overline{OP}$.

19. Construct the bisector of $\angle F$.

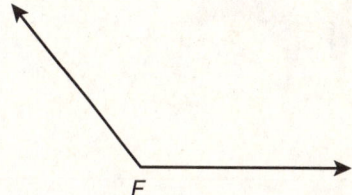

Classify each polygon in as many ways as possible. Then tell if it is a regular polygon.

20.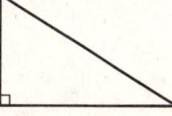

21.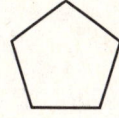

22.

Chapter 9 Test Form B   **107**

23.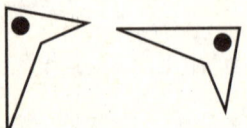

_____

_____

Tell whether the figures in each pair are related by a slide, a flip, or a turn. If a turn, describe it.

24.

_____

25.

_____

Tell if each figure has reflection symmetry, rotational symmetry, or both.

26.

_____

27.

_____

WRITING IN MATH

28. If 2 quadrilaterals are similar and one is a trapezoid, is the other one also a trapezoid? Explain.

_____

_____

_____

_____

_____

29. Compare the figures below. Write two statements about how the figures are alike and one statement about how the figures are different.

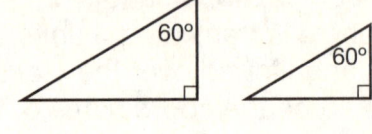

_____

_____

_____

_____

_____

30. Draw a picture to solve the problem.

A submarine is traveling 728 ft below sea level. The peak of an underwater mountain is 5,950 ft above the ocean floor where the ocean is 6,824 ft deep. How far above the peak does the submarine pass?

Chapters 1–9 Cumulative Test

Circle the letter of the correct answer.

1. Find $4 - 2\frac{4}{7}$.
   - A. $6\frac{4}{7}$
   - B. $2\frac{3}{7}$
   - C. $1\frac{3}{7}$
   - D. $1\frac{2}{7}$

2. Find the measure of an angle complementary to an angle with a measure of 58°.
   - A. 32°
   - B. 85°
   - C. 122°
   - D. 148°

3. What is 30% of 90?
   - A. 6
   - B. 18
   - C. 27
   - D. 800

4. Which two lines are parallel?

   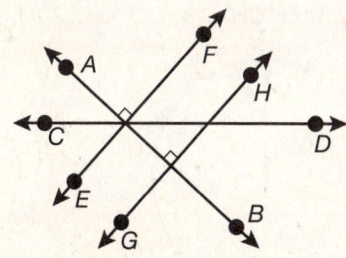

   - A. $\overline{CD}$ and $\overline{EF}$
   - B. $\overline{AB}$ and $\overline{CD}$
   - C. $\overline{EF}$ and $\overline{GH}$
   - D. $\overline{AB}$ and $\overline{GH}$

5. Which integer is the greatest?
   - A. −2
   - B. 0
   - C. −10
   - D. 1

6. Jana bought juice for $1.99 and paid an additional 6.5% for sales tax. How much did Jana pay including sales tax?
   - A. $2.65
   - B. $2.12
   - C. $2.06
   - D. $0.13

7. Coach Taylor needs 35 tennis balls for the tennis tournament. Since tennis balls come 3 in a carton, how many cartons must Coach Taylor buy to have 35 tennis balls?
   - A. 11
   - B. 12
   - C. 18
   - D. 35

8. Which point is located at (−3, 2)?

   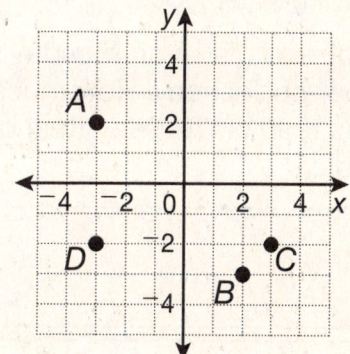

   - A. A
   - B. B
   - C. C
   - D. D

9. In a class, 85% of the students voted to go to a science museum. What fraction of students voted to go to the science museum?
   - A. $\frac{3}{8}$
   - B. $\frac{1}{2}$
   - C. $\frac{17}{20}$
   - D. $\frac{9}{10}$

10. An $80 CD player is on sale for $64. What is the percent of decrease?

A. 8%   C. 25%
B. 20% D. 33%

11. In a jar, there are 6 white balls, 4 green balls, and 6 red balls. What percent of the balls is white and green?

A. 75%   C. 37.5%
B. 62.5% D. 25%

12. What is 1.76 written as a fraction in simplest form?

A. $\frac{19}{25}$ C. $1\frac{19}{25}$
B. $1\frac{3}{4}$ D. $1\frac{38}{50}$

13. Which operation would you use to solve the problem? The picture shows the main idea.

David read $\frac{2}{3}$ hour on Monday and $\frac{11}{12}$ hour on Tuesday. How much longer did he read on Tuesday than on Monday?

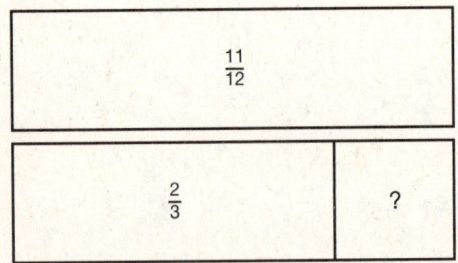

A. Addition   C. Multiplication
B. Subtraction   D. Division

14. Which is the value of 7^3?

A. 14   C. 343
B. 21   D. 2,187

15. Why is 7,569 divisible by 3?

A. The sum of the digits is divisible by 3.
B. The last digit is divisible by 3.
C. The sum of the last two digits is divisible by 3.
D. The ones digit is a 3, 6, or 9.

16. Which statement is false?

A. All squares are rectangles.
B. All parallelograms are trapezoids.
C. All equilateral triangles are regular polygons.
D. Circles are not polygons.

17. Which percent is equivalent to $\frac{3}{8}$?

A. 80%   C. 37.5%
B. 38%   D. 2.67%

18. Find x in the circle.

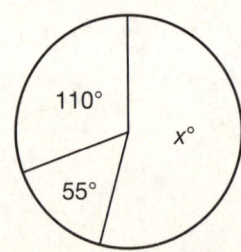

A. 15°   C. 195°
B. 35°   D. 200°

19. Which answer is a negative integer?

A. $2 - (-5)$ C. $14 + (-10)$
B. $72 \div -6$ D. -6×-3

110 Chapters 1–9 Cumulative Test

20. What is the reciprocal of $3\frac{4}{5}$?

   A. $3\frac{5}{4}$ C. $1\frac{9}{5}$
   B. $\frac{19}{5}$ D. $\frac{5}{19}$

21. Which list shows numbers in order from least to greatest?

   A. $0.2; \frac{1}{3}; \frac{3}{5}; -0.4$
   B. $\frac{3}{5}; 0.2; -\frac{1}{3}; 0.4$
   C. $-0.4; 0; 0.2; \frac{1}{3}$
   D. $0.2; -\frac{1}{3}; 0.4; \frac{3}{5}$

22. Which operation do you perform first when evaluating
   $18 - 5 \times 2 + (7 - 3) - 2^2$?

   A. $18 - 5$ C. 5×2
   B. $7 - 3$ D. $2 + 7$

23. Identify the figure below.

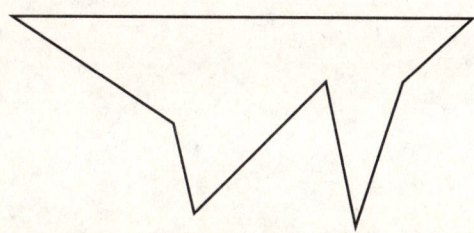

   A. a regular heptagon
   B. an irregular heptagon
   C. a regular hexagon
   D. an irregular hexagon

24. Solve $n + 12 = -9$.

   A. $n = -21$ C. $n = 3$
   B. $n = -12$ D. $n = 21$

25. Write 0.02675 in scientific notation.

   A. 2.675×10^{-3}
   B. 0.2675×10^{-2}
   C. 2.675×10^{-2}
   D. 2.675×10^2

26. A trapezoid on the coordinate grid has vertices at (3, −1), (1, −1), (0, −3), and (3, −3). If the trapezoid is translated 3 units to the left and then flipped over the x-axis, what would be the coordinates of the new trapezoid's vertices?

   A. (0, 1), (−3, 1), (−2, 3), (0, 3)
   B. (0, −1), (0, −3), (−3, −3), (−2, −1)
   C. (0, −1), (−2, 1), (−2, 3), (0, 3)
   D. (0, 1), (−2, 1), (−3, 3), (0, 3)

27. The shapes below are similar. Find x and AB.

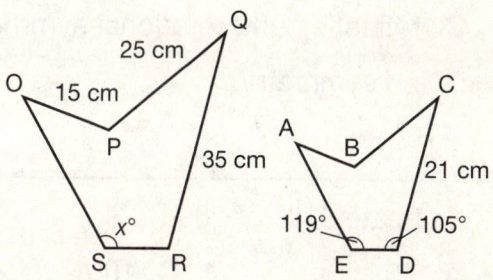

   A. 119°, 9 cm   C. 105°, 9 cm
   B. 119°, 7 cm   D. 105°, 7 cm

28. Solve the proportion
   $\frac{45 \text{ mi}}{2 \text{ hr}} = \frac{270 \text{ mi}}{x \text{ hr}}$.

   A. $x = 12$ hr   C. $x = 6$ hr
   B. $x = 9$ hr   D. $x = 5$ hr

Chapters 1–9 Cumulative Test

29. Which point is NOT located on the line with the equation $y = x + 9$?

    A. $M(4, 13)$ C. $O(-2, -8)$
    B. $N(3, 12)$ D. $P(-5, 4)$

30. Name the next 3 numbers in the pattern.

    0, 1, 3, 7, 15,...

    A. 31, 63, 127
    B. 30, 65, 110
    C. 18, 36, 72
    D. 16, 32, 64

31. The figure below has

    A. reflection symmetry.
    B. rotational symmetry.
    C. reflection and rotational symmetry.
    D. no symmetry.

32. Estimate 33% of 269.

    A. 75   C. 100
    B. 90   D. 110

33. The temperature at noon was 62°F. This was 8°F warmer than at 8:00 A.M. Earlier that same day, the temperature fell 9°F from 1:00 A.M. to 5:00 A.M. Then it rose 7°F from 5:00 A.M. to 8:00 A.M. What was the temperature at 1:00 A.M.?

    A. 68°F   C. 56°F
    B. 66°F   D. 54°F

34. Jerry spent $18 on a book. This was $\frac{1}{3}$ of his total monthly allowance. How much allowance does Jerry get a month?

    A. $30   C. $60
    B. $54   D. $100

35. The scale on a map is 2.5 cm to 30 miles. If the distance between two cities is 120 miles, how far apart are they on the map?

    A. 4 cm   C. 10 cm
    B. 7 cm   D. 15 cm

36. Mia borrows $2,000 at a simple interest rate of 5% a year. If she borrows the money for 3 years, how much interest does she have to pay?

    A. $450   C. $200
    B. $300   D. $100

112 Chapters 1–9 Cumulative Test

Name _____

Chapter 10 Test Form A: Mixed Formats

MULTIPLE CHOICE

Circle the letter of the correct answer.

1. Find the perimeter.

   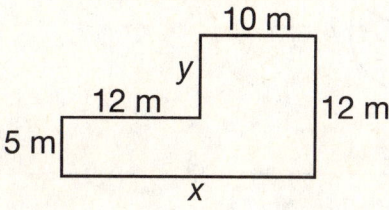

   A. 68 m C. 39 m
   B. 64 m D. 22 m

2. How many gallons are in 34 quarts?

   A. 4.2 gal C. 8.5 gal
   B. 4.25 gal D. 136 gal

3. Which solid figure has 6 vertices?

   A.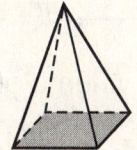

   B.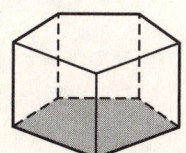

   C.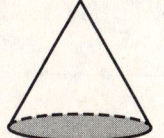

   D.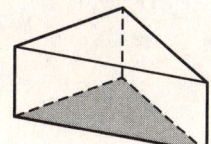

4. Sarah's train ride started at 5:30 P.M. It ended at 7:45 P.M. How long was her train ride?

   A. 1 hr 15 min C. 2 hr 15 min
   B. 1 hr 45 min D. 2 hr 45 min

5. Julian has 34 feet of rope to mark off a rectangle for a flowerbed. He wants the flowerbed to have the greatest area possible. In whole feet, what should be the dimensions of the flowerbed?

   A. 4 ft by 13 ft C. 8 ft by 9 ft
   B. 6 ft by 11 ft D. 10 ft by 7 ft

6. Abby wants to get dirt for her new ant farm. What is the volume of the box that will hold more dirt?

   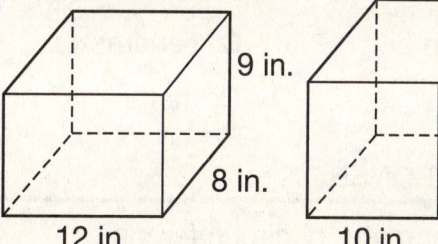

   A. 80 in.^{3} C. 800 in.^{3}
   B. 96 in.^{3} D. 864 in.^{3}

7. What is the capacity of a 2-liter bottle of juice in milliliters?

   A. 20,000 mL C. 200 mL
   B. 2,000 mL D. 0.002 mL

8. Find the surface area of this solid.

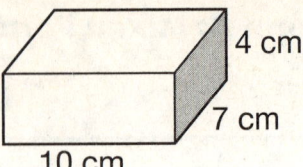

A. 138 cm² C. 276 cm²
B. 220 cm² D. 280 cm²

9. Which net represents a triangular pyramid?

A. 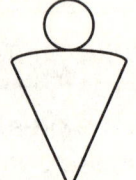   C.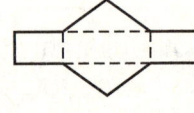

B. 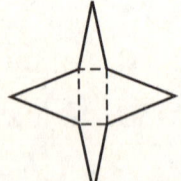   D.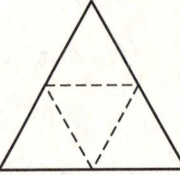

10. Which unit of measure is most precise?

A. inch C. centimeter
B. foot D. meter

FREE RESPONSE

Find the perimeter or circumference of each figure. Then find the area of each figure.

11.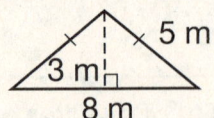

P = _____ A = _____

12.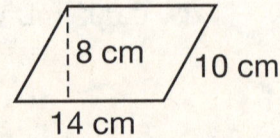

P = _____ A = _____

13.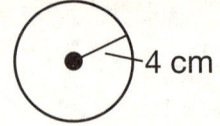

P = _____ A = _____

14.

C ≈ _____ A ≈ _____

Find each missing number.

15. 7.4 m = _____ km
16. 2.5 yd = _____ in.
17. 0.6 L = _____ mL
18. 32 oz = _____ c
19. 105 mL ≈ _____ oz
20. 12.7 cm = _____ in.

Find the surface area and volume of each solid.

21.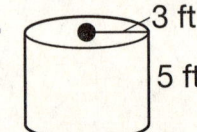

SA ≈ _____

V ≈ _____

22. 3 m is the length of altitude; needs to be on interior of triangle.

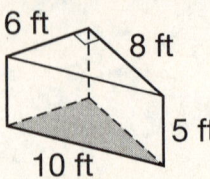

SA = _____

V = _____

114 Chapter 10 Test Form A

WRITING IN MATH

23. Explain how to use logical reasoning and a time zone map to solve the problem. Then, solve.

A flight from Seattle to Philadelphia took 4 hours 35 minutes. If the plane landed in Philadelphia at 7:30 P.M. local time, at what time did it leave Seattle?

24. Explain if the problem has extra or missing information. Solve if you have enough information.

Luke ran around a 100-meter track 5 times. Afterwards, he walked around the track 1.5 times. His walk took him 10 minutes. How many meters can Luke run in an hour?

25. Each edge of a cube is 6 cm long. Explain how to find the surface area and volume of the cube.

Chapter 10 Test Form A **115**

Name _____

Chapter 10 Test Form B: Mixed Formats

MULTIPLE CHOICE

Circle the letter of the correct answer.

1. Find the perimeter.

   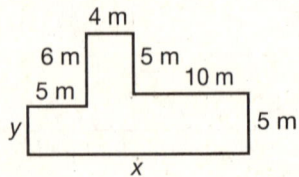

   A. 15 m   C. 54 m
   B. 35 m   D. 58 m

2. How many cups are in 52 fluid ounces?

   A. 416 c   C. 6.5 c
   B. 8 c   D. 4 c

3. Which solid figure has 10 vertices?

   A.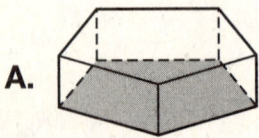

   B.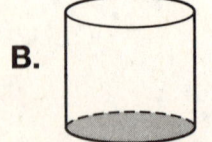

   C.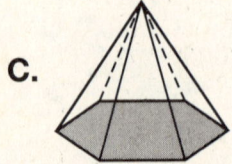

   D.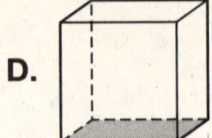

4. Jeannette's bus ride started at 7:15 A.M. It ended at 10:00 A.M. How long was her bus ride?

   A. 2 hr 15 min   C. 3 hr 15 min
   B. 2 hr 45 min   D. 3 hr 45 min

5. Beatrice has 26 feet of fencing to enclose a rectangular garden. She wants the garden to have the greatest area possible. In whole feet, what should be the dimensions of the garden?

   A. 3 ft by 10 ft   C. 5 ft by 8 ft
   B. 4 ft by 9 ft   D. 7 ft by 6 ft

6. Carmen wants to use one of the two boxes shown to plant flowers. What is the volume of the box that holds more dirt?

   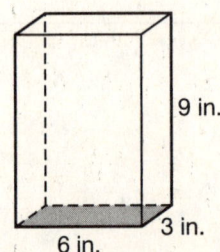 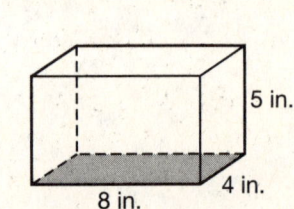

   A. 18 in³   C. 160 in³
   B. 32 in³   D. 162 in³

7. George's dog has a mass of 35.7 kilograms. What is the dog's mass in grams?

   A. 35,700 g   C. 3.57 g
   B. 3,570 g   D. 0.0357 g

116 Chapter 10 Test Form B

8. Find the surface area of this solid.

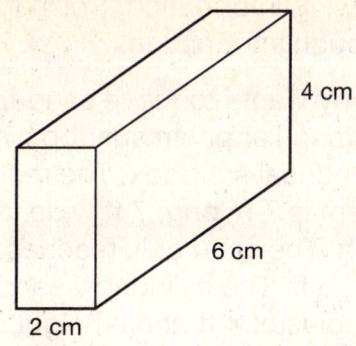

A. 48 cm² C. 74 cm²
B. 64 cm² D. 88 cm²

9. Which net represents a square pyramid?

A.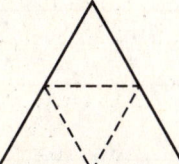
C.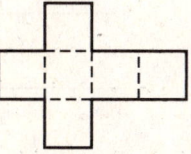
B.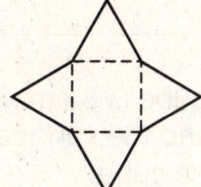
D.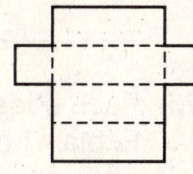

10. Which unit of measure is most precise?

A. liter C. quart
B. milliliter D. cup

FREE RESPONSE

Find the perimeter or circumference of each figure. Then find the area of each figure.

11.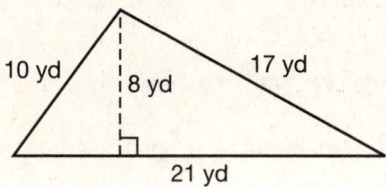

P = _____ A = _____

12.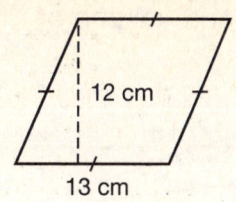

P = _____ A = _____

13.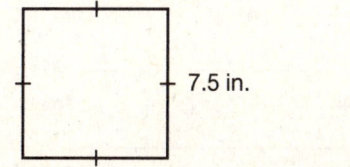

P = _____ A = _____

14.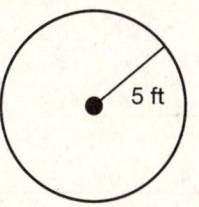

C ≈ _____ A ≈ _____

Find each missing number.

15. 9.3 g = _____ kg

16. 4 yd = _____ in.

17. 0.4 L = _____ mL

18. 4 oz = _____ lb

19. 27 kg ≈ _____ lb

20. 22.86 cm = _____ in.

Find the surface area and volume of each solid.

21.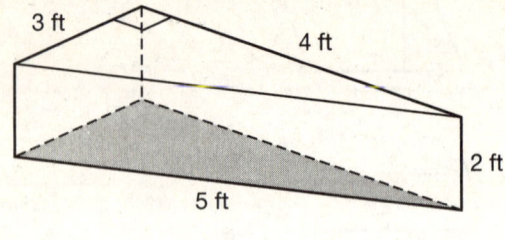

SA ≈ _____

V ≈ _____

22.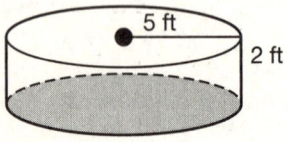

SA ≈ _____

V ≈ _____

WRITING IN MATH

23. Explain how to use logical reasoning and a time zone map to solve this problem. Then, solve.

A flight from Boston to Los Angeles took 5 hours 15 minutes. If the plane landed in Los Angeles at 4:30 P.M. local time, at what time did it leave Boston?

_____
_____
_____
_____
_____
_____
_____

24. Explain if the problem has extra or missing information. Solve if you have enough information.

Cindy wants to move sand from a rectangular prism sandbox into a cylindrical sandbox. The rectangular prism is 7 ft long, 7 ft wide, and 3 ft high. The sand only reaches a height of 2.5 ft. The cylindrical sandbox has a radius of 4 ft and a height of 2 ft. What is the volume of the sand that Cindy has to move?

_____
_____
_____
_____
_____
_____
_____

25. Each edge of a cube is 8 cm long. Explain how to find the surface area and volume of the cube.

_____
_____

118 Chapter 10 Test Form B

Name _____

Chapter 11 Test Form A: Mixed Formats

MULTIPLE CHOICE

Circle the letter of the correct answer.

At a shirt factory, a worker randomly selected 150 shirts. He noticed that 6 shirts were missing buttons.

1. What percent of the shirts produced that day were probably missing buttons?

   A. 2% C. 6%
   B. 4% D. 40%

2. If the factory produced 600 shirts, how many shirts might they expect to have missing buttons?

   A. 6   C. 24
   B. 18 D. 30

3. Find the mean of the data set.
   4, 8, 10, 11, 13, 16, 25, 25

   A. 11 C. 14
   B. 13 D. 25

For 4–5, use the line plot.

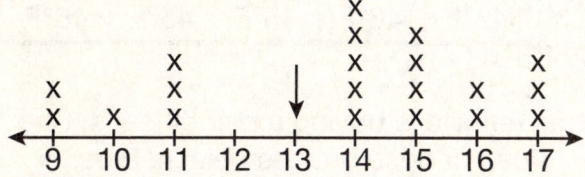

4. Find the median of the data in the line plot.

   A. 12   C. 14.5
   B. 14   D. 15

5. The arrow is pointing to the

   A. gap.   C. outlier.
   B. cluster. D. minimum.

The class scores for a biology test are displayed in the stem-and-leaf plot.

Biology Test Scores

Stem	Leaf
6	3 7
7	2 8 8 9
8	0 1 4 5 7 9
9	0 0 0 1 5 8 8

6. What is the mode of the test scores?

   A. 0   C. 78
   B. 30 D. 90

7. Who has the most baseball and hockey cards combined?

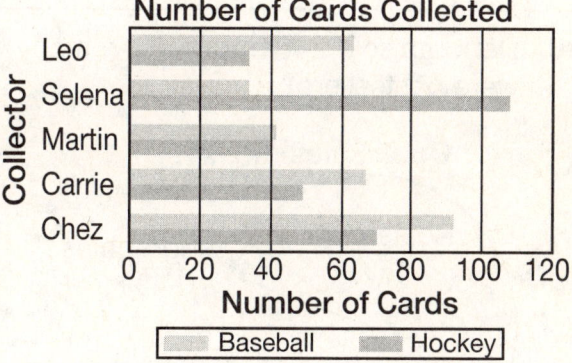

   A. Joe   C. Selena
   B. Carrie D. Chez

Chapter 11 Test Form A **119**

For 8–9, use the double-line graph.

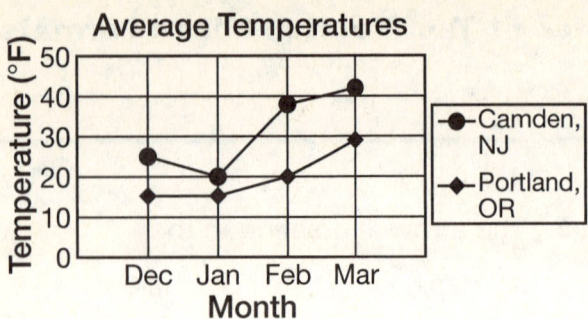

8. During which month is the temperature in Portland the highest?

   A. December   C. February
   B. January   D. March

9. Which statement is TRUE?

   A. The temperature in both cities increases after January.
   B. The temperature in both cities is less than 10° in January.
   C. The temperature in Portland is sometimes higher than the temperature in Camden.
   D. The biggest increase in temperature occurs between February and March for both cities.

10. Deborah sold 240 books. How many were bestsellers?

    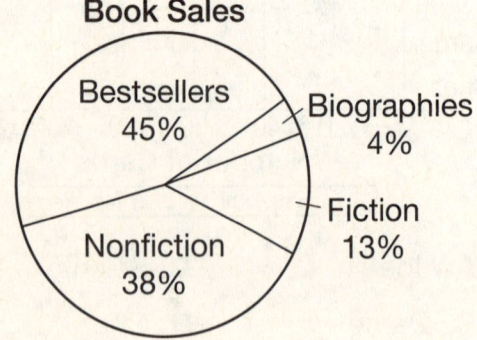

    A. 45   C. 108
    B. 91.2   D. 132

11. Heath is buying a car. He can choose between red, black, or blue, a sunroof or air conditioning, and 2-doors or 4-doors. How many possible combinations are there?

    A. 18   C. 9
    B. 12   D. 8

12. How many different ways can Audrey arrange 5 books on her shelf?

    A. 5   C. 60
    B. 25   D. 120

FREE RESPONSE

Find the mean, median, mode, and range of the data. Round decimal answers to the nearest hundredth.

13. 5, 6, 2, 2, 8, 5, 9, 5

    Mean _____   Median _____

    Mode _____   Range _____

14. Represent the data below in a frequency table and a line plot.

Temperatures				
45°F	41°F	46°F	46°F	42°F
47°F	43°F	45°F	49°F	47°F
43°F	46°F	45°F	45°F	48°F

15. Tennille is buying a pair of jeans. She can choose between black, blue, or beige, boot-cut or flared, and relaxed or regular fit. Make a tree diagram to show all of Tennille's possible choices for a pair of jeans.

16. Jerry has 7 model airplanes. He can only hang 2 of the planes from his ceiling. In how many ways can Jerry choose 2 of the 7 airplanes to display?

_____

For 17–22 use the cards below. Find each probability.

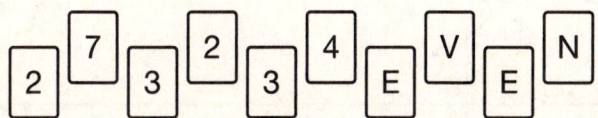

17. P(3) _____

18. P(even number) _____

19. P(2 or a vowel) _____

20. P(N or a number) _____

21. Find P(a vowel, 3) if the first card is replaced before the second is picked.

_____

22. Find P(7, N) if the first card is NOT replaced before the second is picked.

_____

WRITING IN MATH

23. The table shows the results of a survey about favorite shoes. Make and describe the most appropriate graph to show the data.

Favorite Shoes			
Sneakers	115	Boots	95
Slippers	27	Sandals	50
Loafers	79	Flip-flops	62

24. Explain how to make a graph of the Favorite Shoes data using 3 shoes that received the most votes, so it seems like loafers got half as many votes as sneakers.

25. Using the counting principle, explain how to calculate the number of permutations for 5 objects in 3 positions.

Chapter 11 Test Form A **121**

Name _____

Chapter 11 Test Form B: Mixed Formats

MULTIPLE CHOICE

Circle the letter of the correct answer.

At a telephone factory, a worker randomly selected 250 phones. She noticed that 15 phones were missing buttons.

1. What percent of the phones produced that day were probably missing buttons?

   A. 60% C. 6%
   B. 15% D. 0.6%

2. If the factory produced 750 telephones, how many telephones might a worker expect to have missing buttons?

   A. 450 C. 30
   B. 45   D. 3

3. Find the mean of the data set.
   13, 22, 10, 10, 14, 18, 29, 20

   A. 19   C. 16
   B. 17   D. 15.5

For 4–5, use the line plot.

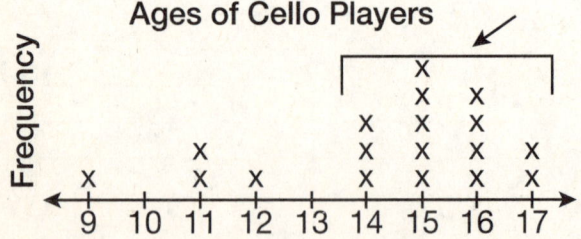

4. Find the median of the data in the line plot.

   A. 13   C. 14.5
   B. 14   D. 15

5. The arrow is pointing to the

   A. gap.   C. outlier.
   B. range. D. cluster.

The class scores for a history test are displayed in the stem-and-leaf plot.

History Test Scores

Stem	Leaf
6	6 8 9
7	3 5 5 8
8	2 2 2 4 6 6 9
9	0 1 3 7 9 9

6. What is the mode of the test scores?

   A. 2   C. 86
   B. 82   D. 99

7. Which day had the greatest movie attendance for afternoon and evening combined?

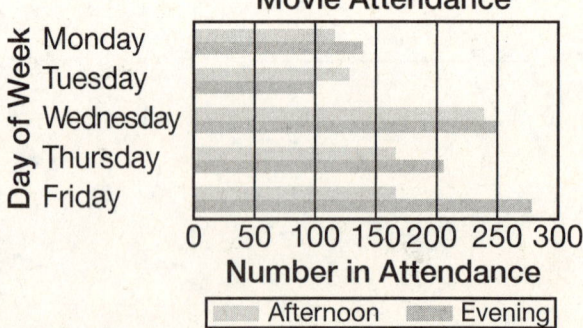

   A. Monday   C. Thursday
   B. Friday   D. Wednesday

122 Chapter 11 Test Form B

For Exercises 8–9, use the double-line graph.

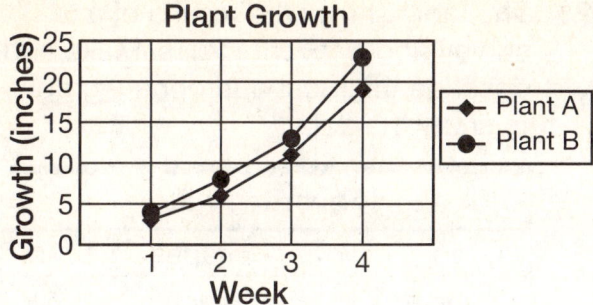

8. During which week did Plant B measure 8 inches tall?

   A. Week 1
   B. Week 2
   C. Week 3
   D. Week 4

9. Which statement is TRUE?

   A. The height of both plants is less than 20 inches in Week 4.
   B. The height of Plant B is sometimes less than the height of Plant A.
   C. The greatest increase in height occurs between Week 3 and Week 4 for both plants.
   D. The height of Plant A decreases from Week 1 to Week 2.

10. Jay's music shop sold 450 items this week. How many of the items sold were CDs?

   A. 20
   B. 62
   C. 90
   D. 279

11. Robyn is buying a hat. She can choose between a baseball cap or a visor, fitted or adjustable, and red, green, yellow, or black. How many possible combinations are there?

   A. 24
   B. 16
   C. 8
   D. 4

12. How many different ways can Phil arrange 4 vases on his shelf?

   A. 4
   B. 12
   C. 16
   D. 24

FREE RESPONSE

Find the mean, median, mode, and range of the data set. Round decimal answers to the nearest hundredth.

13. 4, 5, 6, 9, 6, 2, 6

   Mean _____   Median _____

   Mode _____   Range _____

14. Represent the data below in a frequency table and in a line plot.

High Temperatures				
68°F	65°F	69°F	73°F	68°F
66°F	68°F	68°F	66°F	67°F
72°F	72°F	67°F	71°F	69°F

Temperature	Tally	Frequency

Temperatures

Frequency

65°F 66°F 67°F 68°F 69°F 70°F 71°F 72°F 73°F

Chapter 11 Test Form B   **123**

15. Eugene is buying a watch. He can choose between a metal, leather, or plastic band, and a digital or analog display. The watch can also be waterproof, water-resistant, or neither. Make a tree diagram to show all of Eugene's possible watch choices.

16. Cecilia has 7 wind chimes. She can only hang 2 of the wind chimes on her porch. In how many ways can Cecilia choose 2 of the 7 wind chimes to display?

_____

For 17–22 use the cards below. Find each probability.

[6] [2] [4] [2] [2] [5] [C] [A] [R] [D]

17. $P(2)$ _____

18. $P(\text{odd number})$ _____

19. $P(6 \text{ or a vowel})$ _____

20. $P(5 \text{ or a letter})$ _____

21. Find $P(2, \text{a consonant})$ if the first card is replaced before the second is picked.

_____

22. Find $P(R, 4)$ if the first card is NOT replaced before the second is picked.

_____

WRITING IN MATH

23. The table shows the results of a survey about favorite fruits. Make and describe the most appropriate graph to show the data.

Favorite Fruit			
Apple	77	Grapes	45
Orange	38	Peach	61
Banana	29	Pear	23

_____
_____
_____
_____

24. Explain how to make a graph of the Favorite Fruit data using 3 fruits that received the most votes to make it seem that apples got twice as many votes as grapes.

_____
_____

25. Is the example below an example of a permutation or a combination? How do you know?

How many ways can Brad arrange 4 posters on his wall?

_____
_____

Chapter 12 Test Form A: Mixed Formats

MULTIPLE CHOICE

Circle the letter of the correct answer.

1. Which of the following is NOT a solution of $m \leq 4$?

   A. $m = -5$ **C.** $m = 3$
   B. $m = 0$ **D.** $m = 7$

2. Which inequality is graphed on the number line?

   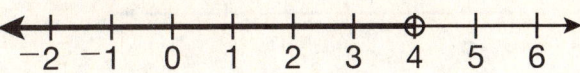

   A. $y \geq 4$ **C.** $y < 4$
   B. $y > 4$ **D.** $y \leq 4$

3. Which property of inequality should you use to solve $a - 4 \geq 3$?

   A. Addition Property of Inequality
   B. Subtraction Property of Inequality
   C. Multiplication Property of Inequality
   D. Division Property of Inequality

4. What is the solution of the inequality $b + 5 > 11$?

   A. $b < 6$ **C.** $b > 6$
   B. $b \leq 6$ **D.** $b \geq 6$

5. Let y represent the number of shoes sold last week. This week the number of shoes sold is 13 less than twice as many as last week. Which expression represents the number of shoes sold this week?

   A. $2(y - 13)$ **C.** $13 - 2y$
   B. $2y - 13$ **D.** $\frac{1}{2}(y - 13)$

6. Which tells the correct order of steps to solve the equation $3p - 9 = 21$?

   A. Subtract 9 from both sides of the equation. Then divide both sides by 3.
   B. Add 9 to both sides of the equation. Then divide both sides by 3.
   C. Add 9 to both sides of the equation. Then multiply both sides by 3.
   D. Divide both sides of the equation by 3. Then add 9 to both sides.

7. Which of the following equations does NOT have a solution of $x = 6$?

   A. $\frac{x}{3} + 1 = 3$ **C.** $3x - 7 = 11$
   B. $5x + 10 = 40$ **D.** $\frac{x}{2} + 3 = 5$

8. Which of the following is the solution of $3x - 7 = 2$?

   A. $x = \frac{1}{3}$ **C.** $x = 0$
   B. $x = \frac{5}{3}$ **D.** $x = 3$

9. The graph of the equation $y = 3x - 4$ is shown below. Which of the following is the correct solution of $-1 = 3x - 4$?

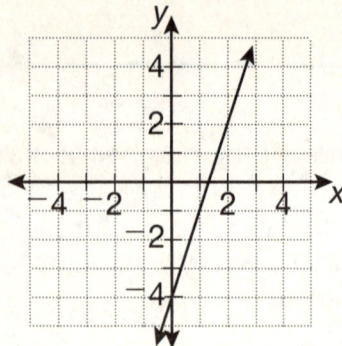

A. $x = -2$ C. $x = 0$
B. $x = -1$ D. $x = 1$

10. It is a cold morning and Shazia notices that the heat is not working in the house. Which of the following is most likely the temperature in the house?

A. 40°C   C. 40°F
B. 78°F   D. 20°C

11. Moore buys a 32-ounce bottle of milk. How many 12-ounce glasses of milk can she drink from the bottle? Use the inequality $12m \leq 32$ to solve.

A. 24 glasses   C. 3 glasses
B. 12 glasses   D. 2 glasses

12. Find $-15°C$ in degrees Fahrenheit. Use the formula $F = \frac{9}{5}C + 32$.

A. 27°F   C. $-5°F$
B. 5°F   D. $-27°F$

FREE RESPONSE

Solve each inequality or equation.

13. $\frac{1}{4}x - 3 = 7$ _____

14. $8x \geq 40$ _____

15. $2x - 7 = 19$ _____

Name three solutions for each inequality, and graph each inequality on a number line.

16. $x > 8$ _____, _____, _____

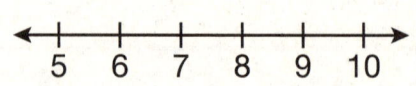

17. $x \leq 7$ _____, _____, _____

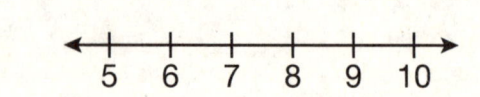

18. What inequality is graphed on the number line below? _____

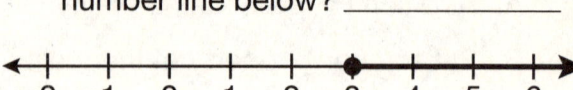

126 Chapter 12 Test Form A

For 19–20, make a T-table. Then graph each equation on a coordinate plane.

19. $y = 2x + 3$

x	y
-2	
-1	
0	

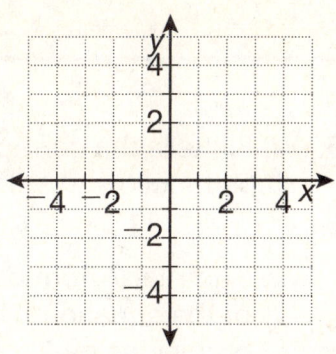

20. $y = 1 - \frac{1}{2}x$

x	y
-2	
0	
2	

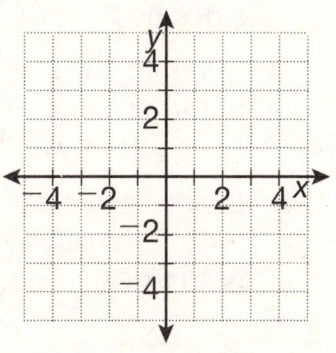

21. Use try, check, and revise to solve this problem.

Pat needs to sell on average 16 T-shirts a week (without rounding) to raise money for a charity. She sold 13 T-shirts in the first week and 20 T-shirts in the second week. How many T-shirts can she sell in the third week to achieve the average?

_____

WRITING IN MATH

22. Write an equation to find the perimeter, P, of a row of 35 hexagons that are joined side by side. Each side is 1 cm long.

Complete the table. Use the pattern in the table to help you write the equation.

Number of Hexagons	1	2	3	4	5	10	35
Perimeter (cm)	6	10	14	18			

_____

23. Explain how you can use inverse operations and the properties of inequality to solve $n - 30 \geq 111$.

_____

_____

_____

_____

_____

_____

_____

24. Explain the steps you would follow to graph the equation $y = 3x + 5$.

_____

_____

_____

_____

_____

_____

Chapter 12 Test Form A

Name _____

Chapter 12 Test Form B: Mixed Formats

MULTIPLE CHOICE

Circle the letter of the correct answer.

1. Which of the following is NOT a solution of $n \geq 7$?

   A. $n = {}^-8$ C. $n = 9.5$
   B. $n = 7$ D. $n = 12$

2. Which inequality is graphed on the number line?

   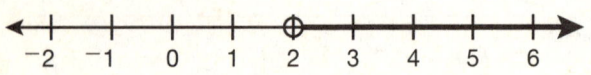

   A. $y \geq 2$ C. $y < 2$
   B. $y > 2$ D. $y \leq 2$

3. Which property of inequality should you use to solve $\frac{b}{4} \geq 5$?

   A. Addition Property of Inequality
   B. Subtraction Property of Inequality
   C. Multiplication Property of Inequality
   D. Division Property of Inequality

4. What is the solution of the inequality $w - 5 < 2$?

   A. $w < 7$ C. $w > 7$
   B. $w \leq 7$ D. $w \geq 7$

5. Let y represent the number of students in the math club last year. This year there are five fewer students than half as many as last year. Which expression represents the number of students in the math club this year?

   A. $5y + \frac{1}{2}$ C. $\frac{1}{2}(y - 5)$
   B. $2(y - 5)$ D. $\frac{1}{2}y - 5$

6. Which tells the correct order of steps to follow to solve the equation $2n + 7 = 11$?

   A. Subtract 7 from both sides of the equation. Then divide both sides by 2.
   B. Add 7 on both sides of the equation. Then divide both sides by 2.
   C. Subtract 7 from both sides of the equation. Then multiply both sides by 2.
   D. Divide both sides of the equation by 2. Then subtract 7 from both sides.

7. Which of the following equations does NOT have the solution of $x = 3$?

   A. $2x - 1 = 5$ C. $\frac{x}{3} + 7 = 8$
   B. $4x + 2 = 15$ D. $5x + 8 = 23$

8. Which of the following is the solution of $3x + 5 = 11$?

   A. $x = 11$ C. $x = 2$
   B. $x = \frac{16}{3}$ D. $x = 0$

128 Chapter 12 Test Form B

9. The graph of the equation $y = 2x + 1$ is shown below. Which of the following is the correct solution of $3 = 2x + 1$?

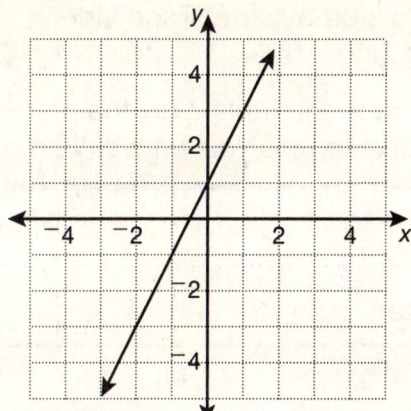

A. $x = ^-1$ C. $x = 1$
B. $x = 0$ D. $x = 3$

10. It is an extremely hot day and Melissa decides to turn on the air conditioner. Which of the following temperatures would she most likely choose?

A. 50°F   C. 74°C
B. 50°C   D. 74°F

11. Fiona bought a 32-ounce bottle of juice. How many 6-ounce glasses of juice can she drink from the bottle? Use the inequality $6m \leq 32$ to solve.

A. 5 glasses   C. 12 glasses
B. 6 glasses   D. 24 glasses

12. Find $^-5$°C in degrees Fahrenheit. Use the formula $F = \frac{9}{5}C + 32$.

A. $^-23$°F   C. 9°F
B. $^-9$°F   D. 23°F

FREE RESPONSE

Solve each inequality or equation.

13. $\frac{1}{3}x - 4 = 3$ _____

14. $7x \geq 56$ _____

15. $3x - 12 = 15$ _____

Name three solutions for each inequality, and graph each inequality on a number line.

16. $x > 6$ _____, _____, _____

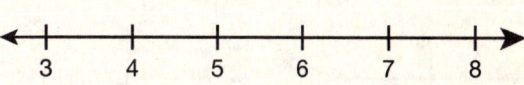

17. $x \leq 13$ _____, _____, _____

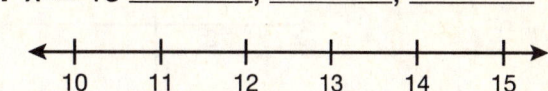

18. What inequality is graphed on the number line below? _____

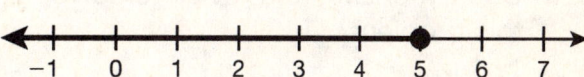

Chapter 12 Test Form B

For 19–20, make a T-table. Then graph each equation on a coordinate plane.

19. $y = 2x + 2$

x	y
⁻1	
0	
1	

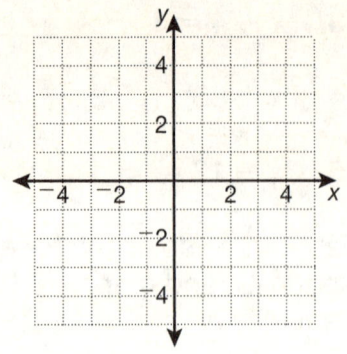

20. $y = 3 - \frac{1}{2}x$

x	y
⁻2	
0	
2	

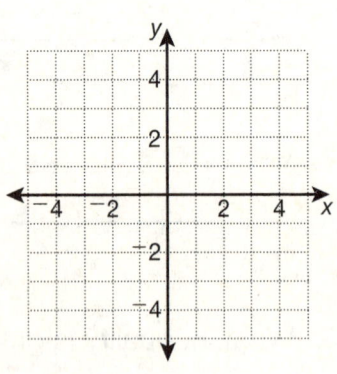

21. Use try, check, and revise to solve this problem.

Marci wants to save an average (without rounding) of $150 a month for the first four months of the year. She saved $110 in January, $175 in February, and $145 in March. How much money does she need to save in April to meet her goal?

_____

WRITING IN MATH

22. Write an equation to find the perimeter, p, of a row of 40 pentagons that are joined side by side. Each side is 1 cm long.

Complete the table. Use the pattern in the table to help you write the equation.

Number of Pentagons	1	2	3	4	5	10	40
Perimeter	5	8	11	14			

_____

23. Explain how you can use inverse operations and the properties of inequality to solve $m + 25 \geq 81$.

_____
_____
_____
_____
_____
_____

24. Explain the steps you would follow to graph the equation $y = 2x + 8$.

_____
_____
_____
_____
_____
_____

Name _____

Chapters 1–12 Cumulative Test

Circle the letter of the correct answer.

1. Find $\frac{5}{8} - \frac{1}{10}$.

   A. $\frac{1}{2}$ C. $\frac{3}{5}$
   B. $\frac{21}{40}$ D. $\frac{29}{40}$

2. Find the measure of an angle supplementary to an angle with a measure of 55°.

   A. 35°   C. 125°
   B. 85°   D. 148°

3. Which net can be used to make a triangular prism?

   A.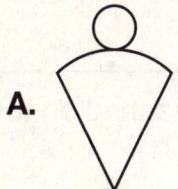

   B.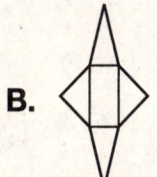

   C.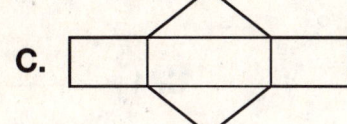

   D.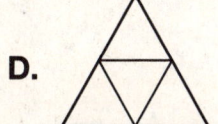

4. Which of the following is the solution of $3x - 8 = 4$?

   A. $x = \frac{-4}{3}$ C. $x = 4$
   B. $x = 3$ D. $x = 6$

5. Pam went to the museum at 3:15 P.M. and left at 6:30 P.M. How much time did she spend at the museum?

   A. 2 hr 45 min   C. 3 hr 45 min
   B. 3 hr 15 min   D. 4 hr 15 min

6. In which quadrant is the point $(-3, -1)$?

   A. I   C. III
   B. II   D. IV

7. Which of the following is NOT a solution of $m \leq 8$?

   A. ⁻8   C. 8
   B. 0   D. 11

8. A $70 watch is on sale for $49. Which is the percent of decrease?

   A. 30%   C. 14%
   B. 21%   D. 7%

9. Which solid figure has 5 vertices?

   A. 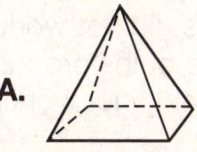   C.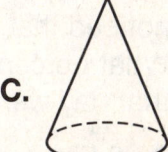

   B. 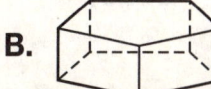   D.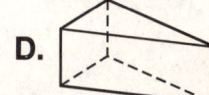

Chapters 1–12 Cumulative Test **131**

10. Find the unit cost of a 5-lb bag of potatoes that costs $3.
    A. $6/lb   C. $1.50/lb
    B. $1.67/lb D. $0.60/lb

11. Find the GCF for 15 and 42.
    A. 3   C. 6
    B. 5   D. 15

12. What is the solution of the inequality $a + 3 \geq 17$?
    A. $a < 14$ C. $a > 14$
    B. $a \leq 14$ D. $a \geq 14$

13. Find $^-25°C$ in degrees Fahrenheit. Use the formula $F = \frac{9}{5}C + 32$.
    A. $^-18°F$ C. $13°F$
    B. $^-13°F$ D. $18°F$

14. How many different ways can Noreen arrange 6 CDs on her shelf?
    A. 20   C. 120
    B. 60   D. 720

15. At a light-bulb factory, a worker randomly selected 120 bulbs. He noticed that 3 bulbs did not work. What percent of the bulbs produced that day were probably not working?
    A. 0.5%   C. 5%
    B. 2.5%   D. 25%

16. The class scores for a science test are displayed in the stem-and-leaf plot. What is the mode of the test scores?

    Science Test Scores

Stem	Leaf
5	4 8
6	1 3 7
7	0 2 4 7 7
8	1 3 3 3 5 9

    A. 89   C. 77
    B. 83   D. 3

17. Das has 12 bricks. This is $\frac{1}{3}$ of the number he needs. How many bricks does he need?
    A. 4 bricks   C. 30 bricks
    B. 24 bricks   D. 36 bricks

18. Which inequality is graphed on the number line?

    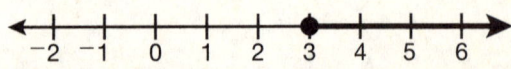

    A. $y \geq 3$ C. $y < 3$
    B. $y > 3$ D. $y \leq 3$

19. Find $4\frac{2}{3} \div 3\frac{1}{9}$.
    A. $\frac{1}{2}$ C. $1\frac{1}{5}$
    B. $\frac{2}{3}$ D. $1\frac{1}{2}$

For 20–21, use the line plot.

Number of Pistachios in a Bag

```
                  X
               X  X
               X  X
               X  X  X
            X  X  X  X
         X  X  X  X  X                    X
         11 12 13 14 15 16 17 18 19
```
Frequency

20. Find the median of the data in the line plot.

A. 11 C. 14.5
B. 14 D. 15

21. The arrow is pointing to the

A. gap. C. outlier.
B. cluster. D. minimum.

22. Calculate the value of $15 \div 3 \times (10 - 2^2)$.

A. 30 C. 40
B. 32 D. 46

23. What is the capacity in milliliters of a 7 liter bottle of juice?

A. 7,000 mL C. 70 mL
B. 700 mL D. 0.007 mL

24. What is 0.00326 in scientific notation?

A. 3.26×10^{-3}
B. 0.326×10^2
C. 3.26×10^{-4}
D. 32.6×10^3

25. Which property of inequality should you use to solve $\frac{a}{7} \geq 3$?

A. Addition Property of Inequality
B. Subtraction Property of Inequality
C. Multiplication Property of Inequality
D. Division Property of Inequality

26. The two triangles are similar. Find the measure of $\angle E$ and AC.

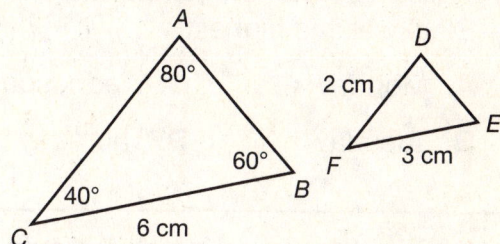

A. 60°, 4 cm C. 80°, 4 cm
B. 60°, 3 cm D. 80°, 3 cm

27. Which of the following equations does NOT have a solution of $x = 9$?

A. $2x + 5 = 23$ C. $3x - 7 = 20$
B. $\frac{x}{3} + 1 = 7$ D. $\frac{x}{3} - 1 = 2$

For 28–29, use the double-line graph.

City Temperatures

28. Which day was the temperature in Blackwell the highest?

A. Monday C. Wednesday
B. Tuesday D. Thursday

29. Which of the following statements is TRUE?

A. The temperature in both cities increased from Monday to Thursday.
B. The lowest temperature for each city occurs on Thursday.
C. The temperature of Blackwell is always higher than Frisco.
D. The temperature for each city falls after Tuesday.

30. Which unit of measure is most precise?

A. inch C. yard
B. millimeter D. centimeter

31. Find the area of this circle.

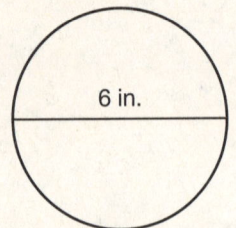

A. 9.42 in² C. 28.26 in²
B. 18.84 in² D. 113.04 in²

32. Mary wants to plant a garden in a rectangular plot with a perimeter of 22 feet. She wants the garden to have the greatest area possible. In whole feet, what should be the dimensions of the garden?

A. 2 ft by 9 ft C. 4 ft by 7 ft
B. 3 ft by 8 ft D. 5 ft by 6 ft

33. If you toss a number cube and flip a coin, what is the probability of tossing a number greater than 5 and having the coin land tails up?

A. $\frac{1}{12}$ C. $\frac{1}{2}$
B. $\frac{1}{6}$ D. $\frac{3}{4}$

34. Hope needs an average score of 84 (without rounding) on her three quizzes. Her scores on the first two quizzes were 96 and 74. What score does she need to get on the last quiz?

A. 86 C. 82
B. 84 D. 80

35. Which is 40% of 120?

A. 80 C. 40
B. 48 D. 24

36. Find the surface area of this solid.

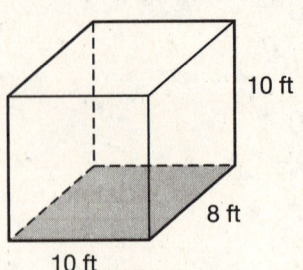

A. 260 ft² C. 520 ft²
B. 360 ft² D. 800 ft²

Basic-Facts Timed Test

Basic-Facts Timed Test 1 (page 27)

Name _____

Give the answer.

1. 2 + 8 = 10
2. 10 − 6 = 4
3. 7 + 1 = 8
4. 5 + 9 = 14
5. 4 + 8 = 12
6. 15 − 8 = 7
7. 9 − 3 = 6
8. 3 + 5 = 8
9. 4 + 3 = 7
10. 6 + 7 = 13
11. 13 − 5 = 8
12. 1 + 8 = 9
13. 9 − 0 = 9
14. 8 − 7 = 1
15. 8 + 3 = 11
16. 12 − 7 = 5
17. 0 + 3 = 3
18. 9 + 7 = 16
19. 16 − 8 = 8
20. 2 + 9 = 11
21. 13 − 6 = 7
22. 3 − 1 = 2
23. 14 − 8 = 6
24. 16 − 7 = 9
25. 6 + 3 = 9
26. 12 − 8 = 4
27. 9 + 5 = 14
28. 4 + 6 = 10
29. 7 − 0 = 7
30. 1 + 6 = 7
31. 5 + 4 = 9
32. 7 + 7 = 14
33. 17 − 9 = 8
34. 12 − 7 = 5
35. 11 − 4 = 7
36. 18 − 9 = 9
37. 6 + 0 = 6
38. 15 − 6 = 9
39. 11 − 9 = 2
40. 8 + 7 = 15
41. 17 − 8 = 9
42. 10 − 4 = 6
43. 8 + 8 = 16
44. 14 − 9 = 5
45. 1 + 9 = 10
46. 10 − 8 = 2
47. 8 + 5 = 13
48. 13 − 9 = 4
49. 9 + 6 = 15
50. 6 + 5 = 11

Basic-Facts Timed Test 2 (page 28)

Name _____

Give the answer.

1. 2 × 8 = 16
2. 16 ÷ 4 = 4
3. 4 × 7 = 28
4. 5 × 9 = 45
5. 18 ÷ 2 = 9
6. 15 ÷ 3 = 5
7. 3 × 6 = 18
8. 72 ÷ 9 = 8
9. 7 × 8 = 56
10. 8 × 9 = 72
11. 54 ÷ 6 = 9
12. 36 ÷ 6 = 6
13. 9 × 2 = 18
14. 25 ÷ 5 = 5
15. 8 × 0 = 0
16. 7 × 7 = 49
17. 81 ÷ 9 = 9
18. 6 × 8 = 48
19. 40 ÷ 5 = 8
20. 63 ÷ 9 = 7
21. 9 × 9 = 81
22. 64 ÷ 8 = 8
23. 2 × 9 = 18
24. 24 ÷ 8 = 3
25. 5 × 8 = 40
26. 1 × 6 = 6
27. 7 × 9 = 63
28. 5 × 4 = 20
29. 45 ÷ 5 = 9
30. 6 × 7 = 42
31. 72 ÷ 8 = 9
32. 56 ÷ 7 = 8
33. 42 ÷ 6 = 7
34. 0 × 8 = 0
35. 35 ÷ 7 = 5
36. 48 ÷ 6 = 8
37. 5 × 0 = 0
38. 0 ÷ 4 = 0
39. 6 × 9 = 54
40. 18 ÷ 6 = 3
41. 36 ÷ 9 = 4
42. 3 × 9 = 27
43. 6 × 4 = 24
44. 7 ÷ 7 = 1
45. 30 ÷ 6 = 5
46. 8 × 7 = 56
47. 9 × 4 = 36
48. 7 ÷ 1 = 7
49. 24 ÷ 6 = 4
50. 6 × 6 = 36

Basic-Facts Timed Test 3 (page 29)

Name _____

Give the answer.

1. 3 + 7 = 10
2. 8 + 5 = 13
3. 7 + 3 = 10
4. 4 + 9 = 13
5. 0 + 4 = 4
6. 10 − 3 = 7
7. 11 − 7 = 4
8. 14 − 5 = 9
9. 6 − 2 = 4
10. 12 − 9 = 3
11. 7 + 5 = 12
12. 6 + 6 = 12
13. 8 + 9 = 17
14. 6 + 4 = 10
15. 4 + 7 = 11
16. 15 − 7 = 8
17. 10 − 7 = 3
18. 15 − 9 = 6
19. 13 − 4 = 9
20. 12 − 6 = 6
21. 6 + 8 = 14
22. 7 + 9 = 16
23. 8 + 6 = 14
24. 4 + 5 = 9
25. 9 + 9 = 18
26. 3 × 4 = 12
27. 8 × 8 = 64
28. 5 × 3 = 15
29. 9 × 7 = 63
30. 2 × 7 = 14
31. 49 ÷ 7 = 7
32. 54 ÷ 9 = 6
33. 14 ÷ 2 = 7
34. 27 ÷ 3 = 9
35. 42 ÷ 7 = 6
36. 1 × 9 = 9
37. 7 × 4 = 28
38. 7 × 6 = 42
39. 3 × 3 = 9
40. 6 × 2 = 12
41. 0 ÷ 7 = 0
42. 32 ÷ 4 = 8
43. 48 ÷ 8 = 6
44. 63 ÷ 7 = 9
45. 21 ÷ 7 = 3
46. 4 × 5 = 20
47. 8 × 1 = 8
48. 8 × 5 = 40
49. 2 × 3 = 6
50. 9 × 8 = 72

Basic-Facts Timed Test 4 (page 30)

Name _____

Give the answer.

1. 4 + 4 = 8
2. 6 + 9 = 15
3. 5 + 6 = 11
4. 2 + 7 = 9
5. 3 + 9 = 12
6. 4 − 3 = 1
7. 12 − 3 = 9
8. 12 − 5 = 7
9. 11 − 8 = 3
10. 9 − 6 = 3
11. 1 + 6 = 7
12. 5 + 7 = 12
13. 8 + 4 = 12
14. 5 + 8 = 13
15. 9 + 1 = 10
16. 5 − 3 = 2
17. 14 − 7 = 7
18. 12 − 8 = 4
19. 16 − 9 = 7
20. 14 − 6 = 8
21. 7 + 8 = 15
22. 3 + 2 = 5
23. 9 + 8 = 17
24. 2 + 5 = 7
25. 8 + 0 = 8
26. 8 × 2 = 16
27. 4 × 9 = 36
28. 6 × 5 = 30
29. 8 × 4 = 32
30. 3 × 8 = 24
31. 8 ÷ 1 = 8
32. 12 ÷ 2 = 6
33. 45 ÷ 9 = 5
34. 56 ÷ 8 = 7
35. 20 ÷ 4 = 5
36. 7 × 0 = 0
37. 9 × 6 = 54
38. 9 × 5 = 45
39. 3 × 7 = 21
40. 8 × 6 = 48
41. 6 ÷ 6 = 1
42. 9 ÷ 3 = 3
43. 16 ÷ 8 = 2
44. 40 ÷ 8 = 5
45. 28 ÷ 7 = 4
46. 9 × 7 = 63
47. 7 × 2 = 14
48. 4 × 3 = 12
49. 5 × 7 = 35
50. 2 × 4 = 8

Basic-Facts Timed Test

Basic-Facts Timed Test 5

Give the answer.

1. 8 × 3 = **24**
2. 9 × 4 = **36**
3. 7 × 8 = **56**
4. 6 × 2 = **12**
5. 5 × 9 = **45**
6. 7 × 4 = **28**
7. 2 × 1 = **2**
8. 3 × 2 = **6**
9. 9 × 9 = **81**
10. 8 × 4 = **32**
11. 2 × 9 = **18**
12. 8 × 5 = **40**
13. 7 × 7 = **49**
14. 7 × 2 = **14**
15. 9 × 3 = **27**
16. 1 × 6 = **6**
17. 3 × 0 = **0**
18. 5 × 7 = **35**
19. 7 × 9 = **63**
20. 9 × 2 = **18**
21. 3 × 3 = **9**
22. 6 × 5 = **30**
23. 5 × 5 = **25**
24. 8 × 2 = **16**
25. 5 × 8 = **40**
26. 16 ÷ 4 = **4**
27. 30 ÷ 5 = **6**
28. 10 ÷ 5 = **2**
29. 24 ÷ 3 = **8**
30. 42 ÷ 7 = **6**
31. 16 ÷ 2 = **8**
32. 6 ÷ 6 = **1**
33. 81 ÷ 9 = **9**
34. 35 ÷ 5 = **7**
35. 0 ÷ 2 = **0**
36. 21 ÷ 3 = **7**
37. 7 ÷ 1 = **7**
38. 56 ÷ 8 = **7**
39. 8 ÷ 2 = **4**
40. 27 ÷ 3 = **9**
41. 48 ÷ 6 = **8**
42. 28 ÷ 4 = **7**
43. 10 ÷ 2 = **5**
44. 15 ÷ 5 = **3**
45. 18 ÷ 3 = **6**
46. 24 ÷ 6 = **4**
47. 2 ÷ 2 = **1**
48. 24 ÷ 4 = **6**
49. 63 ÷ 7 = **9**
50. 36 ÷ 4 = **9**

page 31

Basic-Facts Timed Test 6

Give the answer.

1. 7 × 9 = **63**
2. 9 × 6 = **54**
3. 9 × 9 = **81**
4. 9 × 1 = **9**
5. 4 × 9 = **36**
6. 6 × 9 = **54**
7. 7 × 3 = **21**
8. 3 × 5 = **15**
9. 3 × 6 = **18**
10. 8 × 9 = **72**
11. 5 × 3 = **15**
12. 9 × 2 = **18**
13. 2 × 3 = **6**
14. 5 × 5 = **25**
15. 2 × 7 = **14**
16. 2 × 2 = **4**
17. 7 × 5 = **35**
18. 6 × 3 = **18**
19. 7 × 7 = **49**
20. 2 × 5 = **10**
21. 7 × 6 = **42**
22. 8 × 8 = **64**
23. 9 × 4 = **36**
24. 9 × 3 = **27**
25. 6 × 7 = **42**
26. 8 × 4 = **32**
27. 4 × 2 = **8**
28. 9 × 5 = **45**
29. 8 × 3 = **24**
30. 3 × 7 = **21**
31. 8 × 5 = **40**
32. 4 × 1 = **4**
33. 4 × 6 = **24**
34. 3 × 9 = **27**
35. 3 × 2 = **6**
36. 1 × 8 = **8**
37. 5 × 6 = **30**
38. 7 × 4 = **28**
39. 4 × 5 = **20**
40. 4 × 8 = **32**
41. 6 × 8 = **48**
42. 1 × 6 = **6**
43. 8 × 2 = **16**
44. 2 × 8 = **16**
45. 1 × 3 = **3**
46. 4 × 0 = **0**
47. 1 × 5 = **5**
48. 4 × 4 = **16**
49. 2 × 6 = **12**
50. 1 × 4 = **4**

page 32

Basic-Facts Timed Test 7

Give the answer.

1. 8 + 2 = **10**
2. 3 + 7 = **10**
3. 8 + 8 = **16**
4. 3 + 6 = **9**
5. 5 + 1 = **6**
6. 7 + 6 = **13**
7. 9 + 2 = **11**
8. 7 + 7 = **14**
9. 5 + 3 = **8**
10. 6 + 2 = **8**
11. 4 + 7 = **11**
12. 3 + 8 = **11**
13. 1 + 1 = **2**
14. 9 − 1 = **8**
15. 11 − 7 = **4**
16. 12 − 5 = **7**
17. 9 − 4 = **5**
18. 11 − 3 = **8**
19. 8 − 4 = **4**
20. 13 − 7 = **6**
21. 6 − 2 = **4**
22. 12 − 9 = **3**
23. 6 − 4 = **2**
24. 11 − 6 = **5**
25. 3 − 1 = **2**
26. 2 × 6 = **12**
27. 3 × 4 = **12**
28. 8 × 2 = **16**
29. 6 × 2 = **12**
30. 3 × 9 = **27**
31. 7 × 2 = **14**
32. 8 × 8 = **64**
33. 4 × 6 = **24**
34. 8 × 7 = **56**
35. 7 × 8 = **56**
36. 2 × 5 = **10**
37. 5 × 5 = **25**
38. 5 × 1 = **5**
39. 4 ÷ 4 = **1**
40. 0 ÷ 4 = **0**
41. 12 ÷ 4 = **3**
42. 21 ÷ 3 = **7**
43. 14 ÷ 2 = **7**
44. 5 ÷ 1 = **5**
45. 24 ÷ 4 = **6**
46. 54 ÷ 6 = **9**
47. 20 ÷ 4 = **5**
48. 45 ÷ 5 = **9**
49. 63 ÷ 7 = **9**
50. 18 ÷ 2 = **9**

page 33

Basic-Facts Timed Test 8

Give the answer.

1. 4 + 9 = **13**
2. 2 + 5 = **7**
3. 8 + 2 = **10**
4. 13 − 9 = **4**
5. 9 − 1 = **8**
6. 12 − 4 = **8**
7. 9 + 4 = **13**
8. 8 − 8 = **0**
9. 7 + 1 = **8**
10. 3 − 3 = **0**
11. 12 − 8 = **4**
12. 6 − 5 = **1**
13. 5 + 5 = **10**
14. 7 + 4 = **11**
15. 8 + 9 = **17**
16. 4 + 1 = **5**
17. 2 − 2 = **0**
18. 1 + 7 = **8**
19. 7 + 6 = **13**
20. 2 + 1 = **3**
21. 8 − 7 = **1**
22. 2 + 7 = **9**
23. 16 − 9 = **7**
24. 13 − 4 = **9**
25. 5 + 1 = **6**
26. 7 + 2 = **9**
27. 4 + 8 = **12**
28. 9 + 3 = **12**
29. 15 − 7 = **8**
30. 14 − 7 = **7**
31. 7 − 3 = **4**
32. 9 − 7 = **2**
33. 5 − 0 = **5**
34. 8 + 7 = **15**
35. 4 + 4 = **8**
36. 8 + 3 = **11**
37. 11 − 2 = **9**
38. 6 + 6 = **12**
39. 2 + 6 = **8**
40. 7 + 7 = **14**
41. 7 − 4 = **3**
42. 5 + 9 = **14**
43. 5 − 2 = **3**
44. 11 − 5 = **6**
45. 5 + 3 = **8**
46. 4 − 1 = **3**
47. 4 + 5 = **9**
48. 11 − 9 = **2**
49. 8 − 2 = **6**
50. 3 − 0 = **3**

page 34

Basic-Facts Timed Test

Name _____

Basic-Facts Timed Test 9

Give the answer.

1. 6 × 6 = **36**
2. 4 × 5 = **20**
3. 5 × 2 = **10**
4. 8 × 9 = **72**
5. 5 × 9 = **45**
6. 7 × 2 = **14**
7. 8 × 0 = **0**
8. 4 × 7 = **28**
9. 9 × 6 = **54**
10. 8 × 3 = **24**
11. 8 × 6 = **48**
12. 5 × 8 = **40**
13. 1 × 1 = **1**
14. 1 × 0 = **0**
15. 2 × 7 = **14**
16. 5 × 4 = **20**
17. 5 × 3 = **15**
18. 6 × 4 = **24**
19. 7 × 7 = **49**
20. 2 × 9 = **18**
21. 7 × 5 = **35**
22. 5 × 5 = **25**
23. 4 × 4 = **16**
24. 4 × 3 = **12**
25. 7 × 3 = **21**
26. 9 ÷ 9 = **1**
27. 9 ÷ 3 = **3**
28. 12 ÷ 4 = **3**
29. 9 ÷ 1 = **9**
30. 4 ÷ 2 = **2**
31. 63 ÷ 9 = **7**
32. 27 ÷ 9 = **3**
33. 0 ÷ 8 = **0**
34. 36 ÷ 6 = **6**
35. 36 ÷ 4 = **9**
36. 35 ÷ 5 = **7**
37. 32 ÷ 8 = **4**
38. 72 ÷ 8 = **9**
39. 8 ÷ 4 = **2**
40. 3 ÷ 1 = **3**
41. 10 ÷ 5 = **2**
42. 18 ÷ 3 = **6**
43. 21 ÷ 7 = **3**
44. 8 ÷ 2 = **4**
45. 6 ÷ 1 = **6**
46. 20 ÷ 5 = **4**
47. 30 ÷ 5 = **6**
48. 6 ÷ 2 = **3**
49. 40 ÷ 8 = **5**
50. 28 ÷ 7 = **4**

page 35

Name _____

Basic-Facts Timed Test 10

Give the answer.

1. 9 × 0 = **0**
2. 7 × 6 = **42**
3. 5 × 9 = **45**
4. 3 × 1 = **3**
5. 3 × 9 = **27**
6. 8 × 9 = **72**
7. 6 × 9 = **54**
8. 8 × 7 = **56**
9. 4 × 6 = **24**
10. 7 × 4 = **28**
11. 3 × 3 = **9**
12. 6 × 7 = **42**
13. 1 × 3 = **3**
14. 5 × 5 = **25**
15. 2 × 8 = **16**
16. 9 × 2 = **18**
17. 4 × 8 = **32**
18. 3 × 8 = **24**
19. 7 × 2 = **14**
20. 2 × 2 = **4**
21. 5 × 6 = **30**
22. 0 × 2 = **0**
23. 3 × 4 = **12**
24. 8 × 3 = **24**
25. 3 × 7 = **21**
26. 9 × 4 = **36**
27. 3 × 2 = **6**
28. 3 × 5 = **15**
29. 6 × 3 = **18**
30. 2 × 7 = **14**
31. 7 × 5 = **35**
32. 7 × 1 = **7**
33. 1 × 2 = **2**
34. 5 × 7 = **35**
35. 4 × 2 = **8**
36. 8 × 8 = **64**
37. 9 × 8 = **72**
38. 6 × 4 = **24**
39. 2 × 5 = **10**
40. 4 × 7 = **28**
41. 6 × 6 = **36**
42. 1 × 9 = **9**
43. 8 × 5 = **40**
44. 6 × 8 = **48**
45. 7 × 3 = **21**
46. 4 × 4 = **16**
47. 6 × 5 = **30**
48. 4 × 9 = **36**
49. 2 × 4 = **8**
50. 0 × 4 = **0**

page 36

Name _____

Basic-Facts Timed Test 11

Give the answer.

1. 5 + 2 = **7**
2. 6 + 5 = **11**
3. 16 − 7 = **9**
4. 18 − 9 = **9**
5. 6 − 4 = **2**
6. 16 − 8 = **8**
7. 6 + 9 = **15**
8. 9 − 9 = **0**
9. 2 + 9 = **11**
10. 17 − 9 = **8**
11. 14 − 9 = **5**
12. 6 − 3 = **3**
13. 9 + 2 = **11**
14. 1 + 5 = **6**
15. 4 + 8 = **12**
16. 5 + 7 = **12**
17. 8 − 6 = **2**
18. 1 + 9 = **10**
19. 6 + 8 = **14**
20. 2 + 7 = **9**
21. 9 − 3 = **6**
22. 2 + 6 = **8**
23. 15 − 7 = **8**
24. 9 − 2 = **7**
25. 7 + 9 = **16**
26. 0 + 9 = **9**
27. 4 + 2 = **6**
28. 4 + 3 = **7**
29. 14 − 6 = **8**
30. 10 − 7 = **3**
31. 9 − 8 = **1**
32. 9 + 9 = **18**
33. 8 − 6 = **2**
34. 9 + 7 = **16**
35. 6 + 4 = **10**
36. 2 + 8 = **10**
37. 10 − 5 = **5**
38. 7 + 3 = **10**
39. 9 + 8 = **17**
40. 9 + 6 = **15**
41. 8 − 8 = **0**
42. 7 + 8 = **15**
43. 15 − 9 = **6**
44. 10 − 9 = **1**
45. 6 + 7 = **13**
46. 2 − 1 = **1**
47. 9 + 5 = **14**
48. 13 − 6 = **7**
49. 4 + 6 = **10**
50. 7 − 4 = **3**

page 37

Name _____

Basic-Facts Timed Test 12

Give the answer.

1. 6 × 1 = **6**
2. 8 × 6 = **48**
3. 4 × 9 = **36**
4. 5 × 2 = **10**
5. 5 × 4 = **20**
6. 6 × 9 = **54**
7. 6 × 0 = **0**
8. 7 × 8 = **56**
9. 6 × 6 = **36**
10. 4 × 2 = **8**
11. 1 × 5 = **5**
12. 3 × 7 = **21**
13. 9 × 3 = **27**
14. 1 × 4 = **4**
15. 4 × 7 = **28**
16. 6 × 3 = **18**
17. 8 × 4 = **32**
18. 8 × 7 = **56**
19. 3 × 8 = **24**
20. 9 × 9 = **81**
21. 2 × 9 = **18**
22. 4 × 4 = **16**
23. 9 × 5 = **45**
24. 9 × 8 = **72**
25. 9 × 7 = **63**
26. 8 ÷ 4 = **2**
27. 30 ÷ 5 = **6**
28. 15 ÷ 3 = **5**
29. 21 ÷ 7 = **3**
30. 42 ÷ 6 = **7**
31. 10 ÷ 2 = **5**
32. 64 ÷ 8 = **8**
33. 12 ÷ 2 = **6**
34. 27 ÷ 9 = **3**
35. 35 ÷ 5 = **7**
36. 72 ÷ 9 = **8**
37. 18 ÷ 3 = **6**
38. 8 ÷ 1 = **8**
39. 20 ÷ 5 = **4**
40. 48 ÷ 8 = **6**
41. 32 ÷ 4 = **8**
42. 28 ÷ 4 = **7**
43. 36 ÷ 6 = **6**
44. 56 ÷ 7 = **8**
45. 54 ÷ 6 = **9**
46. 16 ÷ 2 = **8**
47. 20 ÷ 4 = **5**
48. 32 ÷ 8 = **4**
49. 12 ÷ 4 = **3**
50. 45 ÷ 9 = **5**

page 38

Diagnosing Readiness for Grade 6

Name_____

Diagnosing Readiness for Grade 6

Circle the letter of the correct answer.

1. What is the value of the underlined digit in 12.0<u>9</u>4?
   A. nine
   B. nine tenths
   C. nine hundredths ✓
   D. nine thousandths

2. What is the measure of the angle?
   A. 180°
   B. 150°
   C. 90° ✓
   D. 60°

3. Which is the best estimate for 61,089 + 3,112?
   A. 64,000 ✓
   B. 65,000
   C. 74,000
   D. 75,000

4. Find 23.1 − 2.56.
   A. 21.5
   B. 20.6
   C. 20.55
   D. 20.54 ✓

5. Solve $24 = x − 8$.
   A. $x = 3$
   B. $x = 16$
   C. $x = 24$
   D. $x = 32$ ✓

6. What instrument do most of the members of the orchestra play?

   Orchestra Members (pie chart: Other, Woodwinds, Brass, Percussion, Strings)

   A. Brass ✓
   B. Strings
   C. Woodwinds
   D. Percussion

7. Simone is decorating her bedroom. She can buy a red bedspread, a blue bedspread, or an orange bedspread. She can choose either white pillows or black pillows. From how many different combinations of bedspreads and pillows can Simone choose?
   A. 3 combinations
   B. 6 combinations ✓
   C. 9 combinations
   D. 12 combinations

page 43

8. You spin the spinner once. Which of the following best describes the chances that the spinner will land on gray?
   A. certain
   B. more likely
   C. equally likely as black ✓
   D. impossible

9. Which is the most reasonable estimate for $8,914 \div 3$?
   A. 2,800
   B. 3,000 ✓
   C. 3,500
   D. 4,000

10. Which number is NOT divisible by 3?
    A. 42
    B. 139 ✓
    C. 243
    D. 291

11. Which fraction equals 0.8?
    A. $\frac{1}{80}$
    B. $\frac{8}{100}$
    C. $\frac{1}{8}$
    D. $\frac{8}{10}$ ✓

12. Evaluate $x + 5$ for $x = 4$.
    A. 45
    B. 20
    C. 9 ✓
    D. 1

For 13–14, use the solid.

13. Which of the following is the top view of the solid?
    A.
    B. ✓
    C.
    D.

14. Find the volume of the solid.
    A. 6 cubes
    B. 10 cubes ✓
    C. 12 cubes
    D. 27 cubes

15. Which is the most reasonable estimate for $551 \div 63$?
    A. 8
    B. 9 ✓
    C. 80
    D. 90

16. Find the area of a square with each side measuring $4\frac{1}{2}$ feet.
    A. $16\frac{1}{4}$ ft²
    B. $16\frac{1}{2}$ ft²
    C. 18 ft²
    D. $20\frac{1}{4}$ ft² ✓

17. Find $912 \div 38$.
    A. 204
    B. 26
    C. 24 ✓
    D. 2.4

page 44

18. Find the perimeter of the figure.
    (sides: 5.1, 2.8, 2.6, 4.2, 3.4)
    A. 18.1 in.²
    B. 18.1 in. ✓
    C. 19.1 in.²
    D. 19.1 in.

19. Which polygon has 4 sides?
    A. pentagon
    B. hexagon
    C. octagon
    D. quadrilateral ✓

20. Find 5.3×100.
    A. 5.3
    B. 53
    C. 530 ✓
    D. 5,300

21. What fraction of the figure is shaded?
    A. $\frac{3}{7}$ ✓
    B. $\frac{1}{2}$
    C. $\frac{4}{7}$
    D. $\frac{7}{3}$

22. Write a ratio to compare the number of striped triangles to the number of circles.
    A. 5:7 ✓
    B. 5:5
    C. 7:5
    D. 5:12

23. Which is a prime number?
    A. 72
    B. 53 ✓
    C. 35
    D. 27

24. Write $\frac{18}{8}$ as a mixed number in simplest form.
    A. $3\frac{1}{4}$
    B. $2\frac{8}{18}$
    C. $2\frac{1}{4}$ ✓
    D. $2\frac{4}{18}$

25. Find $\frac{7}{10} − \frac{3}{5}$.
    A. $\frac{1}{10}$ ✓
    B. $\frac{5}{10}$
    C. $\frac{4}{5}$
    D. $\frac{10}{10}$

26. Multiply $\frac{3}{4}$ and 24.
    A. 6
    B. 9
    C. 12
    D. 18 ✓

27. Which unit would be most appropriate to measure the width of a house?
    A. millimeter
    B. centimeter
    C. meter ✓
    D. kilometer

28. Round 8.9<u>7</u>1 to the underlined place.
    A. 9.0 ✓
    B. 8.9
    C. 8.8
    D. 8.09

page 45

29. Find $5,600 \div 80$.
    A. 60
    B. 70 ✓
    C. 600
    D. 700

30. Which solid figure does this object resemble?
    A. prism
    B. cylinder ✓
    C. pyramid
    D. cone

31. 5,300 mL = ☐
    A. 5,300,000 L
    B. 53 L
    C. 5.3 L ✓
    D. 0.53 L

32. Find $\$14.80 \div 4$.
    A. \$0.35
    B. \$0.37
    C. \$3.45
    D. \$3.70 ✓

33. Find $3(15 − 9) + 2$.
    A. 38
    B. 30
    C. 24
    D. 20 ✓

34. Which decimal is less than 7.805?
    A. 78.05
    B. 7.850
    C. 7.815
    D. 7.58 ✓

35. Find the least common denominator of $\frac{1}{10}$ and $\frac{5}{6}$.
    A. 6
    B. 30 ✓
    C. 50
    D. 60

36. Find the measure of $\angle S$.
    (triangle with angles 61°, 35°)
    A. 35°
    B. 55°
    C. 84° ✓
    D. 96°

37. What percent is shaded?
    A. 7%
    B. 35%
    C. 70% ✓
    D. 140%

38. Estimate $2\frac{1}{5} + 4\frac{5}{6}$ to the nearest whole number.
    A. 5
    B. 6
    C. 7 ✓
    D. 8

39. Which is the most reasonable estimate for 4.15×3.9?
    A. 8
    B. 12
    C. 16 ✓
    D. 20

40. Name the ordered pair for Point H.
    (coordinate grid with points A, C, H, K, N)
    A. (3, 1)
    B. (1, 3) ✓
    C. (0, 3)
    D. (3, 0)

page 46

138

Chapter 1 Form A and Form B

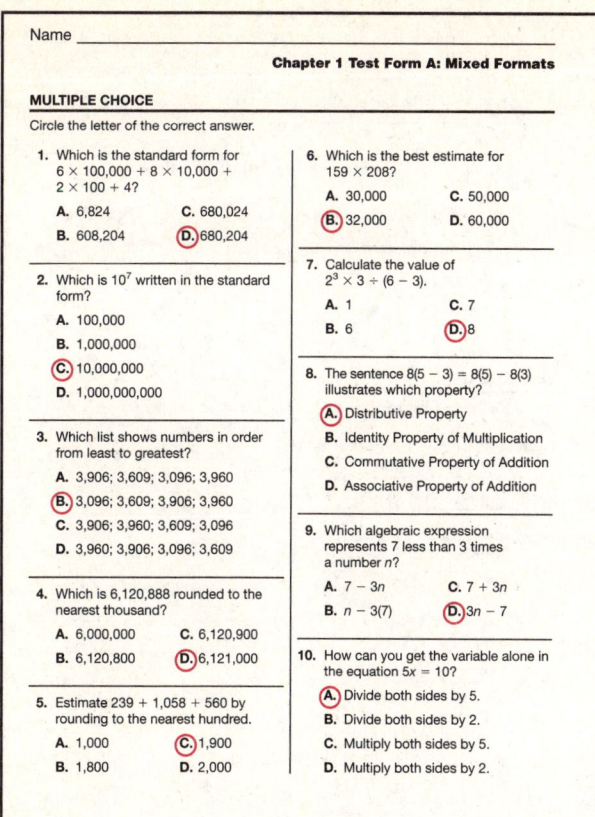

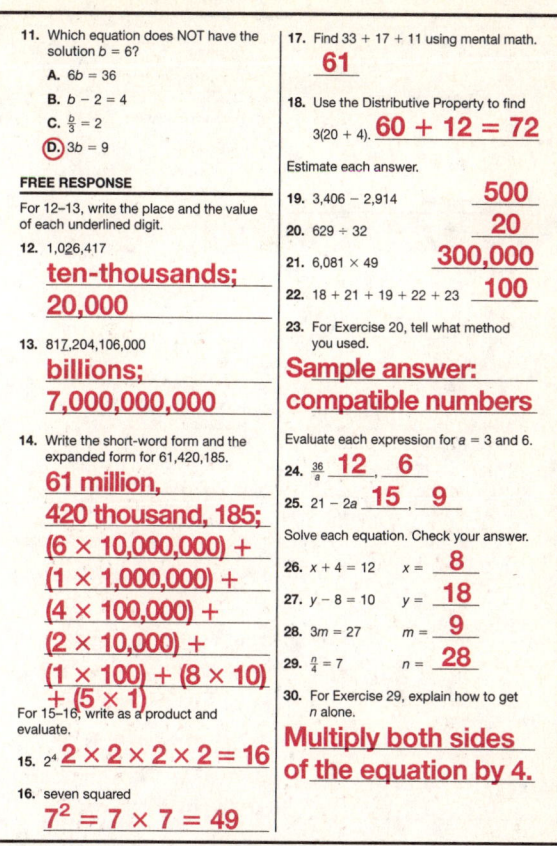

page 47

page 48

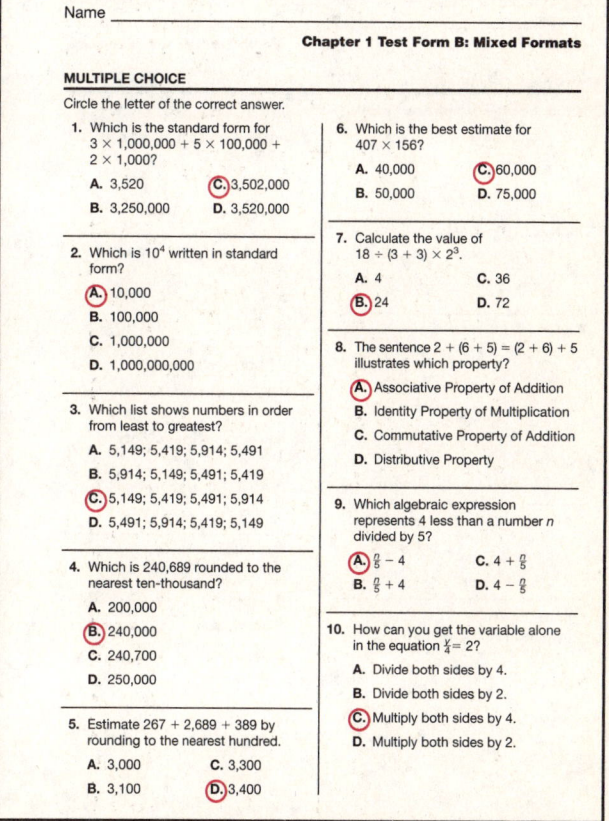

page 49

Form B, page 50

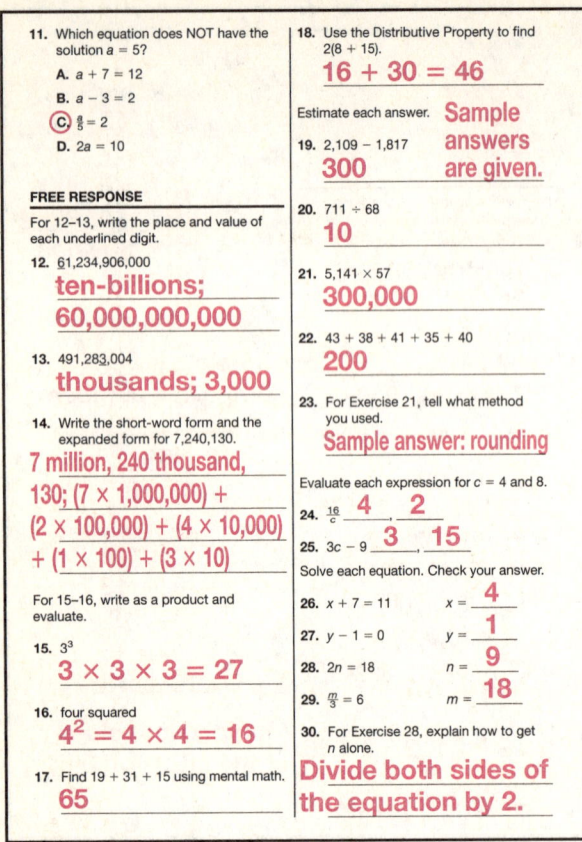
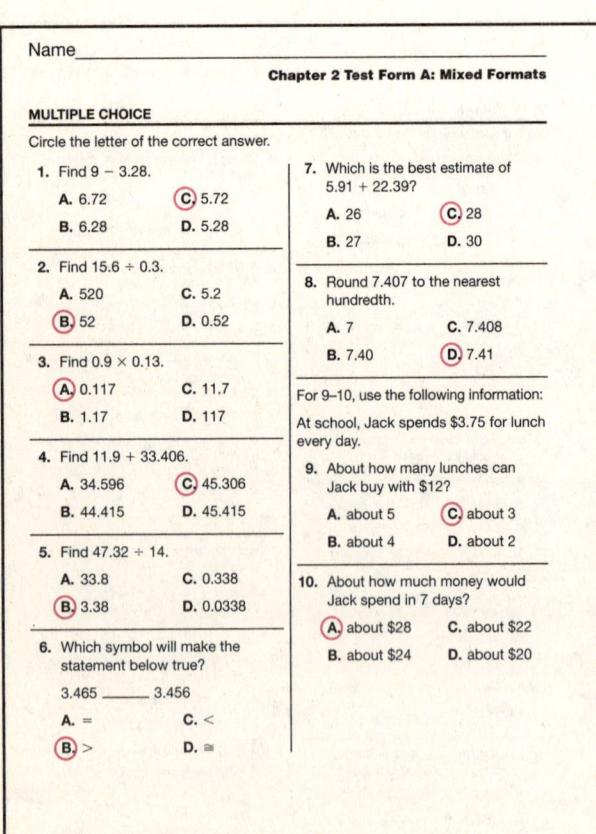
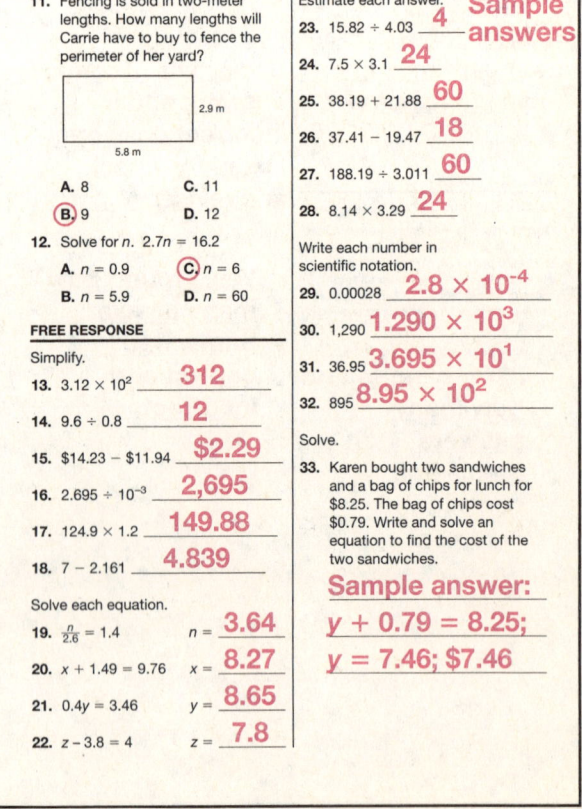

Chapter 2 Form A and Form B

34. Chen works at a local farmer's market. His boss asked him to put 6 bananas in each bag. If all 82 bananas must be put in a bag, how many bags does he need?
14 bags

WRITING IN MATH

35. To divide a decimal number by another decimal number, what is the first step?
Multiply both the dividend and divisor by a power of 10 so that the divisor becomes a whole number.

36. Tell how you know which inverse operation to use when solving the equation below.
$5.4x = 16.2$
Sample answer: Since x is multiplied by 5.4, use the inverse operation which is division.

37. Jerome solved the word problem below. Did he interpret the remainder correctly? Explain why or why not.

A bag of peanuts should contain 3 ounces of peanuts. There are 29 ounces of peanuts. How many bags of peanuts can be made?
$29 \div 3 \approx 9.7$; 9 bags of peanuts can be made. Yes; only 9 bags can be made because each bag should contain 3 ounces.

page 55

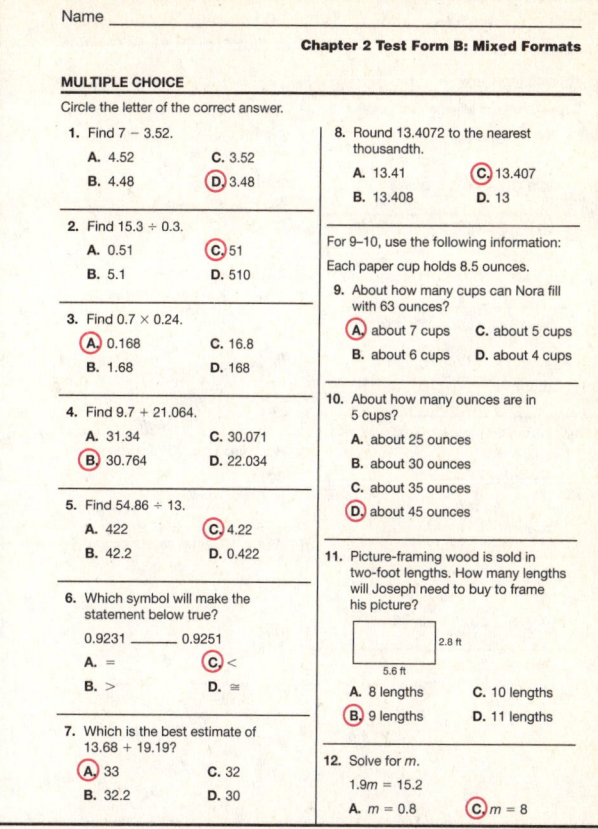

Form B, page 56

FREE RESPONSE
Simplify.

13. 1.06×10^3
1,060

14. $8.825 \div 10^{-2}$
882.5

Solve each equation.

15. $\frac{x}{3.3} = 0.7$ $x =$ **2.31**

16. $y + 0.27 = 3.16$ $y =$ **2.89**

17. $1.8n = 9.9$ $n =$ **5.5**

18. $z - 1.77 = 3$ $z =$ **4.77**

Estimate each answer.

19. $27.84 + 19.41$
50

20. $28.66 - 14.32$
15

21. $146.28 \div 1.84$
73

22. 5.71×4.25
24

Write each number in scientific notation.

23. 0.00104
1.04×10^{-3}

24. $21,020$
2.102×10^4

Solve.

25. Shakil bought a dozen eggs and a loaf of bread for $4.65. The eggs were $1.99. Write and solve an equation to find the cost of the bread.
Sample answer: $y + 1.99 = 4.65$; $y = 2.66$; $2.66

26. Mary's science teacher asked her to make packets containing two ounces of salt. The salt jar contains 23 ounces of salt. How many complete packets can she make?
11 packets

WRITING IN MATH

27. Explain how to add a whole number and a decimal number using the example below.

$27 + 2.67$
Annex a decimal point and 2 zeros to 27; line up the decimal points. Add, starting with the hundredths column. Regroup as needed; 29.67

28. Tell how you know which inverse operation to use when solving the equation $x + 8.4 = 16.8$.
Sample answer: Since 8.4 is added to x, use the inverse operation which is subtraction.

29. Larry solved the word problem below. Did he interpret the remainder correctly? Explain why or why not.

For a party, Faiz ordered 52 muffins. They were delivered in boxes. Each box holds up to 12 muffins. How many boxes were delivered?

$52 \div 12 \approx 4.3$;
4 boxes were delivered.
No; four boxes would not be enough to hold all 52 muffins.

page 57

page 58

Chapter Tests in the Assessment Sourcebook parallel Chapter Tests in the Student Book item for item. See the Teacher Edition for item analysis of these tests.

Chapter 3 Form A and Form B

Name _____

Chapter 3 Test Form A: Mixed Formats

MULTIPLE CHOICE
Circle the correct letter for each answer.

1. Which number is divisible by 6?
   - (A.) 108
   - B. 223
   - C. 301
   - D. 514

2. Which number is a multiple of 4?
   - A. 362
   - (B.) 864
   - C. 1,202
   - D. 2,458

3. Which of the following is a prime number?
   - (A.) 19
   - B. 45
   - C. 129
   - D. 216

4. What is the prime factorization of 117?
   - A. $2 \times 3 \times 13$
   - (B.) $3^2 \times 13$
   - C. $3 \times 5 \times 9$
   - D. 9×13

5. Find the GCF for 21 and 42.
   - A. 7
   - B. 14
   - (C.) 21
   - D. 42

6. Find the LCM for 3, 5, and 6.
   - A. 15
   - B. 18
   - (C.) 30
   - D. 90

7. Which fraction has a decimal equivalent of 0.3?
   - A. $\frac{3}{100}$
   - B. $\frac{1}{8}$
   - C. $\frac{1}{4}$
   - (D.) $\frac{1}{3}$

8. What fraction does the shaded part of this figure represent?
   - A. $\frac{1}{8}$
   - B. $\frac{3}{8}$
   - C. $\frac{7}{1}$
   - (D.) $\frac{5}{8}$

9. Which fraction is NOT equivalent to $\frac{2}{3}$?
   - (A.) $\frac{10}{18}$
   - B. $\frac{4}{6}$
   - C. $\frac{8}{12}$
   - D. $\frac{6}{9}$

10. What is $1\frac{2}{5}$ written as an improper fraction?
    - A. $\frac{3}{5}$
    - B. $\frac{5}{5}$
    - (C.) $\frac{7}{5}$
    - D. $\frac{9}{5}$

11. Which of the following is the best estimate for $\frac{402}{600}$?
    - A. $\frac{3}{4}$
    - (B.) $\frac{2}{3}$
    - C. $\frac{1}{2}$
    - D. $\frac{1}{3}$

12. Which is 0.6 as a fraction in simplest form?
    - A. $\frac{1}{8}$
    - B. $\frac{1}{2}$
    - C. $\frac{6}{10}$
    - (D.) $\frac{3}{5}$

FREE RESPONSE
Compare using >, <, or =.

13. $\frac{2}{5}$ **<** $\frac{1}{2}$
14. $\frac{7}{8}$ **>** $\frac{4}{5}$
15. $\frac{3}{15}$ **<** $\frac{2}{5}$
16. $\frac{4}{12}$ **=** $\frac{3}{9}$

Order from least to greatest.

17. $\frac{9}{7}, 1\frac{1}{4}, 1.3$
    $1\frac{1}{4}, \frac{9}{7}, 1.3$

18. $\frac{4}{5}, 0.75, \frac{2}{3}, 0.5$
    $0.5, \frac{2}{3}, 0.75, \frac{4}{5}$

Find the LCM and GCF for each pair of numbers.

19. 7 and 9 LCM: **63** GCF: **1**
20. 40 and 10 LCM: **40** GCF: **10**

Write each fraction in simplest form.

21. $\frac{9}{4}$ **$2\frac{1}{4}$**
22. $\frac{6}{14}$ **$\frac{3}{7}$**
23. $\frac{45}{60}$ **$\frac{3}{4}$**

24. Tamara and her family picked 108 apples during a day trip to an orchard. She wants to divide all the apples into groups of 5, 7, or 9 and give them to her friends. Which group size can she use?
    Groups of 9.

25. A box of nails contains four different sizes: $\frac{5}{8}$ inch, $\frac{3}{4}$ inch, $\frac{7}{8}$ inch, and $\frac{2}{3}$ inch. Which size nail is the greatest?
    The $\frac{7}{8}$-inch nails are the greatest in size.

26. Which letter on the number line below corresponds to $1\frac{1}{4}$? **A**

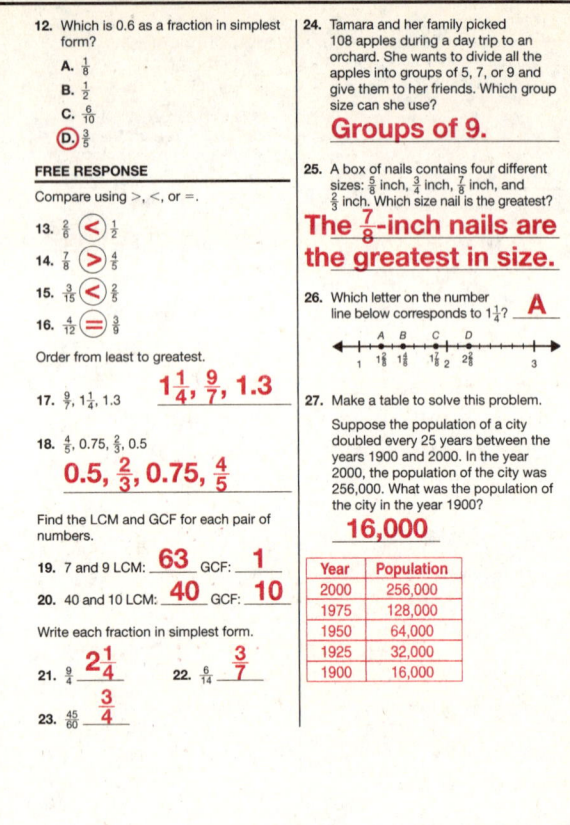

27. Make a table to solve this problem. Suppose the population of a city doubled every 25 years between the years 1900 and 2000. In the year 2000, the population of the city was 256,000. What was the population of the city in the year 1900?
    16,000

Year	Population
2000	256,000
1975	128,000
1950	64,000
1925	32,000
1900	16,000

WRITING IN MATH

28. Explain how to write nine-twelfths as a simplified fraction and as a decimal.
    Divide the numerator and denominator by their GCF, 3, to get $\frac{3}{4}$. Then divide the numerator 3, by the denominator 4, to get 0.75.

29. Without dividing, explain how you can tell whether 143 pencils can be shared equally by 3 people.
    The sum of the digits of 143 is $1 + 4 + 3 = 8$. Since 8 is not divisible by 3, the number 143 is not divisible by 3.

30. Identify and answer any hidden questions in the problem. Then, solve the problem.
    Josh is shopping for tank-top shirts for his school basketball team. The team has five players and three substitutes. Josh wants to get each player two shirts. The shirts come in packs of 8 for $45. How much will the shirts cost?
    How many shirts does Josh need? $2(5 + 3) = 16$ shirts
    How many packs does Josh need? 2 packs
    What is the cost for 16 shirts? **$90**

Name _____

Chapter 3 Test Form B: Mixed Formats

MULTIPLE CHOICE
Circle the letter of the correct answer.

1. Which number is divisible by 9?
   - A. 147
   - (B.) 225
   - C. 335
   - D. 614

2. Which number is a multiple of 7?
   - A. 1,157
   - B. 775
   - C. 324
   - (D.) 63

3. Which of the following is a prime number?
   - A. 15
   - (B.) 23
   - C. 184
   - D. 213

4. What is the prime factorization of 189?
   - (A.) $3^3 \times 7$
   - B. $3 \times 5 \times 11$
   - C. $2 \times 3^2 \times 5$
   - D. $2^2 \times 27$

5. Find the GCF for 15 and 27.
   - A. 1
   - (B.) 3
   - C. 5
   - D. 9

6. Find the LCM for 2, 7, and 10.
   - A. 140
   - (B.) 70
   - C. 35
   - D. 20

7. Which fraction has a decimal equivalent of 0.8?
   - A. $\frac{8}{100}$
   - B. $\frac{1}{8}$
   - C. $\frac{1}{5}$
   - (D.) $\frac{8}{9}$

8. What fraction does the shaded part of this figure represent?
   - A. $\frac{1}{8}$
   - (B.) $\frac{3}{8}$
   - C. $\frac{1}{2}$
   - D. $\frac{5}{8}$

9. Which fraction is NOT equivalent to $\frac{6}{10}$?
   - A. $\frac{3}{5}$
   - B. $\frac{9}{15}$
   - C. $\frac{12}{20}$
   - (D.) $\frac{12}{15}$

10. What is $2\frac{2}{3}$ written as an improper fraction?
    - (A.) $\frac{8}{3}$
    - B. $\frac{6}{3}$
    - C. $\frac{6}{6}$
    - D. $\frac{3}{8}$

11. Which of the following is the best estimate for $\frac{284}{600}$?
    - A. $\frac{1}{2}$
    - B. $\frac{1}{3}$
    - (C.) $\frac{1}{2}$
    - D. $\frac{3}{4}$

12. Write 0.4 as a fraction in simplest form.
    - A. $\frac{1}{5}$
    - B. $\frac{1}{4}$
    - (C.) $\frac{2}{5}$
    - D. $\frac{4}{10}$

Chapter 3 Form B and Chapters 1–3 Cumulative Test

FREE RESPONSE

Compare using >, <, or =.

13. $\frac{3}{9}$ **=** $\frac{4}{12}$
14. $\frac{4}{7}$ **>** $\frac{2}{9}$
15. $\frac{2}{3}$ **<** $\frac{3}{4}$
16. $\frac{3}{8}$ **>** $\frac{2}{6}$

Order from least to greatest.

17. $\frac{4}{3}$, 1.1, $1\frac{2}{3}$

    1.1, $\frac{4}{3}$, $1\frac{2}{3}$

18. $\frac{5}{6}$, 0.9, 0.7, $\frac{3}{4}$

    0.7, $\frac{3}{4}$, $\frac{5}{6}$, 0.9

Find the LCM and GCF for each pair of numbers.

19. 3 and 10 LCM: **30** GCF: **1**
20. 12 and 20 LCM: **60** GCF: **4**

Write each fraction in simplest form.

21. $\frac{11}{4}$ **$2\frac{3}{4}$**
22. $\frac{7}{21}$ **$\frac{1}{3}$**
23. $\frac{15}{55}$ **$\frac{3}{11}$**

24. Deepak works in a bookstore where they received a shipment of 78 copies of a recent bestseller. He has been asked to arrange the books in equal stacks of 6, 7, or 9. Which stack size can he use?

    Stacks of 6

25. Dr. Jones, an entomologist, collected four butterflies during a recent trip. She measured and labeled the length of each butterfly. Butterfly A is $1\frac{7}{8}$ in. long, butterfly B is $1\frac{9}{16}$ in. long, butterfly C is $1\frac{1}{2}$ in. long, and butterfly D is $1\frac{3}{8}$ in. long. Which butterfly is the longest?

    Butterfly A is the longest.

26. Which letter on the number line corresponds to $2\frac{1}{2}$?

    D

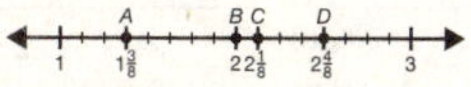

27. Make a table to solve this problem.
    Susan saves $3.50 a week from her pocket money to buy a shirt that costs $21. In how many weeks can she save enough money to buy the shirt?

    6 weeks

Week 1	Week 2	Week 3	Week 4	Week 5	Week 6
$3.50	$7.00	$10.50	$14.00	$17.50	$21.00

WRITING IN MATH

28. Explain how to write fifteen twenty-fifths as a simplified fraction and as a decimal.

    To write $\frac{15}{25}$ as a simplified fraction, divide the numerator and denominator by the GCF of 15 and 25, which is 5; $\frac{15}{25} = \frac{3}{5}$. To write $\frac{15}{25}$ as a decimal, divide 15 by 25. $\frac{15}{25} = 0.6$.

29. Without dividing, explain how you can tell whether 1,516 students can be put into 4 equal groups.

    The last two digits of 1,516 are 16. Since 16 is divisible by 4, the number 1,516 is divisible by 4.

30. Identify and answer any hidden questions in the problem. Then, solve the problem.
    Eugenia is going on a 210-mile car trip. Her gas budget is $12. Gas costs $1.39/gallon and the car gets 30 miles/gallon. Does she have enough money budgeted for gas?

    Yes; How many gallons of gas does Eugenia need to buy? 7 gallons; How much does 7 gallons cost? 7 × $1.39 = $9.73

Chapters 1–3 Cumulative Test: Multiple Choice

Circle the letter of the correct answer.

1. Which is the standard form for 3 × 1,000,000 + 2 × 1,000 + 7 × 100 + 2?
   - **A.** 3,002,702
   - B. 3,020,072
   - C. 3,020,720
   - D. 3,207,002

2. What is the place value of 6 in 1.02364?
   - A. tenths
   - B. hundredths
   - C. thousandths
   - **D.** ten-thousandths

3. Which number is divisible by 6?
   - A. 70
   - **B.** 108
   - C. 214
   - D. 482

4. Write 10^5 in standard form.
   - A. 10,000,000
   - B. 1,000,000
   - **C.** 100,000
   - D. 10,000

5. Which symbol makes this statement true?
   2.409 ◯ 2.490
   - A. =
   - B. >
   - **C.** <
   - D. ≡

6. Round 1.21895 to the nearest ten-thousandth.
   - A. 1.2189
   - **B.** 1.2190
   - C. 1.2191
   - D. 1.2195

7. Which of the following is a prime number?
   - A. 21
   - **B.** 47
   - C. 111
   - D. 302

8. Round 11,617,264 to the nearest ten thousand.
   - A. 11,615,000
   - B. 11,617,000
   - **C.** 11,620,000
   - D. 11,620,300

9. Nikki sold 12 boxes of cookies for $3.25 each to raise money for her soccer team. About how much money did she raise?
   - A. about $30
   - **B.** about $36
   - C. about $44
   - D. about $50

10. What is the prime factorization of 144?
    - **A.** $2^4 \times 3^2$
    - B. $2^3 \times 3^2$
    - C. $2^4 \times 3$
    - D. $2 \times 3 \times 5$

11. Estimate 841 + 1,107 + 1,479 to the nearest hundred.
    - A. 3,600
    - B. 3,550
    - C. 3,500
    - **D.** 3,400

12. Find 8 − 5.19.
    - A. 2.91
    - **B.** 2.81
    - C. 2.69
    - D. 2.19

13. Find the GCF for 18 and 27.
    - A. 54
    - B. 36
    - C. 27
    - **D.** 9

14. Which is the best estimate for 132 × 206?
    - **A.** 26,000
    - B. 30,000
    - C. 32,000
    - D. 35,000

15. Find 0.8 × 0.21.
    - A. 16.8
    - B. 1.68
    - **C.** 0.168
    - D. 0.108

16. Devon bought 3 jars of spaghetti sauce for $11.25. Which equation could you use to find the cost, x, of each jar?
    - **A.** $3x = 11.25$
    - B. $\frac{x}{3} = 11.25$
    - C. $x + 3 = 11.25$
    - D. $x − 3 = 11.25$

17. Which is the best estimate for 254 ÷ 27?
    - **A.** 9
    - B. 10
    - C. 11
    - D. 12

18. Find 31.56 ÷ 12.
    - A. 263
    - B. 26.3
    - **C.** 2.63
    - D. 0.238

19. One day Mary missed 2 classes and attended 5 classes. What fraction of the school day did she miss?
    - A. $\frac{1}{5}$
    - **B.** $\frac{2}{7}$
    - C. $\frac{5}{5}$
    - D. $\frac{5}{7}$

20. Calculate the value of $4^2 \div 2 \times (3 + 1)$.
    - A. 2
    - B. 12
    - **C.** 32
    - D. 40

21. Mira, who owns a local bakery, puts all the unsold cookies in packets of 3 at the end of the day. How many packets can she make if she has 32 cookies left?
    - A. 9
    - **B.** 10
    - C. 11
    - D. 12

22. Which property does the following number sentence illustrate?
    $(2 \times 3) + (4 + 3) = (4 + 3) + (2 \times 3)$
    - A. Distributive Property
    - B. Identity Property of Multiplication
    - **C.** Commutative Property of Addition
    - D. Associative Property of Addition

23. Find 9.81 ÷ 0.3.
    - **A.** 32.7
    - B. 3.27
    - C. 2.27
    - D. 0.227

24. Which fraction is NOT equivalent to $\frac{2}{5}$?
    - **A.** $\frac{2}{10}$
    - B. $\frac{6}{15}$
    - C. $\frac{10}{25}$
    - D. $\frac{8}{20}$

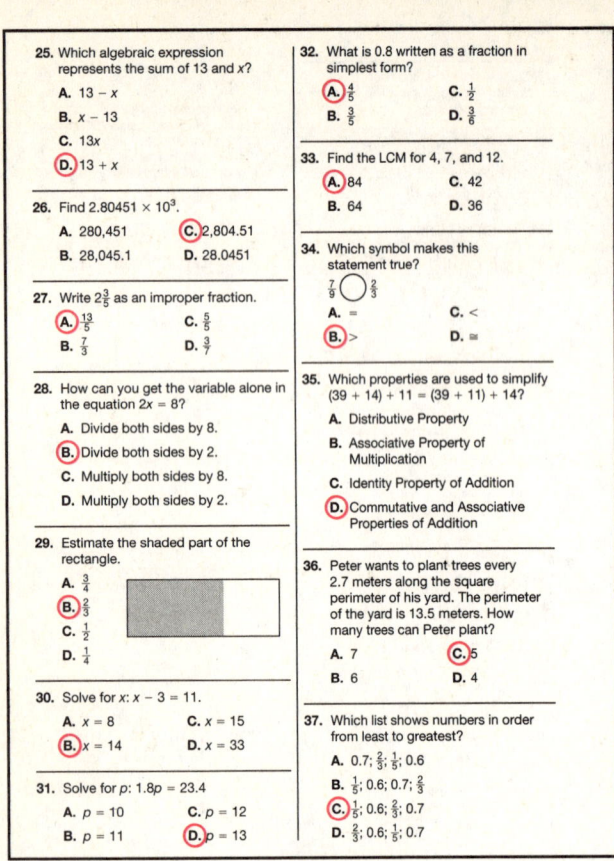
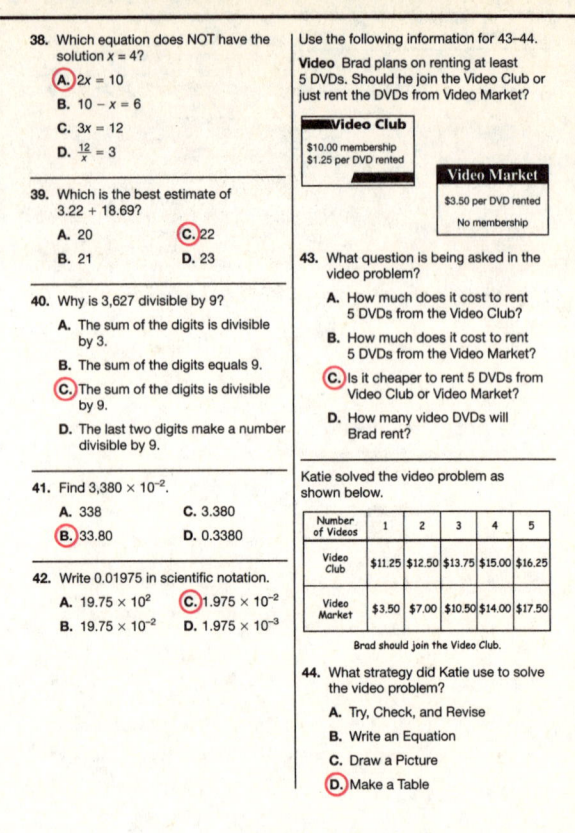
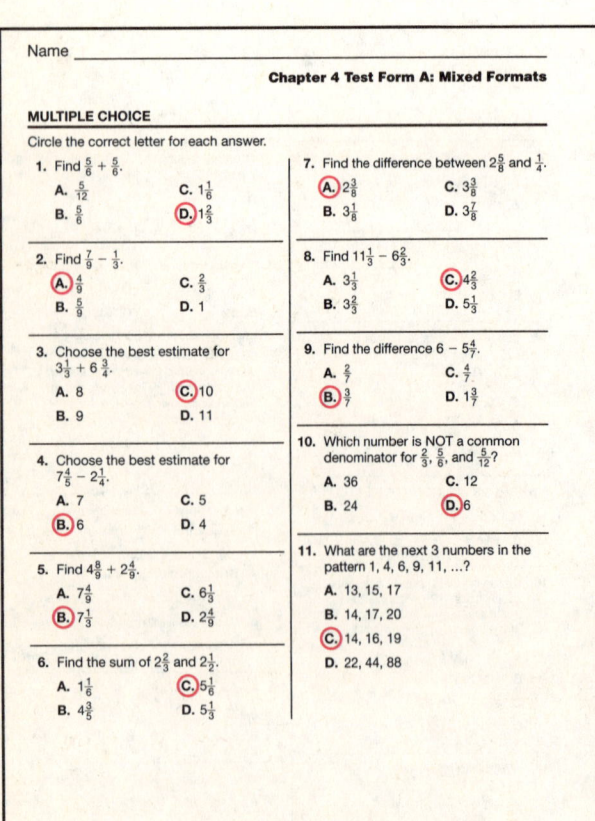
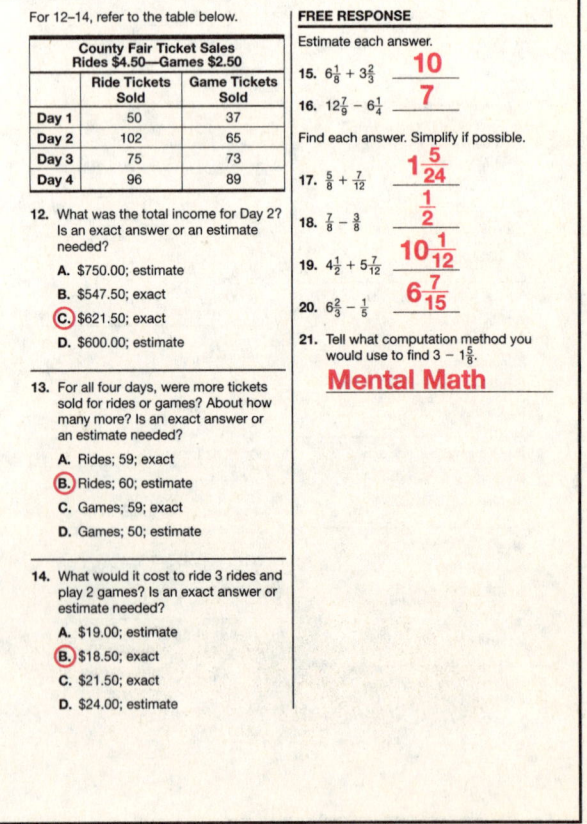

Chapter 4 Form A and Form B

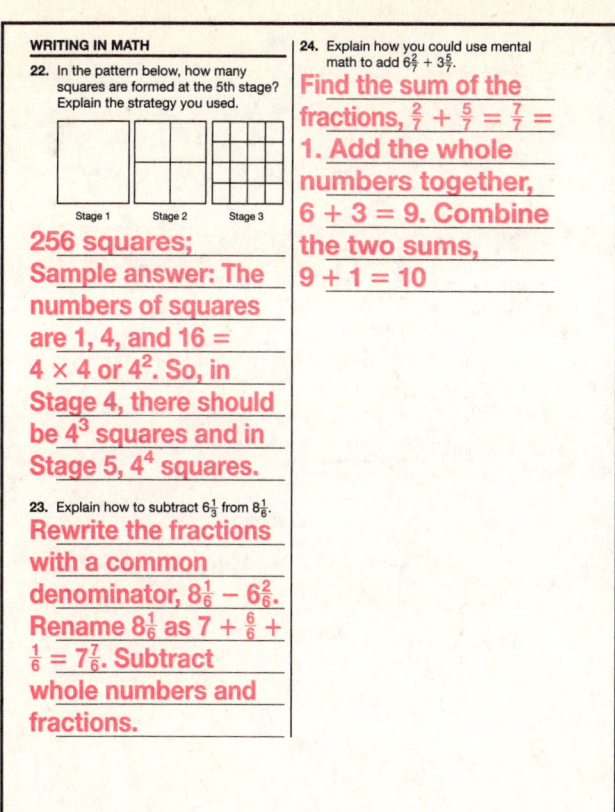

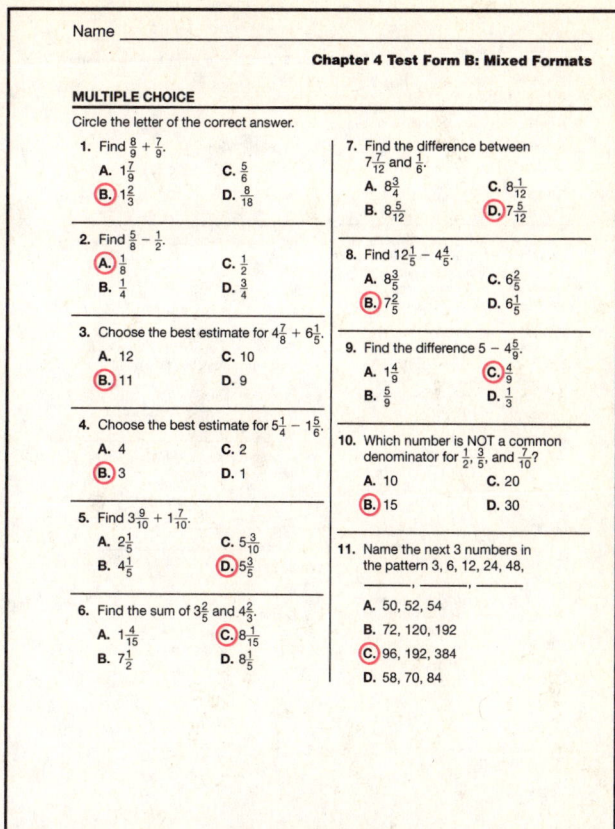

page 71

Form B, page 72

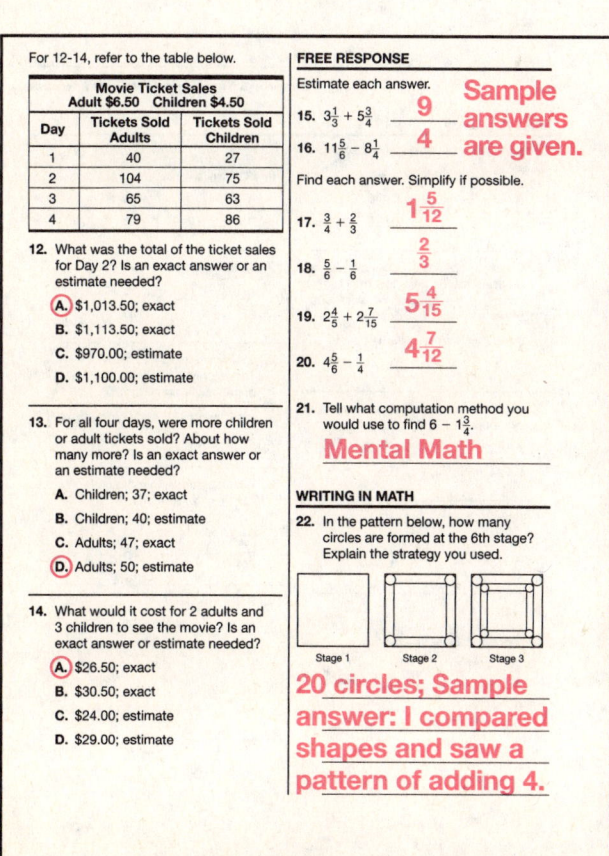

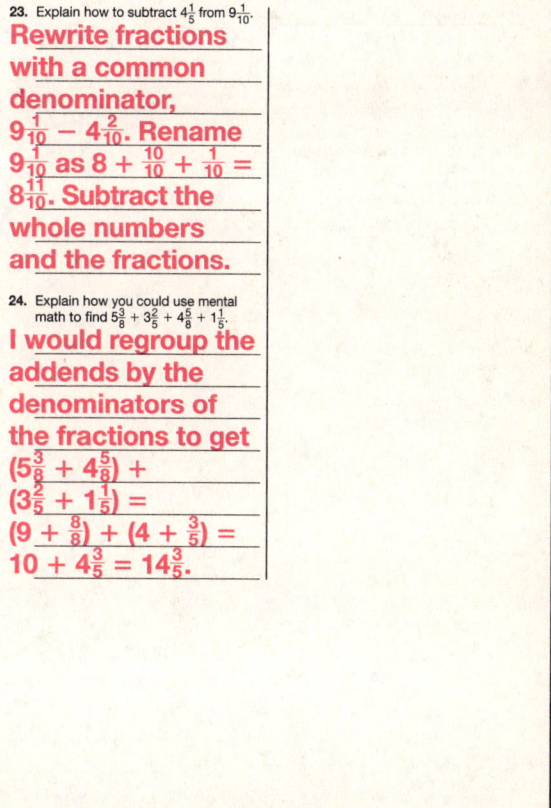

page 73

page 74

Chapter Tests in the Assessment Sourcebook parallel Chapter Tests in the Student Book item for item. See the Teacher Edition for item analysis of these tests.

145

Chapter 5 Form A and Form B

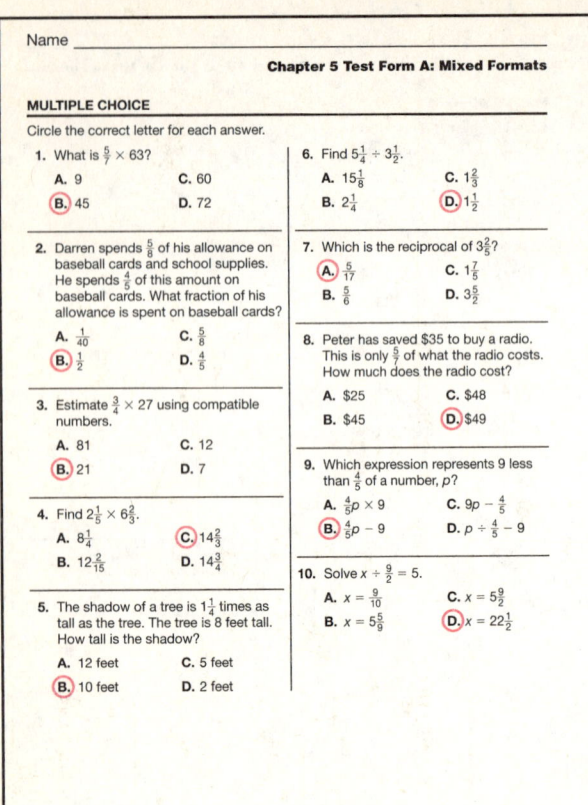

page 75

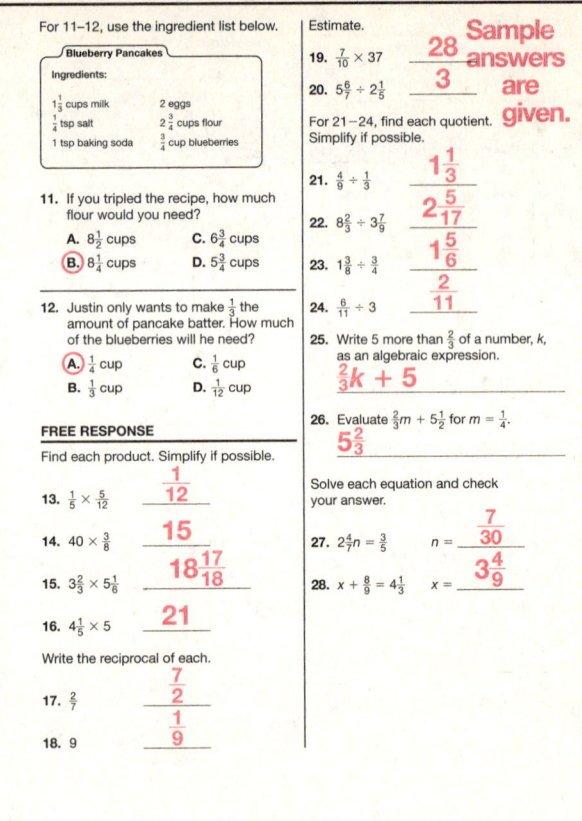

page 76

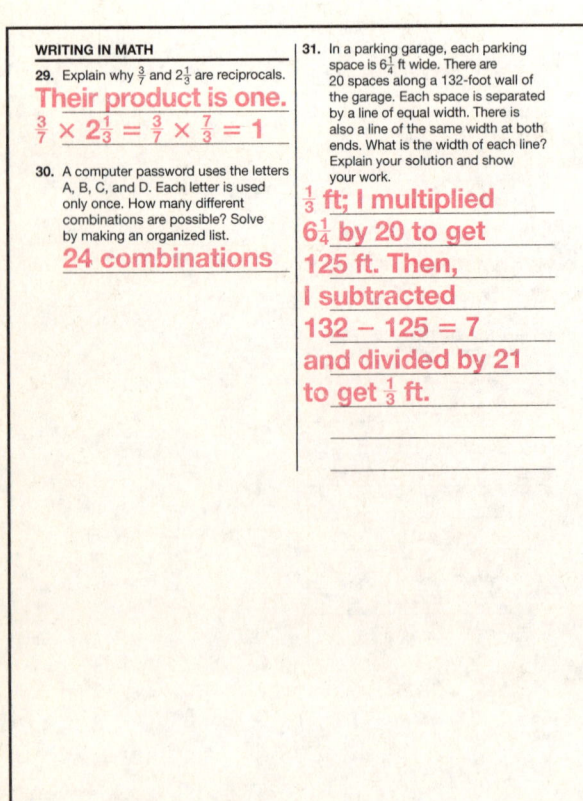

page 77

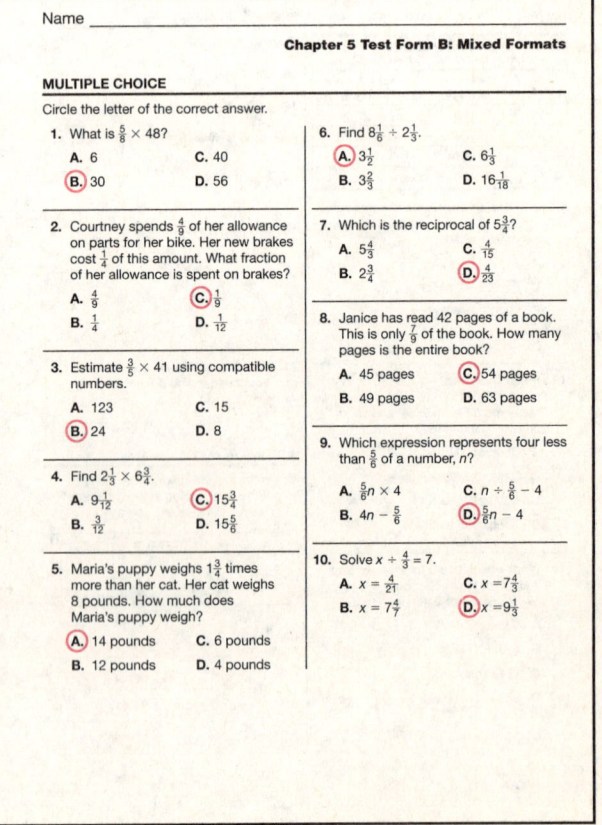

Form B, page 78

For 11–12, use the ingredient list below.

Soap

Ingredients:

$7\frac{1}{2}$ ounces lye
8 ounces cocoa butter
$8\frac{3}{4}$ ounces olive oil
$9\frac{2}{3}$ ounces coconut oil
4 drops rose oil
$\frac{3}{4}$ teaspoon grapefruit extract

11. If you tripled the recipe, how much lye would you need?

(**A.**) $22\frac{1}{2}$ ounces **C.** $21\frac{1}{2}$ ounces
B. $22\frac{1}{4}$ ounces **D.** $10\frac{1}{2}$ ounces

12. Manuel only wants to make $\frac{2}{3}$ the amount of soap. How much of the grapefruit extract will he need?

A. $\frac{2}{3}$ teaspoon **C.** $\frac{1}{2}$ teaspoon
(**B.**) $\frac{1}{2}$ teaspoon **D.** $\frac{1}{6}$ teaspoon

FREE RESPONSE

Find each product. Simplify if possible.

13. $3\frac{1}{4} \times 7\frac{2}{3}$ $24\frac{11}{12}$

14. $3\frac{1}{4} \times 4$ 13

Write the reciprocal of each.

15. $\frac{8}{9}$ $\frac{9}{8}$

16. 7 $\frac{1}{7}$

Estimate. Sample answers are given.

17. $\frac{3}{10} \times 58$ 18

18. $8\frac{2}{9} \div 1\frac{4}{5}$ 4

For 19–20, find each quotient. Simplify if possible.

19. $8\frac{1}{3} \div 5\frac{5}{6}$ $1\frac{3}{7}$

20. $\frac{10}{13} \div 5$ $\frac{2}{13}$

21. Write 3 more than $\frac{2}{5}$ a number, k, as an algebraic expression.

$\frac{2}{5}k + 3$

22. Evaluate $\frac{1}{2}m + 6\frac{1}{2}$ for $m = \frac{3}{4}$.

$6\frac{7}{8}$

Solve each equation and check your answer.

23. $1\frac{1}{4}n = \frac{3}{16}$ $n =$ $\frac{3}{20}$

24. $x + \frac{5}{8} = 6\frac{1}{4}$ $x =$ $5\frac{5}{8}$

WRITING IN MATH

25. Explain why $\frac{4}{9}$ and $2\frac{1}{4}$ are reciprocals.

Their product is one. $\frac{4}{9} \times 2\frac{1}{4} = \frac{4}{9} \times \frac{9}{4} = 1$

26. Amelia wants to make a 4-digit password with her four favorite numbers: 2, 3, 7, and 9. Each number is used only once. How many different combinations are possible? Solve by making an organized list.

24 combinations

page 79

27. A $102\frac{1}{4}$ inch ladder has 8 steps. There are no steps at the top or the bottom, and each step is $2\frac{3}{8}$ inches thick. What is the distance of the space between any two steps? Explain.

$9\frac{1}{4}$ in.; I multiplied $2\frac{3}{8}$ by 8 to get 19 in. Then, I subtracted $102\frac{1}{4} - 19 = 83\frac{1}{4}$ and divided by 9 to get $9\frac{1}{4}$ in.

page 80

Name ______________________

Chapter 6 Test Form A: Mixed Formats

MULTIPLE CHOICE

Circle the letter of the correct answer.

1. Which ratio compares the number of squares to the number of circles?

△□○○△□□○○

(**A.**) 3 to 4 **C.** 2 to 1
B. 4 to 3 **D.** 4 to 2

2. Which ratio is equal to 9:3?

A. 16:3 (**C.**) 12 to 4
B. $\frac{10}{2}$ **D.** $\frac{1}{3}$

3. Which pair below are equal ratios?

A. $\frac{2}{9}$; 18:4 **C.** 3 to 2; $\frac{6}{3}$
(**B.**) $\frac{4}{6}$; 2:3 **D.** 14 to 8; 7 to 2

4. Find the unit rate for running 20 miles in 5 hours.

(**A.**) $\frac{4\text{ mi}}{1\text{ hr}}$ **C.** $\frac{10\text{ mi}}{2\text{ hr}}$
B. $\frac{5\text{ mi}}{1\text{ hr}}$ **D.** $\frac{8\text{ mi}}{1\text{ hr}}$

5. A fruit basket contains 25 pieces of fruit. Two pieces of fruit out of every 5 are oranges. How many oranges are in the fruit basket?

A. 2 **C.** 8
B. 5 (**D.**) 10

6. Which proportion is written correctly?

A. $\frac{5\text{ in.}}{3\text{ ft}} = \frac{2\text{ ft}}{60\text{ in.}}$
(**B.**) $\frac{4\text{ oz}}{2\text{ lb}} = \frac{12\text{ oz}}{6\text{ lb}}$
C. $\frac{2\text{ hr}}{10\text{ min}} = \frac{20\text{ min}}{1\text{ hr}}$
D. $\frac{4\text{ ft}}{6\text{ yd}} = \frac{2\text{ yd}}{15\text{ yd}}$

7. Solve the proportion $\frac{180\text{ mi}}{x\text{ hr}} = \frac{240\text{ mi}}{4\text{ hr}}$

A. $x = 10$ hr (**C.**) $x = 3$ hr
B. $x = 5$ hr **D.** $x = 2.5$ hr

8. Which is the best buy?

A. 6 lb for $3.00
B. 9 lb for $4.50
C. 5 lb for $2.60
(**D.**) 7 lb for $3.36

9. Darren types 55 words per minute. At this rate, how many words will he type in 15 minutes?

A. 610 words **C.** 900 words
(**B.**) 825 words **D.** 1,025 words

10. Kayla can jump 27 inches high. Using the formula $y = \frac{i}{36}$, where y is the number of yards, and i is the number of inches, find how high Kayla can jump in yards.

(**A.**) $y = 0.75$ yd **C.** $y = 7.5$ yd
B. $y = 0.8$ yd **D.** $y = 972$ yd

Form A, page 81

11. What is the actual distance between Percentville and Fractiontown along the road?

A. 6 miles (**C.**) 18 miles
B. 15 miles **D.** 21 miles

FREE RESPONSE

Write a ratio for each comparison.

Color	black	brown	white	red
Number of horses	17	3	15	13

12. white to brown

15 to 3

13. red to all colors

13 to 48

14. black to all other colors

17 to 31

15–18 Sample answers are given.

Give three ratios that are equal to each ratio.

15. $\frac{4}{5}$ $\frac{8}{10}$ $\frac{12}{15}$ $\frac{24}{30}$

16. 6 to 16 3 to 8 12 to 32 24 to 64

17. 18:3 6:1 12:2 36:6

18. $\frac{14}{8}$ $\frac{7}{4}$ $\frac{21}{12}$ $\frac{28}{16}$

Write each ratio in simplest form.

19. $\frac{234}{104}$ $\frac{9}{4}$

20. 4.8 to 0.6 8 to 1

Write each as a unit rate.

21. 18 mi in 3 hr

6 mi per hour

22. $4.64 for 8 gal

$0.58 per gallon

23. 36 cans in 4 cases

9 cans per case

24. 364 mi on 14 gal

26 mi per gallon

Decide if the ratios form a proportion.

25. $\frac{3\text{ ft}}{8\text{ mi}}, \frac{12\text{ ft}}{18\text{ mi}}$ No

26. $\frac{15\text{ oz}}{3\text{ lb}}, \frac{10\text{ oz}}{2\text{ lb}}$ Yes

Solve each proportion.

27. $\frac{176\text{ mi}}{8\text{ gal}} = \frac{x\text{ mi}}{14\text{ gal}}$ $x =$ 308 mi

28. $\frac{6\text{ min}}{21\text{ ft}} = \frac{24\text{ min}}{y\text{ ft}}$ $y =$ 84 ft

29. $\frac{28}{16} = \frac{n}{12}$ $n =$ 21

30. $\frac{18}{32} = \frac{27}{z}$ $z =$ 48

page 82

Chapter Tests in the Assessment Sourcebook parallel Chapter Tests in the Student Book item for item. See the Teacher Edition for item analysis of these tests.

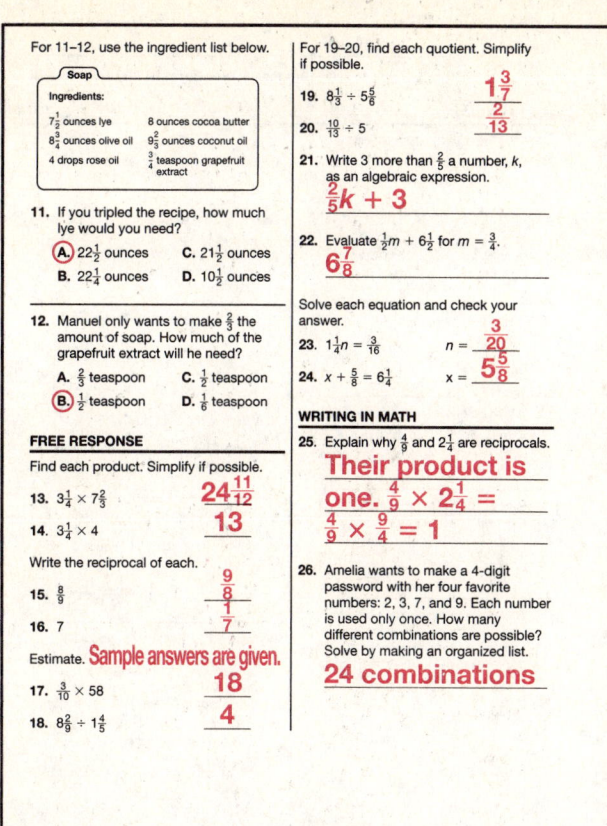

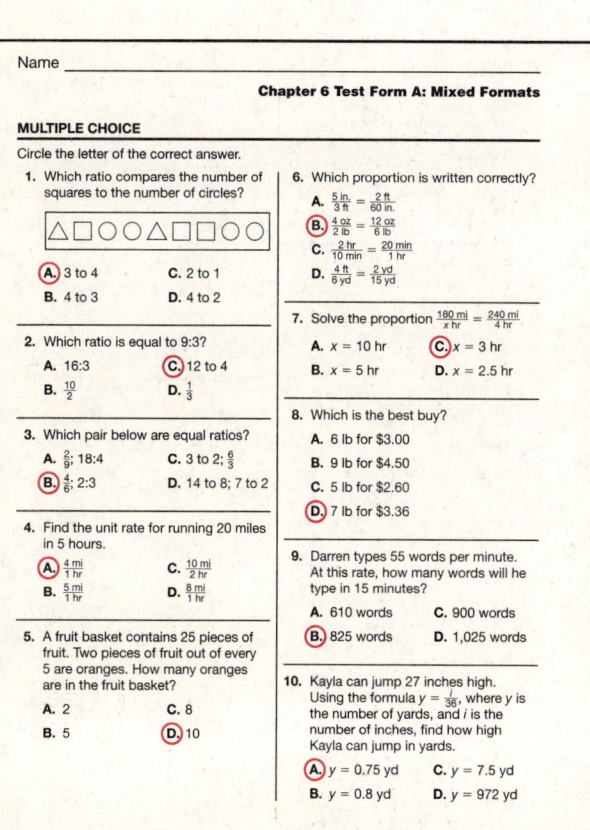

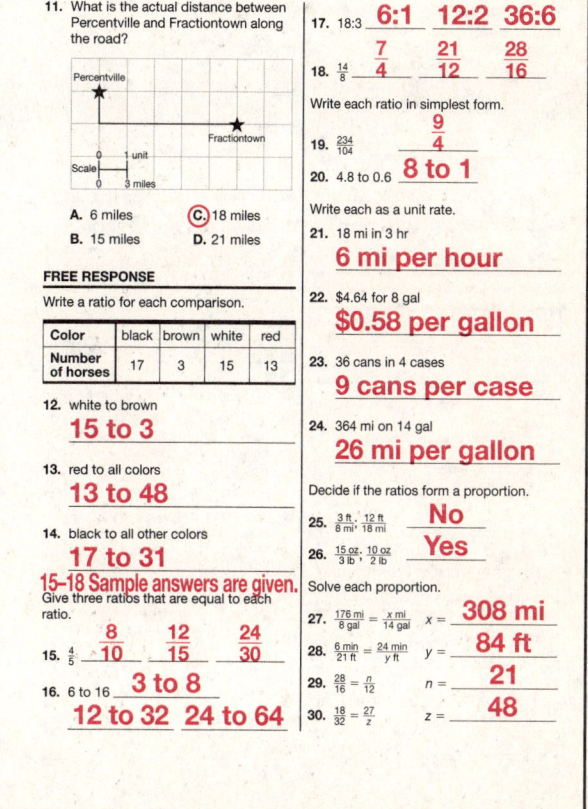

Chapter 6 Form A and Form B

31. Josh drives at a rate of 35 miles per hour for 5 hours. How far does he drive? Use the formula $d = rt$.
175 miles

32. There are about 28.35 grams in an ounce. How many grams are in 1 pound?
453.6 g

33. The scale on a map is 1.5 in. to 24 mi. If two cities are 7 in. apart on the map, what is the actual distance between the two cities?
112 miles

WRITING IN MATH

34. Beginning with the ratio $\frac{2 \text{ in}}{3 \text{ hr}}$, make a table of quantities that vary proportionally. Tell how you know that the values in the table vary proportionally. **Sample answer:**

Inches	2	4	6	8	10
Hours	3	6	9	12	15

The ratios in each column can be simplified to $\frac{2}{3}$.

35. The ratio of fish to turtles in the pond is 26 to 7. If there are 21 turtles, how many fish are there? Solve and explain your reasoning.
78 fish; I solved the proportion $\frac{26}{7} = \frac{x}{21}$. $x = 78$

36. Use objects to solve this problem. Give the answer in a complete sentence.
Three out of every 5 players on a 20-person basketball team can slam dunk. How many players can slam dunk?
Sample answer is given.
☺ = player who can slam dunk
⊘ = player who cannot slam dunk
☺☺☺⊘⊘
☺☺☺⊘⊘
☺☺☺⊘⊘
☺☺☺⊘⊘
There are 12 players who can slam dunk.

page 83

Name _____

Chapter 6 Test Form B: Mixed Formats

MULTIPLE CHOICE
Circle the letter of the correct answer.

1. Which ratio compares the number of triangles to the number of hexagons?
△○○○△△△○
A. 3 to 4 **C. 4 to 3**
B. 1 to 2 D. 4 to 2

2. Which ratio is equal to 6:2?
A. 12 to 2 C. 3 to 9
B. 9:3 D. $\frac{1}{3}$

3. Which pair below are equal ratios?
A. 6 to 21; $\frac{4}{14}$ C. 3 to 2; 5 to 4
B. 8:4; $\frac{4}{8}$ D. 12 to 6; $\frac{4}{3}$

4. Find the unit rate for 16 miles in 4 hours.
A. $\frac{6 \text{ mi}}{1 \text{ hr}}$ C. $\frac{8 \text{ mi}}{2 \text{ hr}}$
B. $\frac{4 \text{ mi}}{1 \text{ hr}}$ D. $\frac{1 \text{ mi}}{4 \text{ hr}}$

5. There are 56 passengers on a plane. Five out of every 8 passengers are carrying a suitcase. How many passengers are carrying a suitcase?
A. 35 C. 16
B. 30 D. 7

6. Which proportion is written correctly?
A. $\frac{7 \text{ ft}}{3 \text{ in.}} = \frac{35 \text{ ft}}{15 \text{ in.}}$
B. $\frac{30 \text{ min}}{2 \text{ hr}} = \frac{45 \text{ min}}{240 \text{ min}}$
C. $\frac{3 \text{ yd}}{4 \text{ ft}} = \frac{9 \text{ ft}}{4 \text{ yd}}$
D. $\frac{3 \text{ lb}}{15 \text{ oz}} = \frac{3,000 \text{ lb}}{2 \text{ T}}$

7. Solve the proportion $\frac{280 \text{ mi}}{x \text{ hr}} = \frac{210 \text{ mi}}{3 \text{ hr}}$.
A. $x = 10$ hr C. $x = 4.5$ hr
B. $x = 5$ hr **D. $x = 4$ hr**

8. Which is the best buy?
A. 4 oz for $3.76 C. 3 oz for $2.88
B. 6 oz for $5.70 D. 2 oz for $1.92

9. A toy robot walks 42 inches per minute. At this rate, how many inches will it walk in 7 minutes?
A. 6 in. **C. 294 in.**
B. 49 in. D. 840 in.

10. Matt put 2 milliliters of chocolate syrup into a cup of milk. Using the formula $t = 4.93m$, where t is the number of teaspoons, and m is the number of milliliters, find the amount of syrup Matt used in teaspoons.
A. $t = 98.6$ tsp C. $t = 10$ tsp
B. $t = 9.86$ tsp D. $t = 2.465$ tsp

Form B, page 84

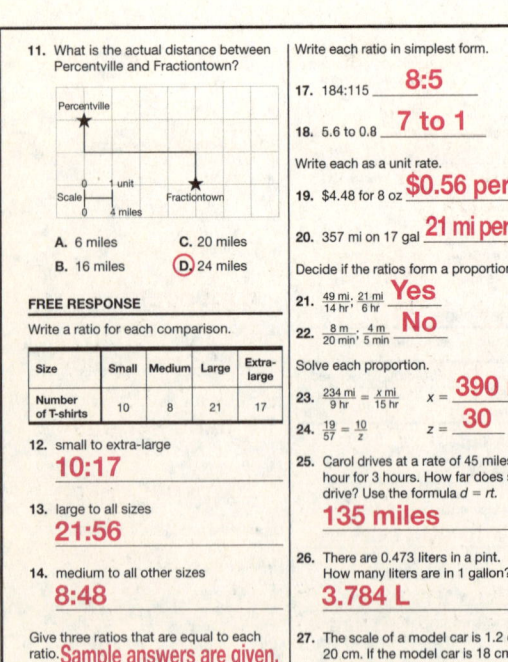

11. What is the actual distance between Percentville and Fractiontown?
A. 6 miles C. 20 miles
B. 16 miles **D. 24 miles**

FREE RESPONSE
Write a ratio for each comparison.

Size	Small	Medium	Large	Extra-large
Number of T-shirts	10	8	21	17

12. small to extra-large
10:17

13. large to all sizes
21:56

14. medium to all other sizes
8:48

Give three ratios that are equal to each ratio. **Sample answers are given.**

15. 9:15   **3:5   6:10   18:30**

16. $\frac{5}{6}$ $\frac{10}{12}$ $\frac{15}{18}$ $\frac{20}{24}$

Write each ratio in simplest form.

17. 184:115   **8:5**

18. 5.6 to 0.8   **7 to 1**

Write each as a unit rate.

19. $4.48 for 8 oz   **$0.56 per oz**

20. 357 mi on 17 gal   **21 mi per gal**

Decide if the ratios form a proportion.

21. $\frac{49 \text{ mi}}{14 \text{ hr}}$, $\frac{21 \text{ mi}}{6 \text{ hr}}$ **Yes**

22. $\frac{8 \text{ m}}{20 \text{ min}}$, $\frac{4 \text{ m}}{5 \text{ min}}$ **No**

Solve each proportion.

23. $\frac{234 \text{ mi}}{9 \text{ hr}} = \frac{x \text{ mi}}{15 \text{ hr}}$ $x =$ **390 mi**

24. $\frac{19}{57} = \frac{10}{z}$ $z =$ **30**

25. Carol drives at a rate of 45 miles per hour for 3 hours. How far does she drive? Use the formula $d = rt$.
135 miles

26. There are 0.473 liters in a pint. How many liters are in 1 gallon?
3.784 L

27. The scale of a model car is 1.2 cm to 20 cm. If the model car is 18 cm long, what is the length of the real car?
300 cm

page 85

WRITING IN MATH

28. Beginning with the ratio $\frac{3 \text{ ft}}{4 \text{ hr}}$, make a table of quantities that vary proportionally. Tell how you know that the values in the table vary proportionally. **Sample answer:**

Feet	3	6	9	12	15
Hours	4	8	12	16	20

The ratios in each column can be simplified to $\frac{3}{4}$.

29. The ratio of kittens to puppies is 14 to 9. If there are 27 puppies, how many kittens are there? Solve and explain your reasoning.
42 kittens; I solved the proportion $\frac{14}{9} = \frac{x}{27}$; $x = 42$

30. Explain how to use objects to solve this problem. Give the answer in a complete sentence.
Four out of every 5 cheerleaders on a 20-person cheer squad can do a back flip. How many cheerleaders can do a back flip?
Use counters in two colors. Show 4 of one color for the cheerleaders who can do a back flip and 1 of another color for the other. Keep adding groups until there are 20 counters in all.

page 86

Chapters 1–6 Cumulative Test

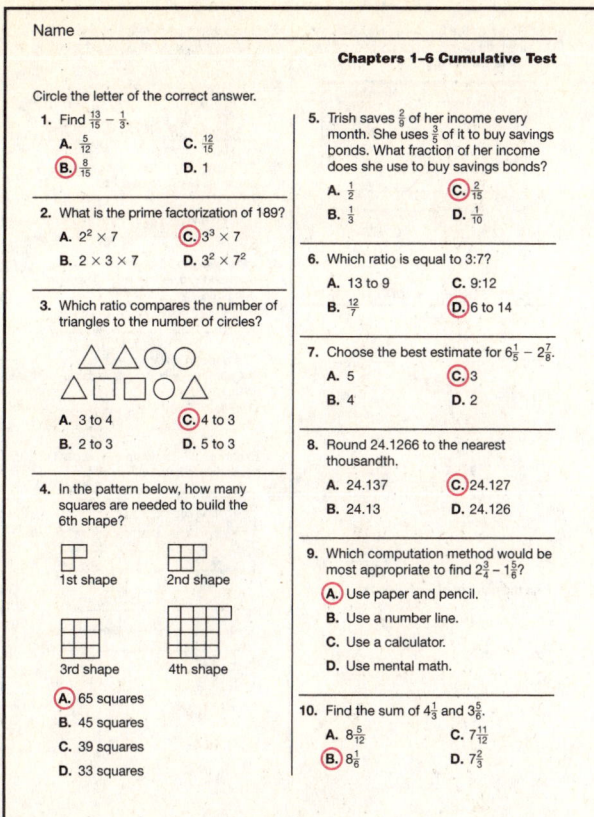

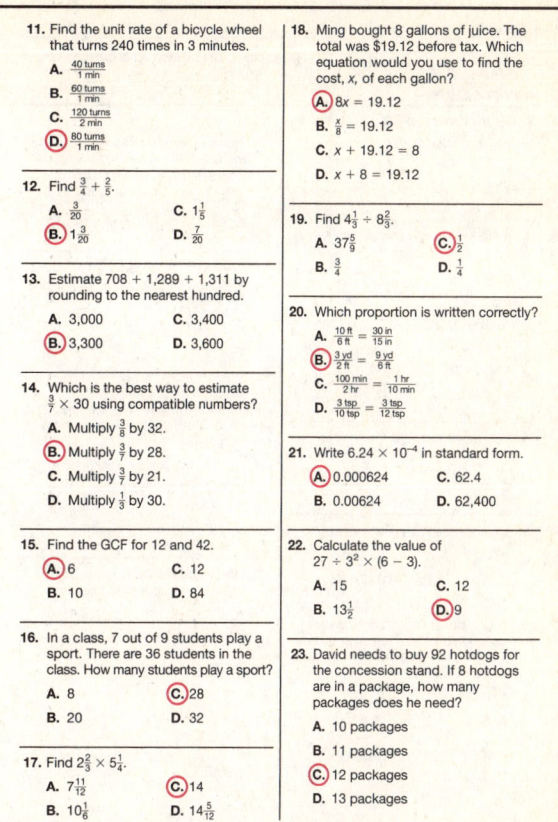

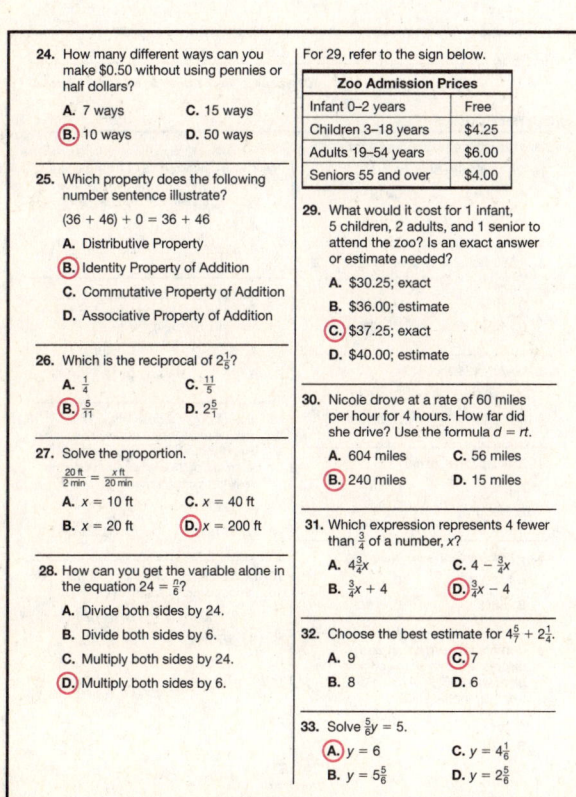

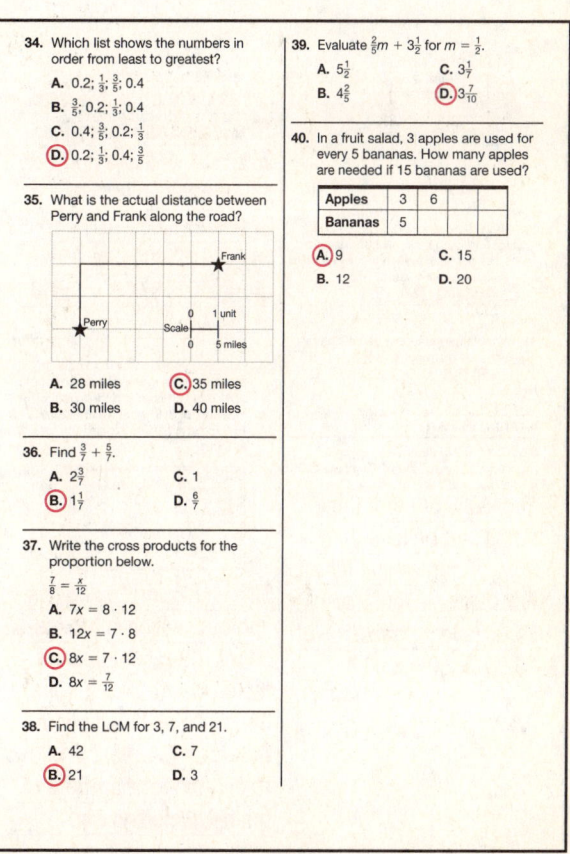

149

Chapter 7 Form A and Form B

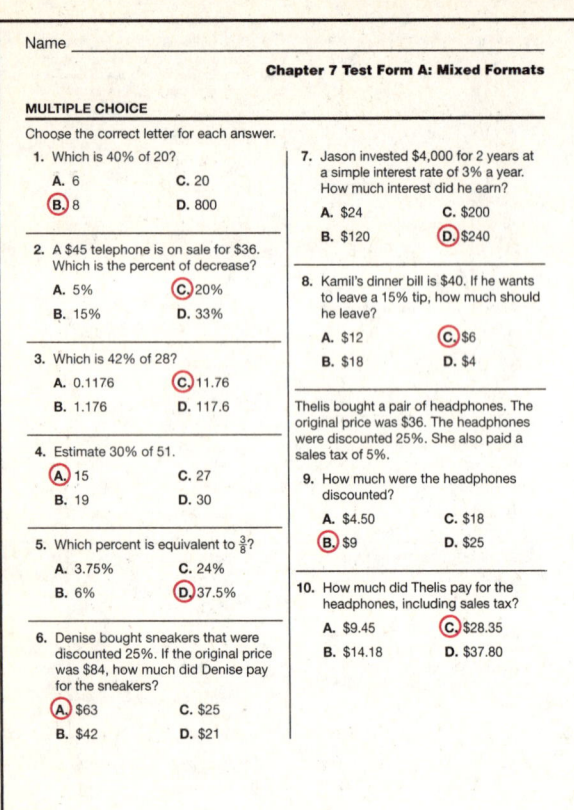

page 91

FREE RESPONSE Samples:
Write each in two other ways.
12. 73% **0.73** **73/100**
13. 60% **0.60** **3/5**
14. 0.84 **84%** **21/25**
15. 17/20 **0.85** **85%**
16. 4.5% **0.045** **4.5/100**
17. 0.03 **3%** **3/100**

Find the percent of each number.
18. 33% of 410 **135.3**
19. 90% of 70 **63**
20. 40% of 260 **104**
21. 30% of 65 **19.5**
22. 27% of 675 **182.25**
23. 2% of 55 **1.1**

Find the percent of increase or decrease. If necessary, round to the nearest tenth of a percent.
24. The temperature drops from 24°F to 16°F.
33.3% decrease
25. The worm population in Soren's compost bin increases from 75 to 105.
40% increase
26. A calf weighs 90 pounds when it is born and grows into a 1,800 pound adult cow.
1900% increase
27. The price of a watermelon is $3 in the summer and increases to $7 in the winter.
133.3% increase

For Exercises 28–29, write the percent of the figure that is shaded.

28.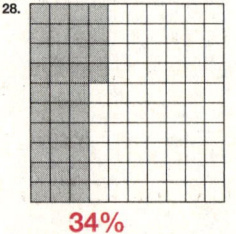
34%

page 92

29.
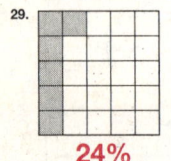
24%

30. Maya deposited $450 into a savings account with a simple interest rate of 6.1% per year. How much money did she have after 4 years?
$559.80

31. What is the total cost of a $23 item with a sales tax of 4.75%?
$24.09

WRITING IN MATH
32. Can 50% of Jack's allowance be something less than 25% of Marcia's allowance? Why or why not?
Yes. 50% of something small can be less than 25% of something larger. For example, 50% of $1.00 is less than 25% of $4.00 ($.50 < $1.00).

33. Explain how to use the strategy solve a simpler problem to find 35% of $24,000.
Break 35% into 25% and 10%. It is easy to find 25% and 10% of a number. 25% of 24,000 is 1/4 of 24,000 or 6,000. 10% of 24,000 is 2,400. So, 35% of 24,000 is 6,000 + 2,400, or $8,400.

34. Nate bought the following items at the store. If he received a discount of 15% off each item and then paid a sales tax of 3%, what was his total bill? Explain how you found the total amount.

batteries	$6.75
notebook	$2.50
box of pens	$5.25
calendar	$12.50
Subtotal	$27.00
Discount: 15%	
Sales Tax: 3%	
Total	

$23.64; I found 15% of the subtotal, which is the discount. Then I subtracted the discount ($4.05) from the subtotal. I multiplied the result ($22.95) by 1.03 to find the total amount of the bill, including tax.

page 93

Name _____
Chapter 7 Test Form B: Mixed Formats

MULTIPLE CHOICE
Circle the letter of the correct answer.

1. Which is 30% of 40?
   A. 1,200   **C. 12**
   B. 120   D. 7

2. A $55 jacket is on sale for $33. Which is the percent of decrease?
   A. 45%   C. 35%
   B. 40%   D. 22%

3. Which is 36% of 47?
   A. 169.2   C. 1.692
   B. 16.92   D. 0.1692

4. Estimate 20% of 69.
   A. 20   C. 16
   B. 19   **D. 14**

5. Which percent is equivalent to 7/8?
   A. 87.5%   C. 8.55%
   B. 56%   D. 5.6%

6. Don bought a shirt that was discounted 20%. If the original price was $45, how much did Don pay for the shirt?
   A. $9   **C. $36**
   B. $20   D. $54

7. Kristine invested $3,000 for 3 years at a simple interest rate of 5% per year. How much interest did she earn?
   A. $45   C. $300
   B. $150   **D. $450**

8. Rochelle's cab fare is $20. If she wants to give the driver a 15% tip, how much should she give?
   A. $2   C. $6
   B. $3   D. $9

9. Victor bought a desk lamp. The original price was $28. The desk lamp was discounted 25%. He also paid a sales tax of 6%. How much was the desk lamp discounted?
   A. $21   **C. $7**
   B. $14   D. $3.50

10. How much did Victor pay for the desk lamp, including sales tax?
    A. $40.28   C. $11.28
    B. $22.26   D. $7.42

Form B, page 94

Chapter 7 Form B and Chapter 8 Form A

page 95

page 96

Form A, page 97

page 98

151

Chapter 8 Form A and Form B

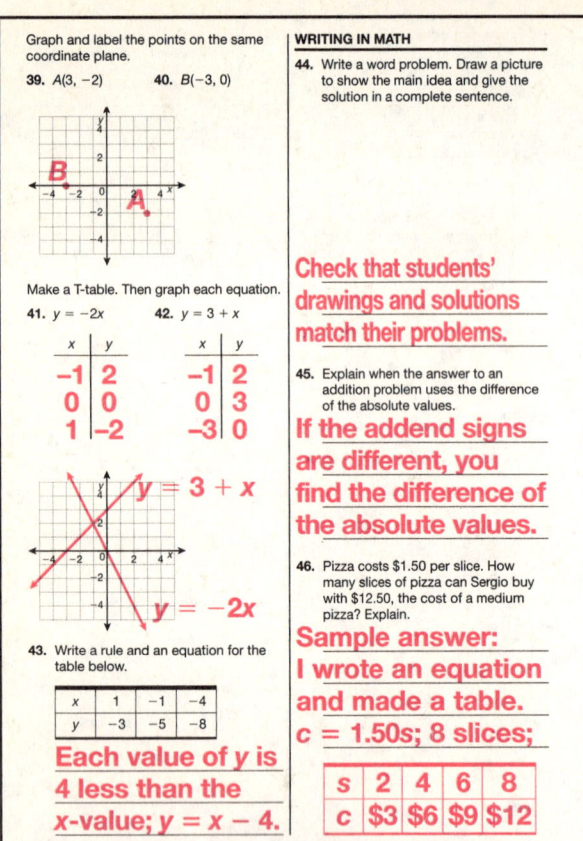

page 99

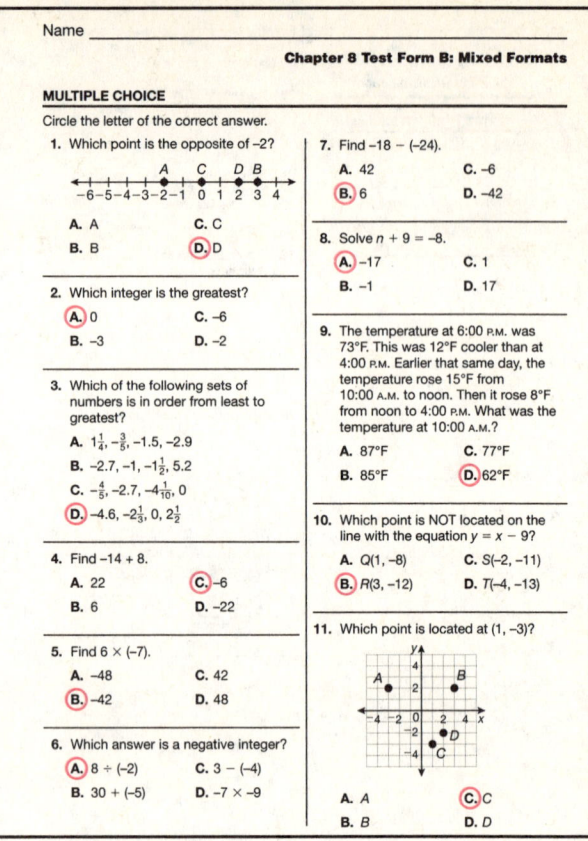

Form B, page 100

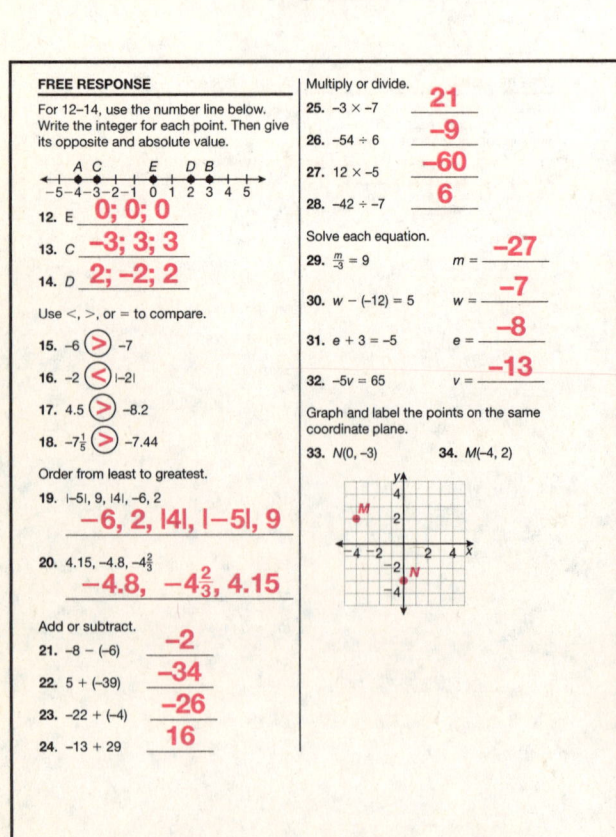

page 101

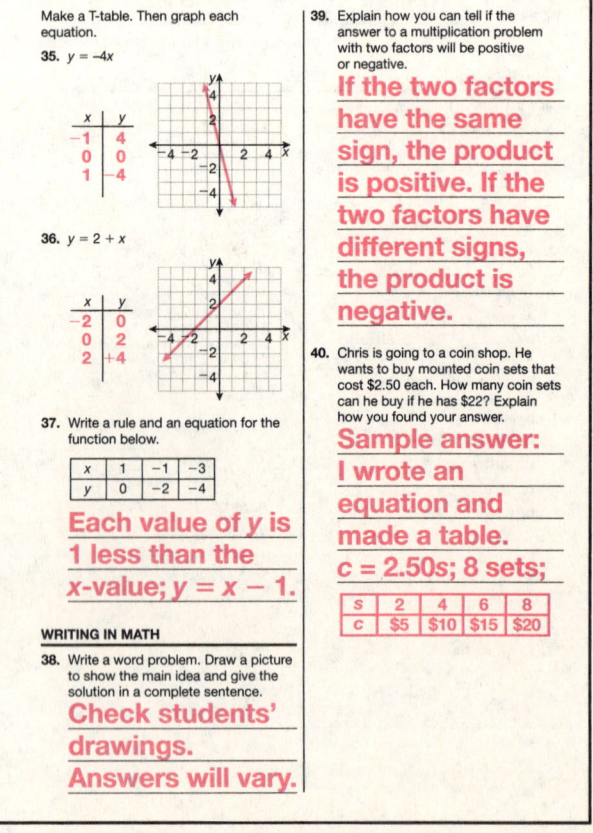

page 102

Chapter 9 Form A and Form B

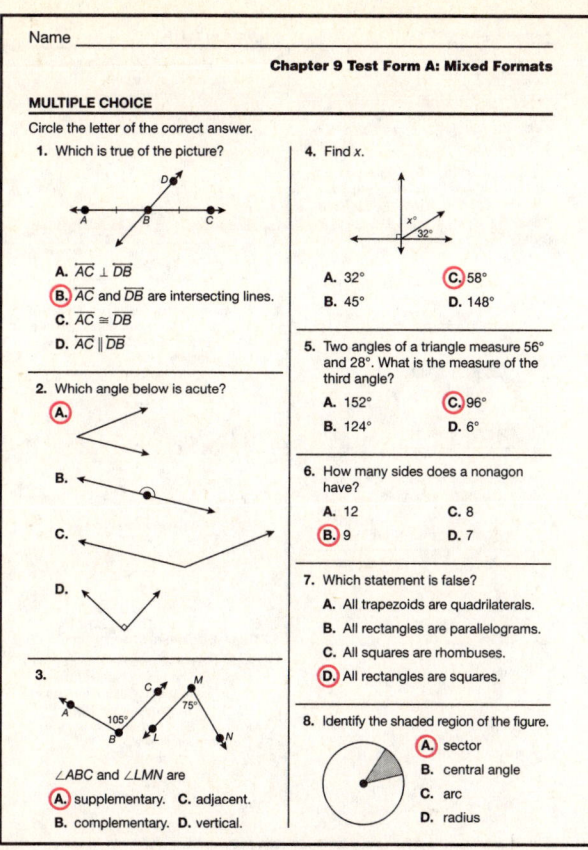

page 103

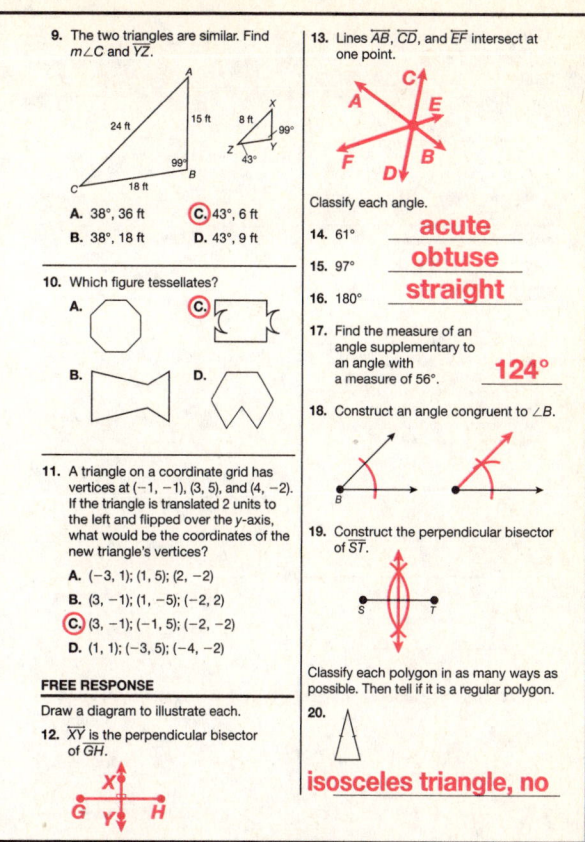

page 104

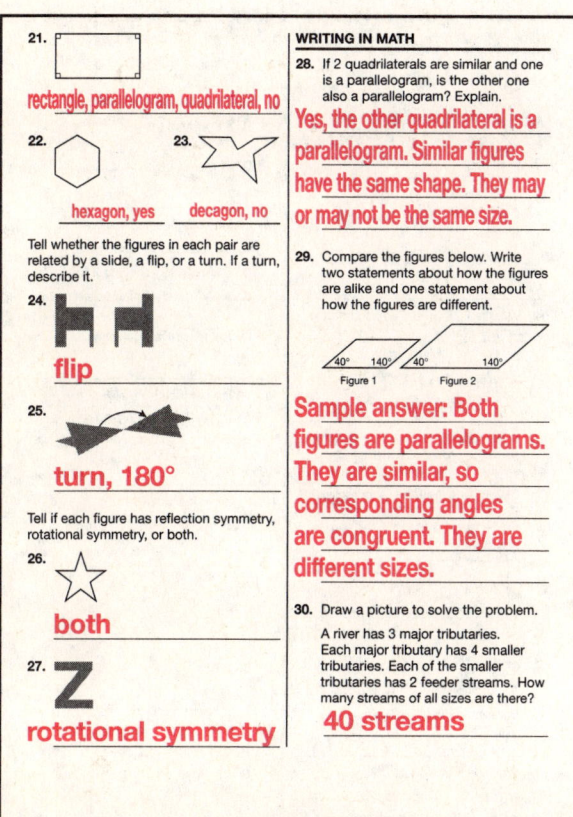

page 105

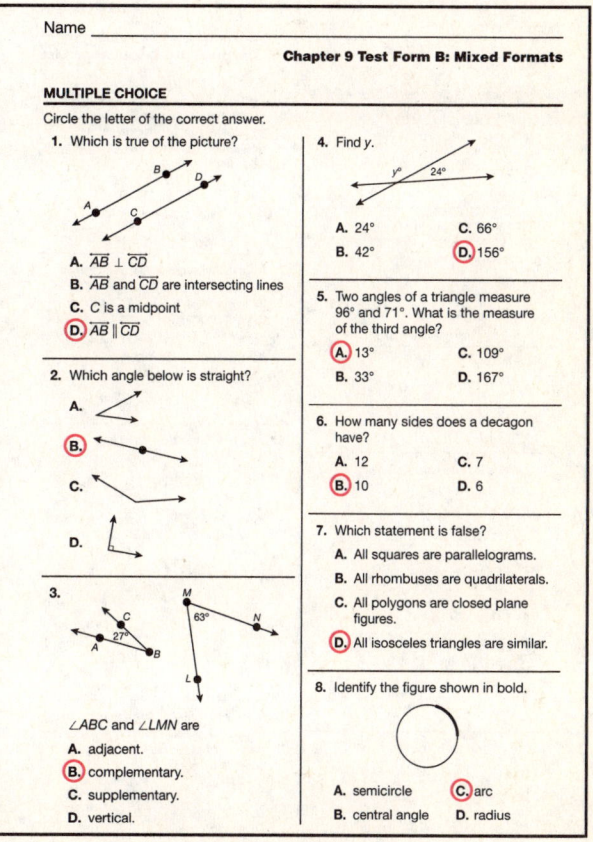

Form B, page 106

Chapter 9 Form B and Chapters 1–9 Cumulative Test

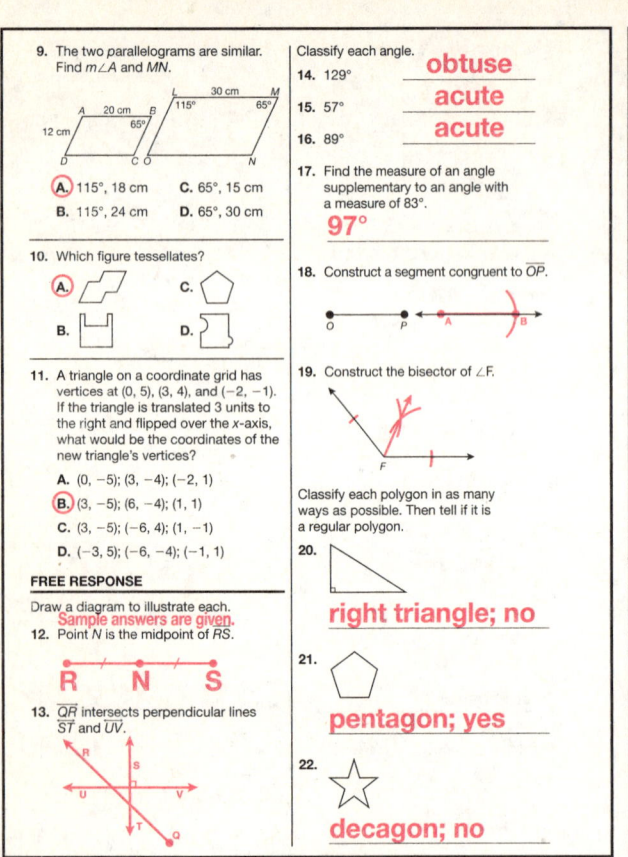

page 107

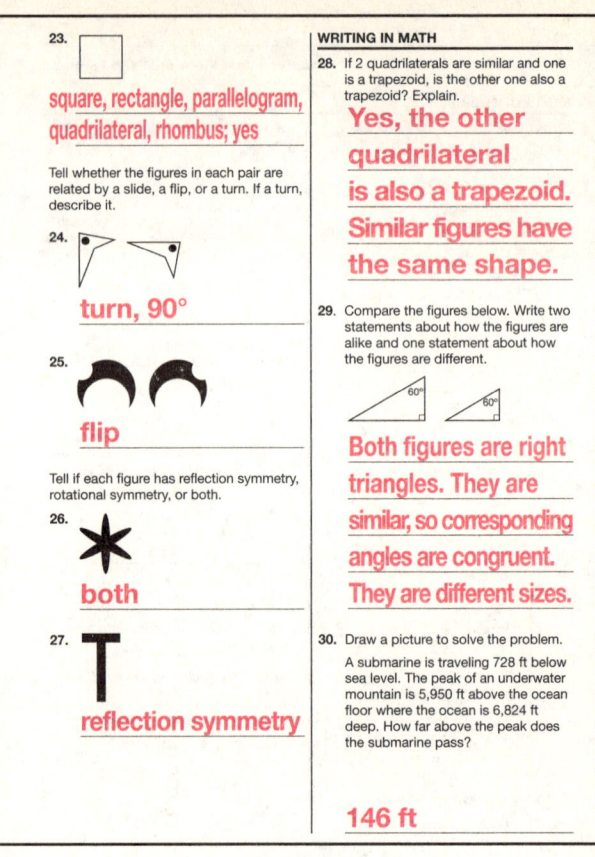

page 108

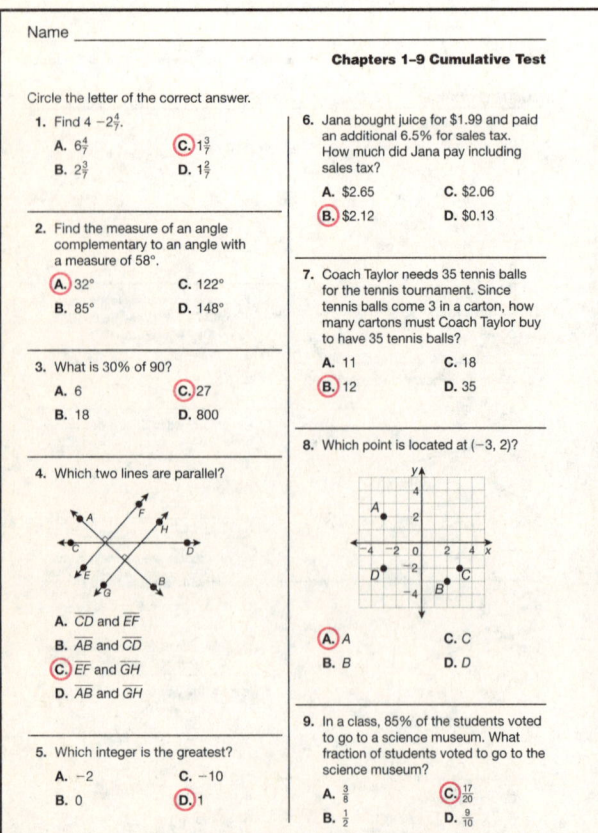

Cumulative Test, page 109

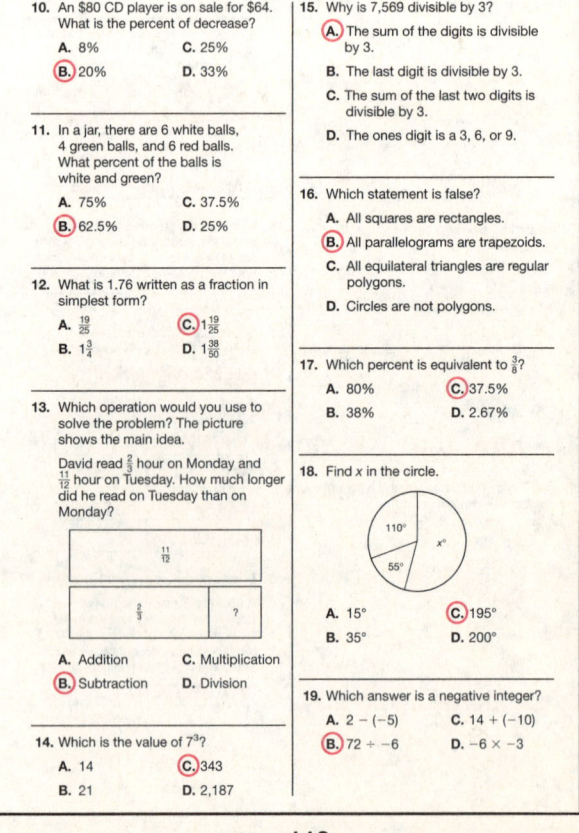

page 110

Chapters 1–9 Cumulative Test and Chapter 10 Form A

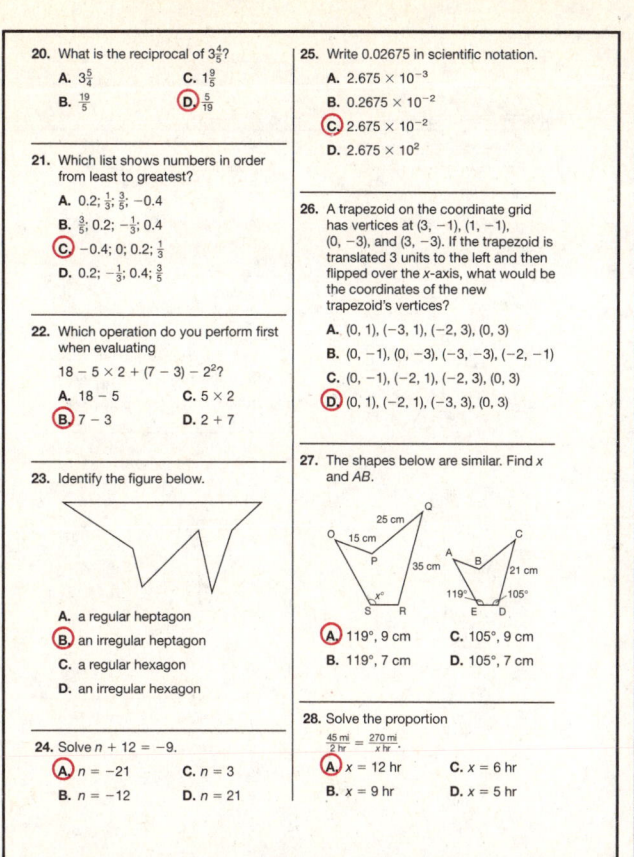

page 111

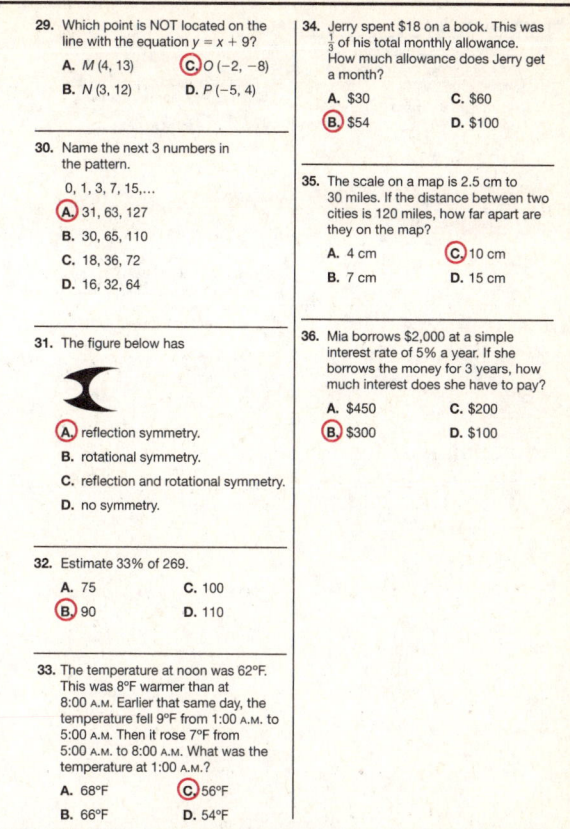

page 112

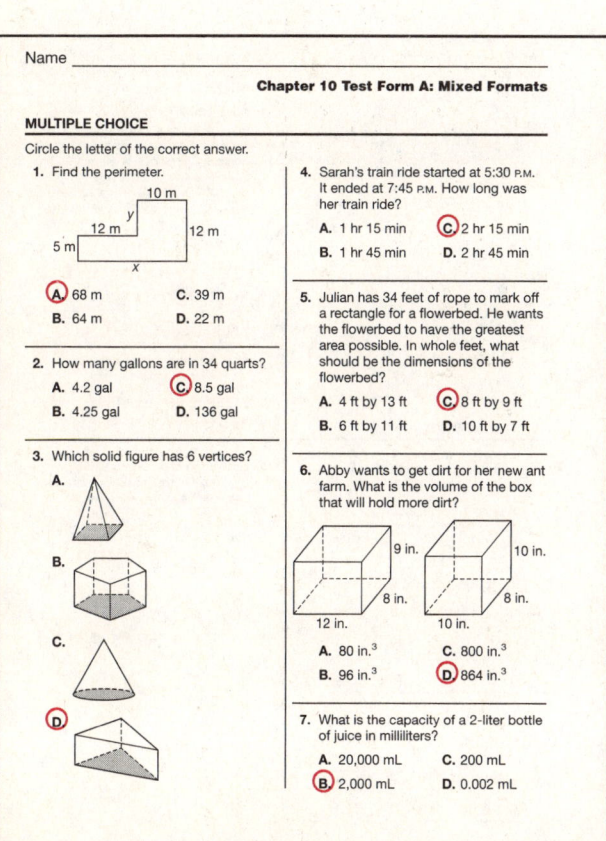

page 113

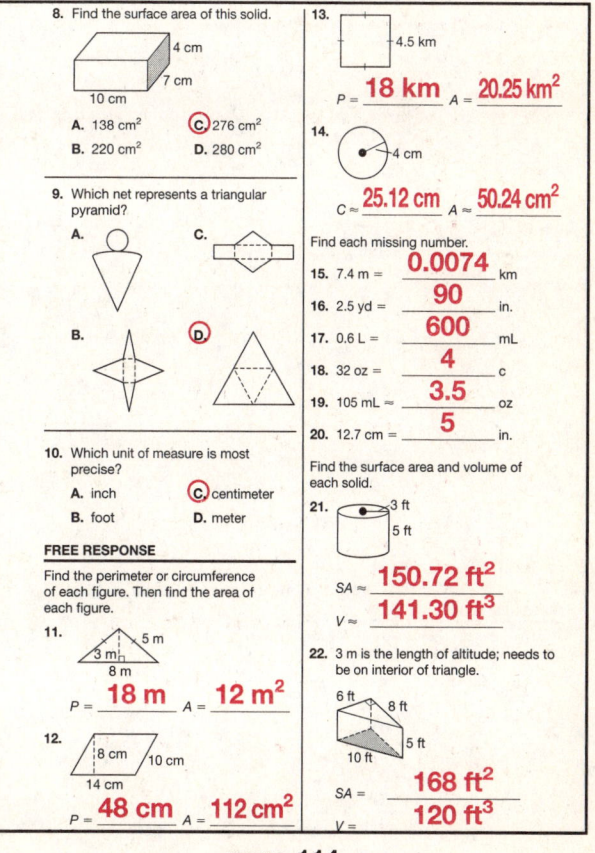

page 114

Chapter 10 Form A and Form B

page 115

WRITING IN MATH

23. Explain how to use logical reasoning and a time zone map to solve the problem. Then, solve.

A flight from Seattle to Philadelphia took 4 hours 35 minutes. If the plane landed in Philadelphia at 7:30 P.M. local time, at what time did it leave Seattle?

11:55 A.M.; The plane left Seattle at 2:55 P.M. Philadelphia time. The time in Seattle is 3 hours earlier than the time in Philadelphia. If it is 2:55 P.M. in Philadelphia, it is 11:55 A.M. in Seattle.

24. Explain if the problem has extra or missing information. Solve if you have enough information.

Luke ran around a 100-meter track 5 times. Afterwards, he walked around the track 1.5 times. His walk took him 10 minutes. How many meters can Luke run in an hour?

Missing information: time it took Luke to run 500 m

25. Each edge of a cube is 6 cm long. Explain how to find the surface area and volume of the cube.

$SA = 6 \times 6^2 = 216$ cm^2
$V = 6^3 = 216$ cm^3

Form B, page 116

Name _____

Chapter 10 Test Form B: Mixed Formats

MULTIPLE CHOICE

Circle the letter of the correct answer.

1. Find the perimeter.

   A. 15 m   C. 54 m
   B. 35 m   (D.) 58 m

2. How many cups are in 52 fluid ounces?

   A. 416 c   (C.) 6.5 c
   B. 8 c   D. 4 c

3. Which solid figure has 10 vertices?

   (A.)
   B.
   C.
   D.

4. Jeannette's bus ride started at 7:15 A.M. It ended at 10:00 A.M. How long was her bus ride?

   A. 2 hr 15 min   C. 3 hr 15 min
   (B.) 2 hr 45 min   D. 3 hr 45 min

5. Beatrice has 26 feet of fencing to enclose a rectangular garden. She wants the garden to have the greatest area possible. In whole feet, what should be the dimensions of the garden?

   A. 3 ft by 10 ft   C. 5 ft by 8 ft
   B. 4 ft by 9 ft   (D.) 7 ft by 6 ft

6. Carmen wants to use one of the two boxes shown to plant flowers. What is the volume of the box that holds more dirt?

   A. 18 in^3 C. 160 in^3
   B. 32 in^3 (D.) 162 in^3

7. George's dog has a mass of 35.7 kilograms. What is the dog's mass in grams?

   (A.) 35,700 g   C. 3.57 g
   B. 3,570 g   D. 0.0357 g

page 117

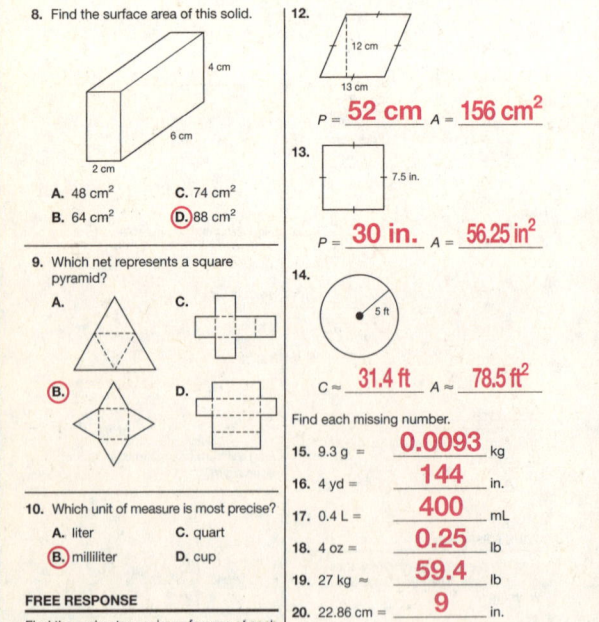

8. Find the surface area of this solid.

   A. 48 cm^2 C. 74 cm^2
   B. 64 cm^2 (D.) 88 cm^2

9. Which net represents a square pyramid?

   A.   (B.)   C.   D.

10. Which unit of measure is most precise?

    A. liter   C. quart
    (B.) milliliter   D. cup

FREE RESPONSE

Find the perimeter or circumference of each figure. Then find the area of each figure.

11. $P = $ **48 yd** $A = $ **84 yd^2**

12. $P = $ **52 cm** $A = $ **156 cm^2**

13. $P = $ **30 in.** $A = $ **56.25 in^2**

14. $C \approx $ **31.4 ft** $A \approx $ **78.5 ft^2**

Find each missing number.

15. 9.3 g = **0.0093** kg
16. 4 yd = **144** in.
17. 0.4 L = **400** mL
18. 4 oz = **0.25** lb
19. 27 kg ≈ **59.4** lb
20. 22.86 cm = **9** in.

page 118

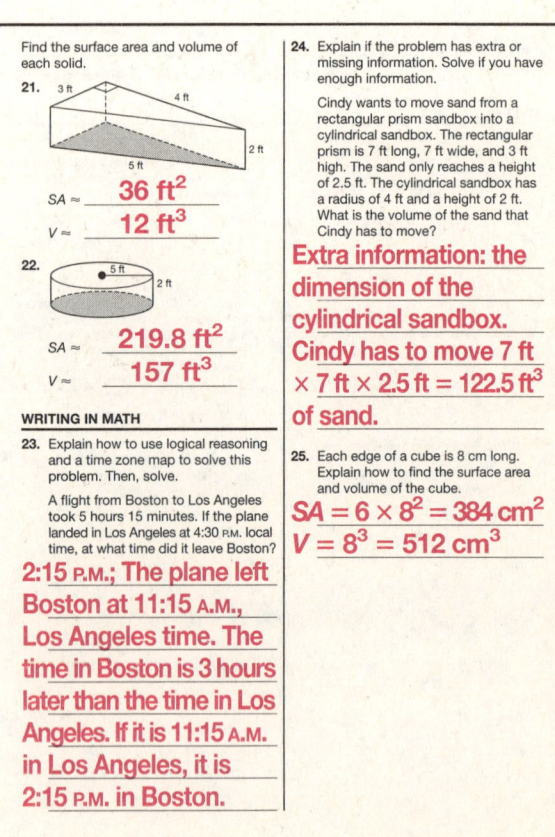

Find the surface area and volume of each solid.

21. $SA \approx $ **36 ft^2**
    $V \approx $ **12 ft^3**

22. $SA \approx $ **219.8 ft^2**
    $V \approx $ **157 ft^3**

WRITING IN MATH

23. Explain how to use logical reasoning and a time zone map to solve this problem. Then, solve.

A flight from Boston to Los Angeles took 5 hours 15 minutes. If the plane landed in Los Angeles at 4:30 P.M. local time, at what time did it leave Boston?

2:15 P.M.; The plane left Boston at 11:15 A.M., Los Angeles time. The time in Boston is 3 hours later than the time in Los Angeles. If it is 11:15 A.M. in Los Angeles, it is 2:15 P.M. in Boston.

24. Explain if the problem has extra or missing information. Solve if you have enough information.

Cindy wants to move sand from a rectangular prism sandbox into a cylindrical sandbox. The rectangular prism is 7 ft long, 7 ft wide, and 3 ft high. The sand only reaches a height of 2.5 ft. The cylindrical sandbox has a radius of 4 ft and a height of 2 ft. What is the volume of the sand that Cindy has to move?

Extra information: the dimension of the cylindrical sandbox. Cindy has to move 7 ft × 7 ft × 2.5 ft = 122.5 ft^3 of sand.

25. Each edge of a cube is 8 cm long. Explain how to find the surface area and volume of the cube.

$SA = 6 \times 8^2 = 384$ cm^2
$V = 8^3 = 512$ cm^3

Chapter 11 Form A and Form B

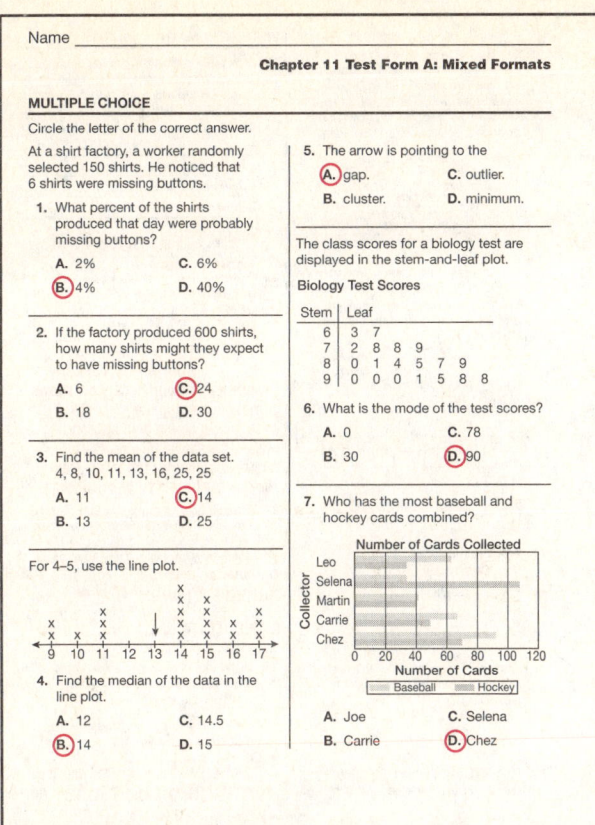

page 119

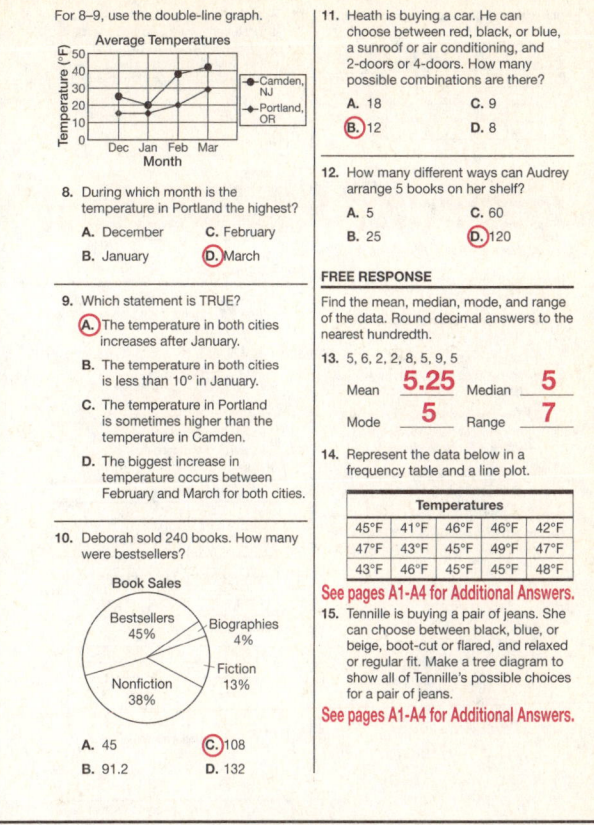

page 120

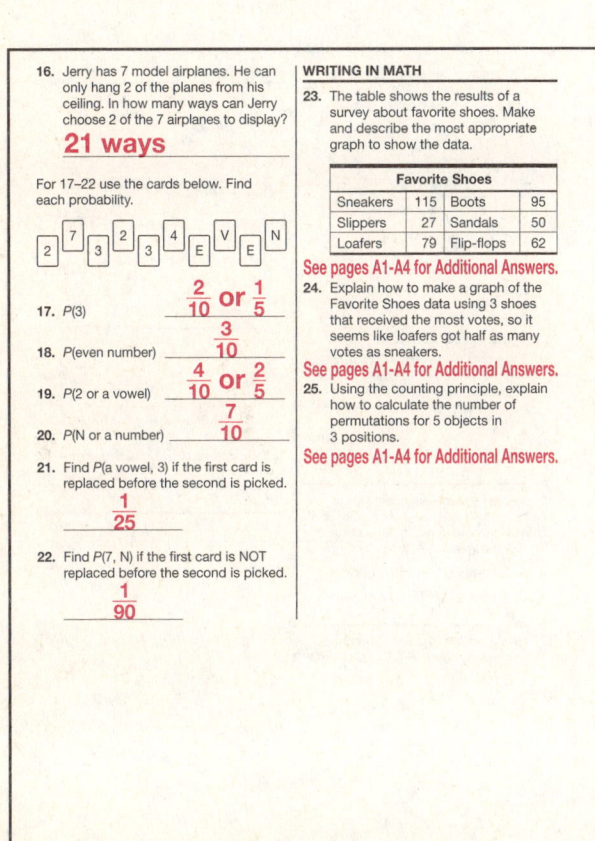

page 121

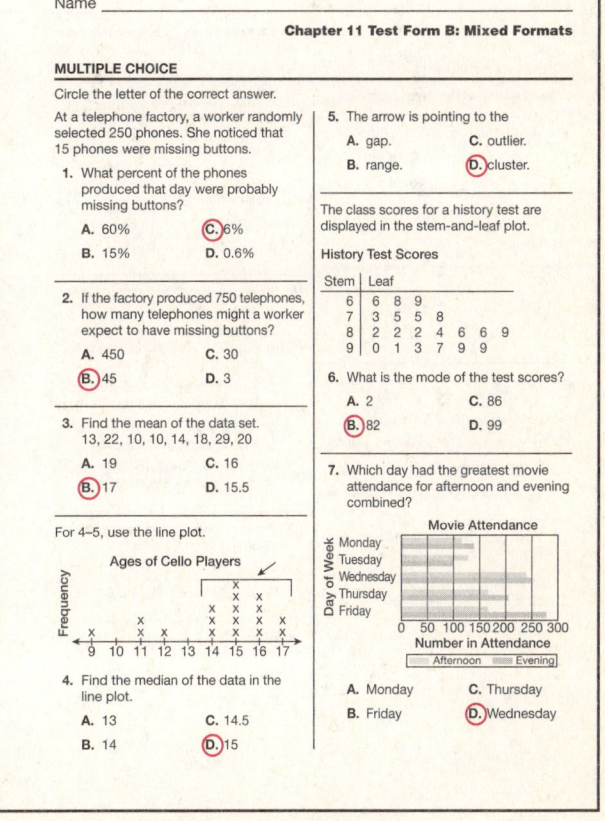

Form B, page 122

For Exercises 8–9, use the double-line graph.

8. During which week did Plant B measure 8 inches tall?

A. Week 1
(B.) Week 2
C. Week 3
D. Week 4

9. Which statement is TRUE?

A. The height of both plants is less than 20 inches in Week 4.
B. The height of Plant B is sometimes less than the height of Plant A.
(C.) The greatest increase in height occurs between Week 3 and Week 4 for both plants.
D. The height of Plant A decreases from Week 1 to Week 2.

10. Jay's music shop sold 450 items this week. How many of the items sold were CDs?

A. 20
B. 62
C. 90
(D.) 279

11. Robyn is buying a hat. She can choose between a baseball cap or a visor, fitted or adjustable, and red, green, yellow, or black. How many possible combinations are there?

A. 24
(B.) 16
C. 8
D. 4

12. How many different ways can Phil arrange 4 vases on his shelf?

A. 4
B. 12
C. 16
(D.) 24

FREE RESPONSE

Find the mean, median, mode, and range of the data set. Round decimal answers to the nearest hundredth.

13. 4, 5, 6, 9, 6, 2, 6

Mean **5.43** Median **6**
Mode **6** Range **7**

14. Represent the data below in a frequency table and in a line plot.

High Temperatures				
68°F	65°F	69°F	73°F	68°F
66°F	68°F	68°F	66°F	67°F
72°F	72°F	67°F	71°F	69°F

Temperature	Tally	Frequency
65°F	/	1
66°F	//	2
67°F	//	2
68°F	////	4
69°F	//	2
70°F		0
71°F	/	1
72°F	//	2
73°F	/	1

page 123

15. Eugene is buying a watch. He can choose between a metal, leather, or plastic band, a digital or analog display. The watch can also be waterproof, water-resistant, or neither. Make a tree diagram to show all of Eugene's possible watch choices.

16. Cecilia has 7 wind chimes. She can only hang 2 of the wind chimes on her porch. In how many ways can Cecilia choose 2 of the 7 wind chimes to display?

21 ways

For 17–22 use the cards below. Find each probability.

6 | 2 | 4 | 2 | 2 | 5 | C | A | R | D

17. $P(2)$ **$\frac{3}{10}$**

18. P(odd number) **$\frac{1}{10}$**

19. P(6 or a vowel) **$\frac{2}{10}$ or $\frac{1}{5}$**

20. P(5 or a letter) **$\frac{5}{10}$ or $\frac{1}{2}$**

21. Find P(2, a consonant) if the first card is replaced before the second is picked.

$\frac{9}{100}$

22. Find P(R, 4) if the first card is NOT replaced before the second is picked.

$\frac{1}{90}$

WRITING IN MATH

23. The table shows the results of a survey about favorite fruits. Make and describe the most appropriate graph to show the data.

Favorite Fruit			
Apple	77	Grapes	45
Orange	38	Peach	61
Banana	29	Pear	23

I chose a bar graph because it shows comparisons of numerical data. A circle graph would be inappropriate because it shows how parts are related to a whole, and a line graph shows how data changes over time.

24. Explain how to make a graph of the Favorite Fruit data using 3 fruits that received the most votes to make it seem that apples got twice as many votes as grapes.

Sample answer: Make the scale from 20 to 100 by 10.

25. Is the example below an example of a permutation or a combination? How do you know?

How many ways can Brad arrange 4 posters on his wall?

This is an example of a permutation because order is important.

page 124

Name ______________________

Chapter 12 Test Form A: Mixed Formats

MULTIPLE CHOICE

Circle the letter of the correct answer.

1. Which of the following is NOT a solution of $m \le 4$?

A. $m = -5$
B. $m = 0$
C. $m = 3$
(D.) $m = 7$

2. Which inequality is graphed on the number line?

A. $y \ge 4$
B. $y > 4$
(C.) $y < 4$
D. $y \le 4$

3. Which property of inequality should you use to solve $a - 4 \ge 3$?

(A.) Addition Property of Inequality
B. Subtraction Property of Inequality
C. Multiplication Property of Inequality
D. Division Property of Inequality

4. What is the solution of the inequality $b + 5 > 11$?

A. $b < 6$
B. $b \le 6$
(C.) $b > 6$
D. $b \ge 6$

5. Let y represent the number of shoes sold last week. This week the number of shoes sold is 13 less than twice as many as last week. Which expression represents the number of shoes sold this week?

A. $2(y - 13)$
(B.) $2y - 13$
C. $13 - 2y$
D. $\frac{1}{2}(y - 13)$

6. Which tells the correct order of steps to solve the equation $3p - 9 = 21$?

A. Subtract 9 from both sides of the equation. Then divide both sides by 3.
(B.) Add 9 to both sides of the equation. Then divide both sides by 3.
C. Add 9 to both sides of the equation. Then multiply both sides by 3.
D. Divide both sides of the equation by 3. Then add 9 to both sides.

7. Which of the following equations does NOT have a solution of $x = 6$?

A. $\frac{x}{3} + 1 = 3$
B. $5x + 10 = 40$
C. $3x - 7 = 11$
(D.) $\frac{x}{2} + 3 = 5$

8. Which of the following is the solution of $3x - 7 = 2$?

A. $x = \frac{1}{3}$
B. $x = \frac{5}{3}$
C. $x = 0$
(D.) $x = 3$

Form A, page 125

9. The graph of the equation $y = 3x - 4$ is shown below. Which of the following is the correct solution of $-1 = 3x - 4$?

A. $x = -2$
B. $x = -1$
C. $x = 0$
(D.) $x = 1$

10. It is a cold morning and Shazia notices that the heat is not working in the house. Which of the following is most likely the temperature in the house?

A. 40°C
B. 78°F
(C.) 40°F
D. 20°C

11. Moore buys a 32-ounce bottle of milk. How many 12-ounce glasses of milk can she drink from the bottle? Use the inequality $12m \le 32$ to solve.

A. 24 glasses
B. 12 glasses
C. 3 glasses
(D.) 2 glasses

12. Find −15°C in degrees Fahrenheit. Use the formula $F = \frac{9}{5}C + 32$.

A. 27°F
(B.) 5°F
C. −5°F
D. −27°F

FREE RESPONSE

Solve each inequality or equation.

13. $\frac{1}{4}x - 3 = 7$ **$x = 40$**

14. $8x \ge 40$ **$x \ge 5$**

15. $2x - 7 = 19$ **$x = 13$**

Name three solutions for each inequality, and graph each inequality on a number line. **Sample solutions are shown.**

16. $x > 8$ **9**, **12**, **13**

17. $x \le 7$ **7**, **0**, **−2**

18. What inequality is graphed on the number line below? **$x \ge 3$**

page 126

 Chapter Tests in the Assessment Sourcebook parallel Chapter Tests in the Student Book item for item. See the Teacher Edition for item analysis of these tests.

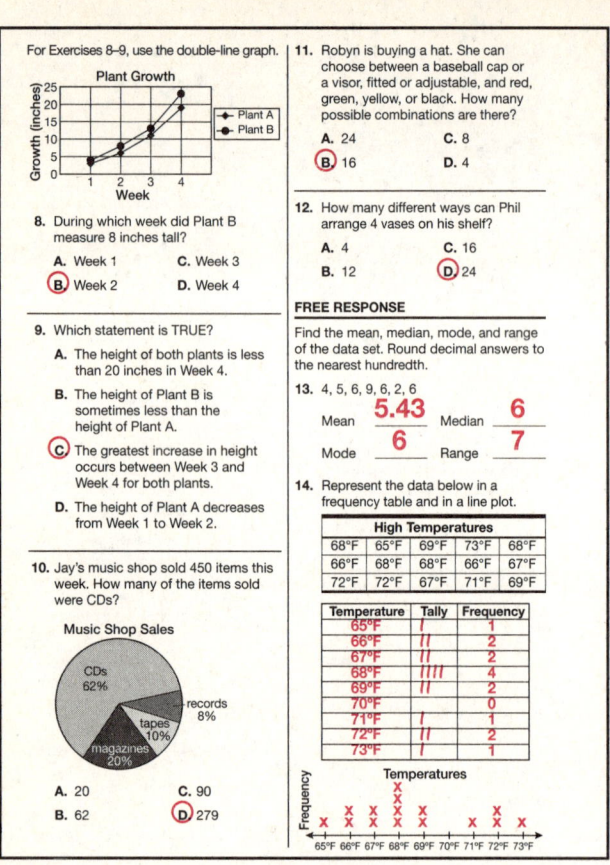

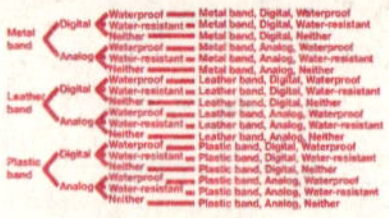

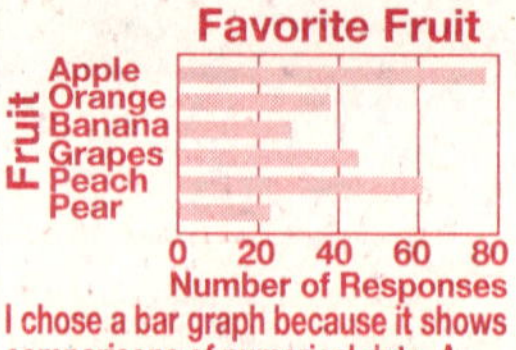

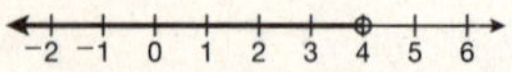

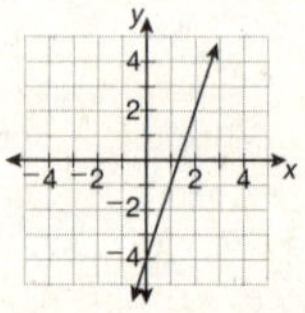

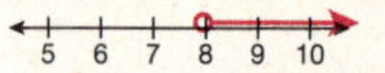

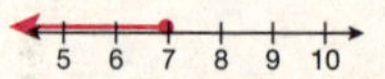

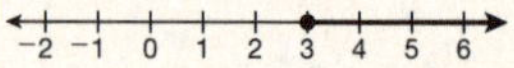

Chapter 12 Form A and Form B

page 127

For 19–20, make a T-table. Then graph each equation on a coordinate plane.

19. $y = 2x + 3$

x	y
-2	**-1**
-1	**1**
0	**3**

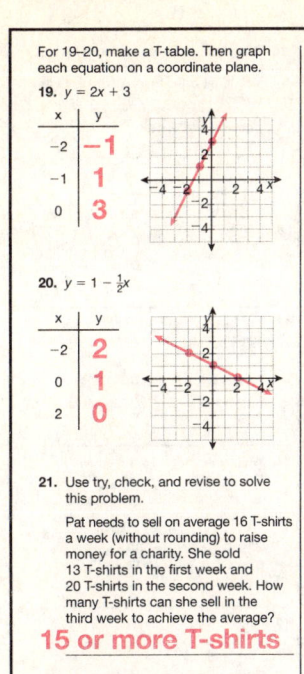

20. $y = 1 - \frac{1}{2}x$

x	y
-2	**2**
0	**1**
2	**0**

21. Use try, check, and revise to solve this problem.

Pat needs to sell on average 16 T-shirts a week (without rounding) to raise money for a charity. She sold 13 T-shirts in the first week and 20 T-shirts in the second week. How many T-shirts can she sell in the third week to achieve the average?

15 or more T-shirts

WRITING IN MATH

22. Write an equation to find the perimeter, P, of a row of 35 hexagons that are joined side by side. Each side is 1 cm long.

Complete the table. Use the pattern in the table to help you write the equation.

Number of Hexagons	1	2	3	4	5	10	35
Perimeter (cm)	6	10	14	18	**22**	**42**	**142**

$P = 4n + 2$, where n = number of hexagons in the row.

23. Explain how you can use inverse operations and the properties of inequality to solve $n - 30 \geq 111$.

Use the Addition Property of Inequality to undo the subtraction. Add 30 to both sides of the inequality to get $n \geq 141$.

24. Explain the steps you would follow to graph the equation $y = 3x + 5$.

Sample answer: Make a T-table with x-values −1, 0, and 1. Find y-values and graph the equation.

Form B, page 128

Name _____

Chapter 12 Test Form B: Mixed Formats

MULTIPLE CHOICE
Circle the letter of the correct answer.

1. Which of the following is NOT a solution of $n \geq 7$?
   - **A.** $n = -8$
   - B. $n = 7$
   - C. $n = 9.5$
   - D. $n = 12$

2. Which inequality is graphed on the number line?

   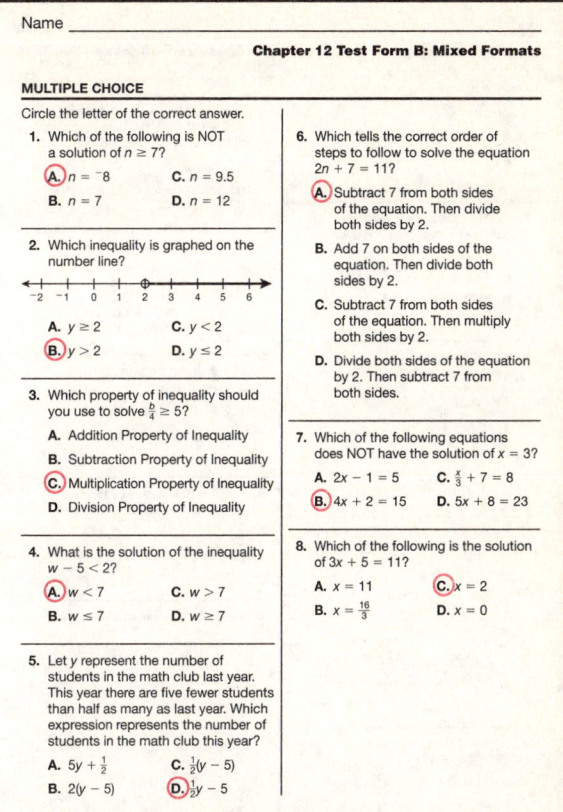

   - A. $y \geq 2$
   - **B.** $y > 2$
   - C. $y < 2$
   - D. $y \leq 2$

3. Which property of inequality should you use to solve $\frac{b}{4} \geq 5$?
   - A. Addition Property of Inequality
   - B. Subtraction Property of Inequality
   - **C.** Multiplication Property of Inequality
   - D. Division Property of Inequality

4. What is the solution of the inequality $w - 5 < 2$?
   - **A.** $w < 7$
   - B. $w \leq 7$
   - C. $w > 7$
   - D. $w \geq 7$

5. Let y represent the number of students in the math club last year. This year there are five fewer students than half as many as last year. Which expression represents the number of students in the math club this year?
   - A. $5y + \frac{1}{2}$
   - B. $2(y - 5)$
   - C. $\frac{1}{2}(y - 5)$
   - **D.** $\frac{1}{2}y - 5$

6. Which tells the correct order of steps to follow to solve the equation $2n + 7 = 11$?
   - **A.** Subtract 7 from both sides of the equation. Then divide both sides by 2.
   - B. Add 7 on both sides of the equation. Then divide both sides by 2.
   - C. Subtract 7 from both sides of the equation. Then multiply both sides by 2.
   - D. Divide both sides of the equation by 2. Then subtract 7 from both sides.

7. Which of the following equations does NOT have the solution of $x = 3$?
   - A. $2x - 1 = 5$
   - **B.** $4x + 2 = 15$
   - C. $\frac{x}{3} + 7 = 8$
   - D. $5x + 8 = 23$

8. Which of the following is the solution of $3x + 5 = 11$?
   - A. $x = 11$
   - B. $x = \frac{16}{3}$
   - **C.** $x = 2$
   - D. $x = 0$

page 129

9. The graph of the equation $y = 2x + 1$ is shown below. Which of the following is the correct solution of $3 = 2x + 1$?

   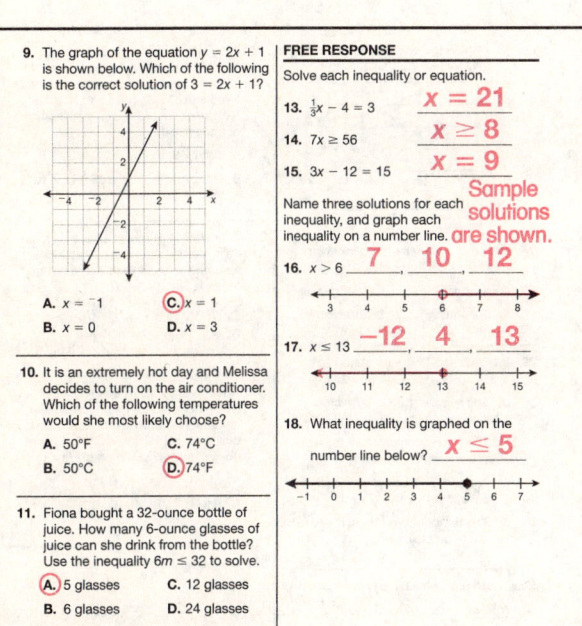

   - A. $x = -1$
   - B. $x = 0$
   - **C.** $x = 1$
   - D. $x = 3$

10. It is an extremely hot day and Melissa decides to turn on the air conditioner. Which of the following temperatures would she most likely choose?
    - A. 50°F
    - B. 50°C
    - C. 74°C
    - **D.** 74°F

11. Fiona bought a 32-ounce bottle of juice. How many 6-ounce glasses of juice can she drink from the bottle? Use the inequality $6m \leq 32$ to solve.
    - **A.** 5 glasses
    - B. 6 glasses
    - C. 12 glasses
    - D. 24 glasses

12. Find −5°C in degrees Fahrenheit. Use the formula $F = \frac{9}{5}C + 32$.
    - A. −23°F
    - B. −9°F
    - C. 9°F
    - **D.** 23°F

FREE RESPONSE
Solve each inequality or equation.

13. $\frac{1}{3}x - 4 = 3$ **$x = 21$**

14. $7x \geq 56$ **$x \geq 8$**

15. $3x - 12 = 15$ **$x = 9$**

Name three solutions for each inequality, and graph each inequality on a number line. **Sample solutions are shown.**

16. $x > 6$ **7 10 12**

17. $x \leq 13$ **−12 4 13**

18. What inequality is graphed on the number line below? **$x \leq 5$**

page 130

For 19–20, make a T-table. Then graph each equation on a coordinate plane.

19. $y = 2x + 2$

x	y
-1	**0**
0	**2**
1	**4**

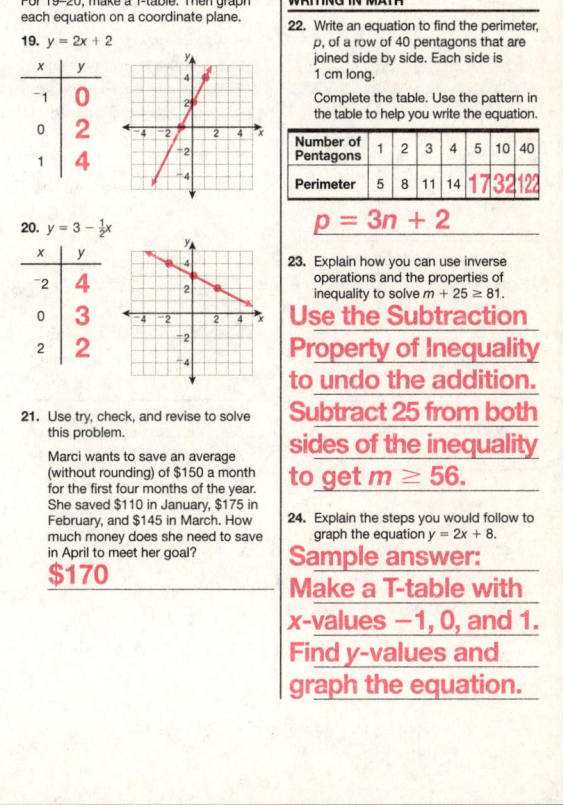

20. $y = 3 - \frac{1}{2}x$

x	y
-2	**4**
0	**3**
2	**2**

21. Use try, check, and revise to solve this problem.

Marci wants to save an average (without rounding) of $150 a month for the first four months of the year. She saved $110 in January, $175 in February, and $145 in March. How much money does she need to save in April to meet her goal?

$170

WRITING IN MATH

22. Write an equation to find the perimeter, p, of a row of 40 pentagons that are joined side by side. Each side is 1 cm long.

Complete the table. Use the pattern in the table to help you write the equation.

Number of Pentagons	1	2	3	4	5	10	40
Perimeter	5	8	11	14	**17**	**32**	**122**

$p = 3n + 2$

23. Explain how you can use inverse operations and the properties of inequality to solve $m + 25 \geq 81$.

Use the Subtraction Property of Inequality to undo the addition. Subtract 25 from both sides of the inequality to get $m \geq 56$.

24. Explain the steps you would follow to graph the equation $y = 2x + 8$.

Sample answer: Make a T-table with x-values −1, 0, and 1. Find y-values and graph the equation.

Chapters 1–12 Cumulative Test

Name _____

Chapters 1–12 Cumulative Test

Circle the letter of the correct answer.

1. Find $\frac{5}{8} - \frac{1}{10}$.
   A. $\frac{1}{2}$ C. $\frac{3}{5}$
   B. $\frac{21}{40}$ D. $\frac{29}{40}$

2. Find the measure of an angle supplementary to an angle with a measure of 55°.
   A. 35°   **C. 125°**
   B. 85°   D. 148°

3. Which net can be used to make a triangular prism?
   A.
   B.
   C.
   D.

4. Which of the following is the solution of $3x - 8 = 4$?
   A. $x = -\frac{4}{3}$ **C. $x = 4$**
   B. $x = 3$ D. $x = 6$

5. Pam went to the museum at 3:15 P.M. and left at 6:30 P.M. How much time did she spend at the museum?
   A. 2 hr 45 min   C. 3 hr 45 min
   B. 3 hr 15 min   D. 4 hr 15 min

6. In which quadrant is the point $(-3, -1)$?
   A. I   **C. III**
   B. II   D. IV

7. Which of the following is NOT a solution of $m \leq 8$?
   A. $^-8$ C. 8
   B. 0   **D. 11**

8. A $70 watch is on sale for $49. Which is the percent of decrease?
   A. 30%   C. 14%
   B. 21%   D. 7%

9. Which solid figure has 5 vertices?
   A.
   B.
   C.
   D.

10. Find the unit cost of a 5-lb bag of potatoes that costs $3.
    A. $6/lb   C. $1.50/lb
    B. $1.67/lb   **D. $0.60/lb**

11. Find the GCF for 15 and 42.
    A. 3   C. 6
    B. 5   D. 15

12. What is the solution of the inequality $a + 3 \geq 17$?
    A. $a < 14$ C. $a > 14$
    B. $a \leq 14$ **D. $a \geq 14$**

13. Find $^-25°C$ in degrees Fahrenheit. Use the formula $F = \frac{9}{5}C + 32$.
    A. $^-18°F$ C. $13°F$
    B. $^-13°F$ D. $18°F$

14. How many different ways can Noreen arrange 6 CDs on her shelf?
    A. 20   C. 120
    B. 60   **D. 720**

15. At a light-bulb factory, a worker randomly selected 120 bulbs. He noticed that 3 bulbs did not work. What percent of the bulbs produced that day were probably not working?
    A. 0.5%   C. 5%
    B. 2.5%   D. 25%

16. The class scores for a science test are displayed in the stem-and-leaf plot. What is the mode of the test scores?

    Science Test Scores
Stem	Leaf
5	4 8
6	1 3 7
7	0 2 4 7 7
8	1 3 3 5 9

    A. 89   C. 77
    B. 83   D. 3

17. Das has 12 bricks. This is $\frac{1}{3}$ of the number he needs. How many bricks does he need?
    A. 4 bricks   C. 30 bricks
    B. 24 bricks   **D. 36 bricks**

18. Which inequality is graphed on the number line?

    A. $y \geq 3$ C. $y < 3$
    B. $y > 3$ D. $y \leq 3$

19. Find $4\frac{2}{3} \div 3\frac{1}{9}$.
    A. $\frac{1}{2}$ C. $1\frac{1}{5}$
    B. $\frac{2}{3}$ **D. $1\frac{1}{2}$**

page 131   page 132

For 20–21, use the line plot.

Number of Pistachios in a Bag

20. Find the median of the data in the line plot.
    A. 11   C. 14.5
    B. 14   D. 15

21. The arrow is pointing to the
    A. gap.   **C. outlier.**
    B. cluster.   D. minimum.

22. Calculate the value of $15 \div 3 \times (10 - 2^2)$.
    A. 30   C. 40
    B. 32   D. 46

23. What is the capacity in milliliters of a 7 liter bottle of juice?
    A. 7,000 mL   C. 70 mL
    B. 700 mL   D. 0.007 mL

24. What is 0.00326 in scientific notation?
    A. 3.26×10^{-3}
    B. 0.326×10^2
    C. 3.26×10^{-4}
    D. 32.6×10^3

25. Which property of inequality should you use to solve $\frac{a}{7} \geq 3$?
    A. Addition Property of Inequality
    B. Subtraction Property of Inequality
    C. Multiplication Property of Inequality
    D. Division Property of Inequality

26. The two triangles are similar. Find the measure of $\angle E$ and AC.

    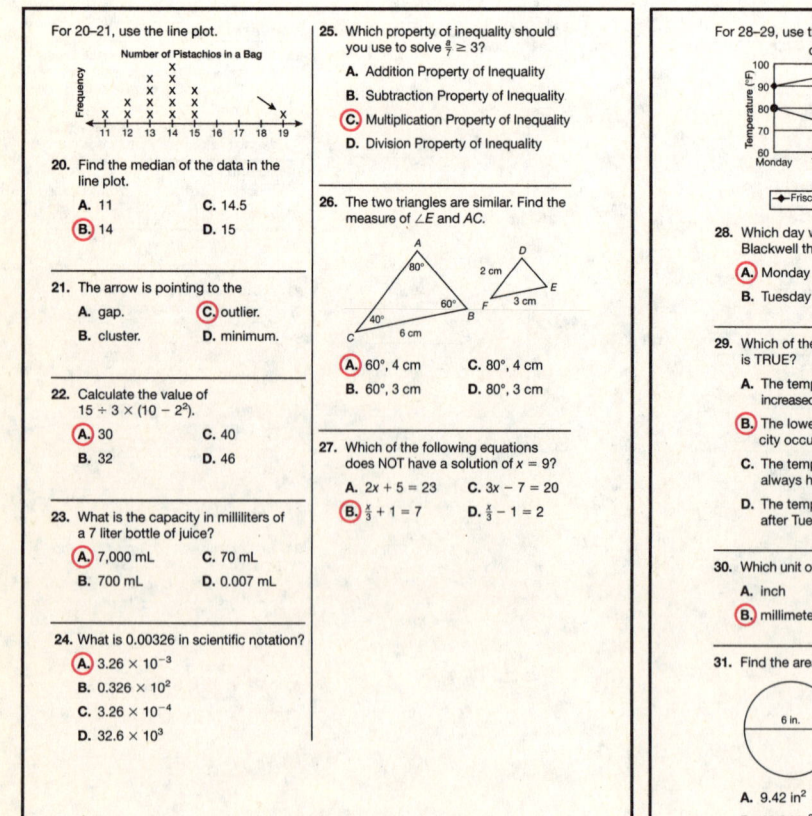

    A. 60°, 4 cm   C. 80°, 4 cm
    B. 60°, 3 cm   D. 80°, 3 cm

27. Which of the following equations does NOT have a solution of $x = 9$?
    A. $2x + 5 = 23$ C. $3x - 7 = 20$
    B. $\frac{x}{3} + 1 = 7$ D. $\frac{x}{3} - 1 = 2$

For 28–29, use the double-line graph.

City Temperatures

28. Which day was the temperature in Blackwell the highest?
    A. Monday   C. Wednesday
    B. Tuesday   D. Thursday

29. Which of the following statements is TRUE?
    A. The temperature in both cities increased from Monday to Thursday.
    B. The lowest temperature for each city occurs on Thursday.
    C. The temperature of Blackwell is always higher than Frisco.
    D. The temperature for each city falls after Tuesday.

30. Which unit of measure is most precise?
    A. inch   C. yard
    B. millimeter   D. centimeter

31. Find the area of this circle.

    6 in.

    A. 9.42 in²   **C. 28.26 in²**
    B. 18.84 in²   D. 113.04 in²

32. Mary wants to plant a garden in a rectangular plot with a perimeter of 22 feet. She wants the garden to have the greatest area possible. In whole feet, what should be the dimensions of the garden?
    A. 2 ft by 9 ft   C. 4 ft by 7 ft
    B. 3 ft by 8 ft   **D. 5 ft by 6 ft**

33. If you toss a number cube and flip a coin, what is the probability of tossing a number greater than 5 and having the coin land tails up?
    A. $\frac{1}{12}$ C. $\frac{1}{2}$
    B. $\frac{1}{6}$ D. $\frac{3}{4}$

34. Hope needs an average score of 84 (without rounding) on her three quizzes. Her scores on the first two quizzes were 96 and 74. What score does she need to get on the last quiz?
    A. 86   **C. 82**
    B. 84   D. 80

35. Which is 40% of 120?
    A. 80   C. 40
    B. 48   D. 24

36. Find the surface area of this solid.

    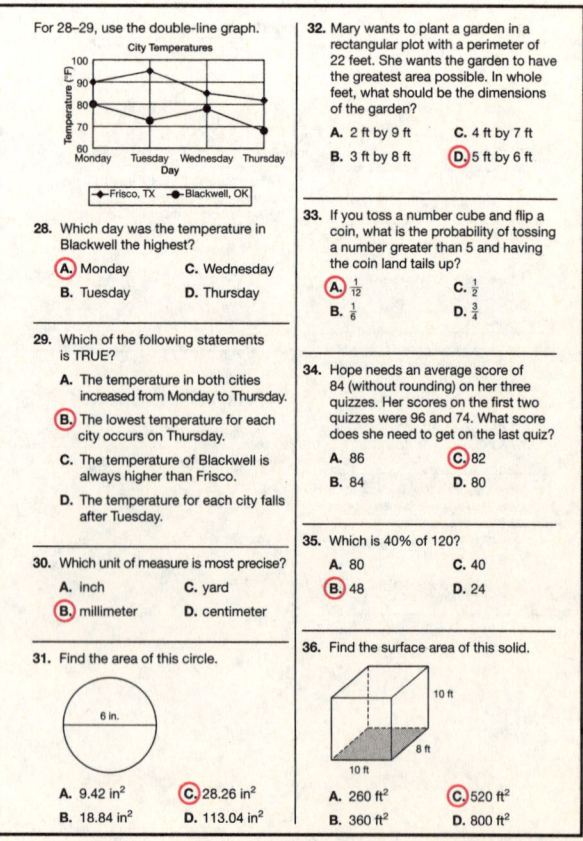

    A. 260 ft²   **C. 520 ft²**
    B. 360 ft²   D. 800 ft²

page 133   page 134

Additional Answers

Chapter 11 Performance Assessment
Page 22

3. $\frac{4}{10}$ or $\frac{2}{5}$; Four out of 10 students chose math; $\frac{1}{15}$; Sample response: To find P(History, Science) find the probability of each and multiply. P(History) $\times$ P(Science) $= \frac{3}{10} \times \frac{2}{9} = \frac{1}{15}$

4.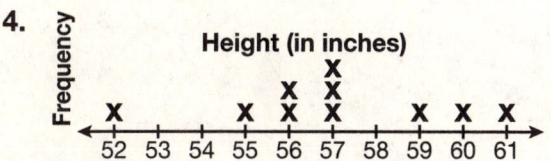

   There is a gap from 52 to 55 and a cluster from 55 to 57.

5. mean: 57; median: 57; mode: 57; range: 9

Chapter 11 Test Form A
Page 120

14.
Temperature	Tally	Frequency
41°F	I	1
42°F	I	1
43°F	II	2
44°F		0
45°F	IIII	4
46°F	III	3
47°F	II	2
48°F	I	1
49°F	I	1

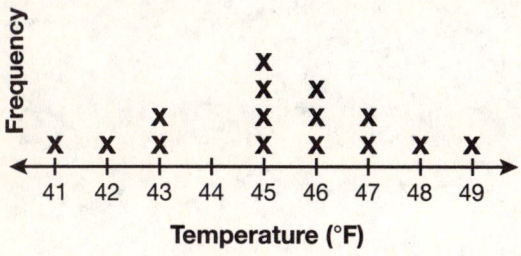

15.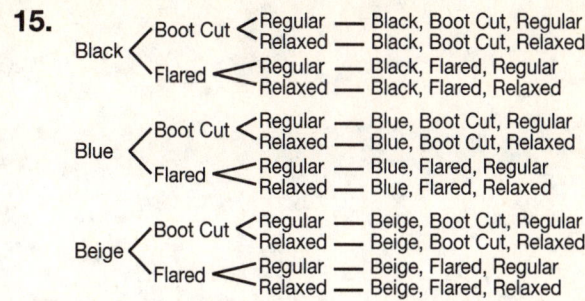

Page 121

23.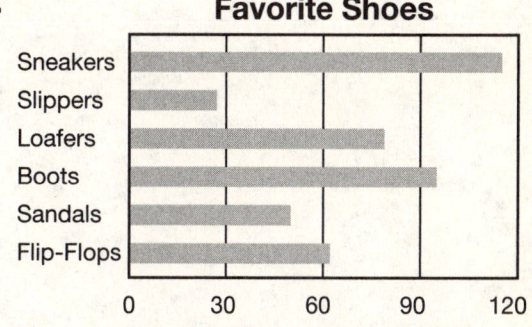

I chose a bar graph because it shows comparisons of numerical data. A circle graph would be inappropriate because it shows how parts are related to a whole, and a line graph shows how data changes over time.

24. Sample answer: Make the scale from 60 to 140 by 20.

25. When counting permutations, order is important. In the first position, there are 5 choices. In the second position, there are 4 choices; in the third, 3 choices. The total number of ways to choose is the product of the number of choices for each position: $5 \times 4 \times 3 = 60$ permutations.